AN AMERICAN DILEMMA

An American Dilemma

Vietnam, 1964–1973

Edited by

Dennis E. Showalter and John G. Albert

Imprint Publications
Chicago
1993

Library of Congress Catalog Card Number 93-061150
ISBN 1-879176-15-7 (Paper)

Military History Symposium Series of the United States Air Force Academy, Vol. 1
Carl W. Reddel, Series Editor

Printed in the United States of America

To the graduates of the Air Force Academy,
especially those who died in the service of their country

Contents

Contributors

Dennis E. Showalter obtained his B.A. from St. John's University, and his M.A. and Ph.D. from the University of Minnesota. Since 1968 he has served on the faculty of Colorado College, where he is Professor of History. From 1991 to 1993 he was Distinguished Visiting Professor of history at the U.S. Air Force Academy. His publications include *Railroads and Rifles: Soldiers, Technology, and the Unification of Germany* (1975), *German Military History Since 1648: A Critical Bibliography* (1982), *Little Man, What Now?: Der Stürmer in the Weimar Republic* (1982), and *Tannenberg: Clash of Empires* (1991).

John G. Albert, Lieutenant Colonel, U.S. Air Force, is a Defense Advisor at the U.S. Mission to NATO. During the editing of this work, he was the Director of World History and Area Studies at the USAF Academy. He is a master navigator and has served two tours at the U.S. Air Force Academy as an instructor. He received his B.S. from the Academy in 1973, his M.A. from Indiana University in 1974, and his Ph.D. from Oxford University in 1987.

Norman A. Graebner was born in Kingman, Kans. in 1915. He studied at Wisconsin State Teachers College, Milwaukee, receiving his B.S. in 1939, and the University of Oklahoma, where he received his M.A. in 1940. He received his Ph.D. from the University of Chicago in 1949. During a long and distinguished career he wrote numerous scholarly works, including *Empire on the Pacific* (1955), *Cold War Diplomacy* (1962), *Ideas and Diplomacy* (1964), *A History of the United States* (1970), *A History of the American People* (1970), *Age of Global Power* (1979), and his most recent work, *The National Security: Its Theory and Practice, 1945–1960* (1986). He is Randolph P. Compton Professor of History and Public Affairs Emeritus at the University of Virginia, Charlottesville.

Phillip B. Davidson, Lieutenant General, U.S. Army, retired, was born in Hachita, N.M. in 1915. He entered the U.S. Military Academy in 1935. Graduating in 1939 as a Second Lieutenant of Cavalry, he joined the 2nd Cavalry Regiment (Horse) at Fort Riley, Kans. In World War II, he was a Squadron Commander and a Regimental Executive Officer in the 3rd Cavalry Reconnaissance Group (Mechanized), participating in four campaigns. During the Korean War, he was a member of General MacArthur's intelligence staff. In Vietnam, Davidson spent two years (1967–69) as a member of the MACV Staff, serving Generals Westmoreland and Abrams as their Chief Intelligence Officer. His decorations include the Distinguished Service Medal (O.L.C.), Silver Star, Legion of Merit (3 O.L.C.), Bronze Star, Purple Heart, and the French *Croix de Guerre.* He also served as an Associate Professor of Military History at West Point and authored three books, *Intelligence is for Commanders* (co-authored with Major General Robert R. Glass, 1948), *Vietnam at War: The His-*

tory, 1946–1975 (1988), and *The Secrets of the Vietnam War* (1990). General Davidson lives in San Antonio, Texas.

George C. Herring was born in Blacksburg, Va. in 1936. He studied at Roanoke College, receiving his B.A. in 1957, and at the University of Virginia, where he received his M.A. in 1962 and his Ph.D. in 1965. Before completing his M.A. and Ph.D. degrees, Herring served in the U.S. Navy from 1958 to 1960. He is an internationally recognized expert on Vietnam and has examined America's involvement in the war from all aspects of the conflict—military, political, diplomatic, economic, and social. His book, *America's Longest War: The United States and Vietnam, 1950–1975* (1985) is the most concise analysis of the Vietnam War yet produced. Other works include *Aid to Russia, 1941–1946: Strategy, Diplomacy, the Origins of the Cold War* (1973), *The Diaries of Edward R. Settinius, Jr., 1943–1946* (co-edited with Thomas M. Campbell, 1975), *The Secret Diplomacy of the Vietnam War: The "Negotiating Volumes" of the Pentagon Papers* (1983), *The Central American Crisis: Sources of Conflict and the Failure of U.S. Policy* (co-edited with Kenneth M. Coleman, 1985), *Modern American Diplomacy* (co-edited with John M. Carroll, 1986), and his most recent work, *Vietnam War: Lessons from Yesterday for Today* (co-authored with Kevin Simon, 1988). Herring is currently Professor of History at the University of Kentucky.

Andrew F. Krepinevich, Lieutenant Colonel, U.S. Army, is the Military Assistant to the Director, Net Assessment, Office of the Secretary of Defense. He was graduated from the U.S. Military Academy in 1972 and continued his education at Harvard University, earning an M.P.A. in 1980 and a Ph.D. in 1984. Krepinevich was Assistant Professor for National Security Affairs, Department of Social Sciences, at the U.S. Military Academy from 1980 to 1984. His publications on Vietnam include *The Army and Vietnam* (1986) and "Low-Intensity Conflict and the U.S. Army's Adaptability in Doctrine and Force Structure," in *Democracy, Strategy, and Vietnam* (1989). Krepinevich is an Adjunct Professor at George Mason University and at the Johns Hopkins School of Advanced International Studies.

Larry Cable completed a Ph.D. with distinction at the University of Houston in 1984 after seventeen years of service with military and civilian components of the national security community including sixty-three months in a variety of unconventional warfare assignments in Southeast Asia. The author of *Conflict of Myths: The Development of American Counterinsurgency Doctrine and the Vietnam War* (1986), *Unholy Grail: The US and the Wars in Vietnam, 1965–1968* (1991), and the forthcoming *Self Inflicted Wound: The US, Indochina and Global Policy, 1940–1975,* as well as articles and papers on the Vietnam War, intelligence, and associated subjects, he is currently at the University of North Carolina–Wilmington as an Associate Professor of History. In addition, he is Adjunct Professor of History at the USAF Special Operations School, and lectures regularly at various military service schools.

Jeffrey J. Clarke, born in East Orange, N.J. in 1942, received his A.B. from Gettysburg College in 1964 and his Ph.D. from Duke University in 1968. Between 1968 and 1970 he served as an officer in the U.S. Army, commanding a Military History Detachment in Vietnam, and is currently a lieutenant colonel in the U.S. Army Reserve. Clarke joined the U.S. Army Center of Military History in 1972 and was recently appointed Chief Historian at the Center. He has also taught history during the past twenty years at Rutgers University and the University of Maryland. His publications include *Advice and Support: The Final Years* (1988), a volume in the Army's official history of the Vietnam War, and *Riviera to the Rhine* (1993), the Army's last operational history of the World War II.

Mark Clodfelter, Major, U.S. Air Force, was graduated from the U.S. Air Force Academy in 1977 and served as an air weapons controller at Myrtle Beach Air Force Base, S.C., and Osan Air Base, Korea. In 1983, after receiving an M.A. from the University of Nebraska, he returned to the Academy as an Instructor in the Department of History. He left the Academy in 1984 to obtain a Ph.D. at the University of North Carolina. Returning to the Academy in 1987, Clodfelter served as Executive Director of the Department of History's Thirteenth Military History Symposium and as the Department's Director of Military History. He is currently Professor of Airpower History at Air University's School of Advanced Airpower Studies, and is the author of *The Limits of Air Power: The American Bombing of North Vietnam* (1989).

Joan Hoff studied at the University of Montana, receiving a B.A. in 1957, at Cornell University, receiving an M.A. in 1959, and at the University of California, receiving a Ph.D. in 1966. Hoff is the former Executive Secretary of the Organization of American Historians, Editor of the *Journal of Women's History,* and Professor of History at Indiana University. Her major writings include *American Business and Foreign Policy, 1920–1923* (1971), *Ideology and Economics: United States Relations with the Soviet Union, 1918–1933* (1974), *Herbert Hoover: Forgotten Progressive* (1975), *Law, Gender and Justice: Legal History of U.S. Women* (1991), and her reevaluation of the Nixon presidency entitled, *Nixon Without Watergate: A Presidency Reconsidered* (forthcoming).

Foreword

This volume developed from the Fourteenth Military History Symposium, held at the United States Air Force Academy, 17–19 October 1990. Fifteen years after the collapse of the Republic of South Vietnam, the symposium brought together government officials, military officers, and the best scholars on the Vietnam War to explore if the passage of time was leading to some consensus about the meaning of this divisive period in American history, to determine American thinking on the war, and to suggest possible directions for future scholarship.

Formal presentations were only the tip of an intellectual iceberg. The meeting assembled the most significant group of prominent Vietnam scholars in recent years and concentrated them in one large room for three days. The Military History Symposium Series is unusual among academic gatherings in two ways. It has no competing panels. Each conference has a single agenda. All attendees share a common experience. There is no possibility of seeking out the most congenial session among three or four offered at the same time. Opportunities for direct interchange of ideas are further enhanced by the symposium's location. The United States Air Force Academy is fifteen miles away from the restaurants and cocktail lounges that encourage separatism at most other academic meetings. Participants are usually bused to the academy in the morning and returned to their hotels late at night, thereby creating a captive audience in the most positive sense. With nowhere to go, those attending the conference are not only compelled to listen to contrary opinions, but also to spend time *nolens volens* with people whose intellectual positions they deplore or despise.

A better climate for systematic interaction can scarcely be imagined. Those who attended the Fourteenth Military History Symposium will vividly remember the intense exchanges among panelists, between panelists and audience, and not least within the audience itself, as officers, officials, scholars, and veterans of both the war and the antiwar movements discussed or eviscerated the presentations. The debates went on over coffee and doughnuts, at lunch, and even at the formal banquet. The impact on the papers was substantial. None of the articles presented here escaped significant revision in the context of those three days of formal and informal critiques. Even more important was the weakening of the intellectual limitations which "tribalism"—to use the term proposed in the Introduction—invariably imposes upon understanding. No one would mistake the Fourteenth Military History Symposium for an intellectual love-feast. Its sharp exchanges, however, generated some remarkable contributions to an understanding of a war that refuses to end, and its impact on an America that two decades later remains "still in Saigon, in our minds."

The Military History Symposium Series at the United States Air Force Academy began in 1967 as an annual event, sponsored by the Academy and its Association of Graduates, with the Department of History as the planning and directing agency.

Since 1970, the symposia have been held biennially. The purpose of the series is to provide a forum in which recognized scholars may present the results of their research in the field of military affairs. The Academy hopes in this way to encourage interest in a vital subject among civilian and military scholars, members of the armed forces, and the cadets who will be the future leaders of the United States Air Force.

The Fourteenth Military History Symposium benefitted greatly from the generous financial support received from the Association of Graduates, the George and Carol Olmsted Foundation, and the Major Donald R. Backlund Memorial Fund. Generous contributions from the Falcon Foundation also played an important role in the success of the symposium.

The editors also wish to acknowledge the debt this volume owes to a number of members and former members of the Department of History at the United States Air Force Academy. Under the leadership of the department's head, Col. Carl Reddel, the symposia have become a world-renowned gathering of outstanding scholars, high-ranking military officers, and important policy-makers interested in achieving a keener understanding of the military past. Maj. Mark Clodfelter, the Academy's Director of Military History, provided the intellectual leadership for the conference. He carried the primary responsibility for deciding what topics would be covered, and for recommending the distinguished scholars whose articles appear in this volume. The editors have built upon and refined the product that he crafted, but this volume is ultimately the product of his vision. The index was prepared by Capt. David Stilwell.

Two other names that stand out in the production of this book are Maj. John Farrell and Pam Hiller. John provided expert advice in the early stages of editing. He spent long hours poring over the original submissions and transcriptions. His recommendations for additions, deletions, and revisions were always on the mark. When he left the Academy in the summer of 1991, the foundations for the volume were well established. Pam, meanwhile, efficiently transcribed oral commentaries from the symposium, typed the bulk of the manuscript and endnotes, and cheerfully oversaw a myriad of administrative duties related to the conference. Any errors that remain after her meticulous work are solely the responsibility of the editors.

The Editors

Introduction

Dennis E. Showalter and John G. Albert

After more than a quarter century the historiography of the Vietnam War is just beginning to emerge from its tribal stage. In this as in so many other ways, Vietnam is unique in the U.S. experience. The country's earlier major conflicts, the Revolutionary and Civil Wars, World Wars I and II, initially generated consensus history, dominated by a structure of recognized mainstream works reflecting a fairly broad spectrum of agreement on the purpose, course, and nature of the recently completed experience. Only later did more detailed evidence, increased hindsight, and personal and professional disagreements combine to generate alternative perspectives. Serious revisionist histories of World War I required a decade to make either an intellectual or public impact. Cold War revisionism, with its emphasis on American culpability as opposed to Soviet expansionism, took even longer to develop. Not for twenty years did interpretations developed in the late 1940s face a comprehensive challenge that in turn gave way to a currently dominant "post-revisionism" stressing the Cold War as a general consequence of World War II rather than a function of specific state behaviors.

Vietnam was different—utterly different. From the early stages of American involvement, writing about the war presented evidence in the context of authors' value systems. This phenomenon in part reflected not merely the neglect of Southeast Asia by the American academic community, but the nonexistence, for all practical purposes, of any institutional matrix for understanding Vietnam. No major universities offered doctorates in Vietnamese history or sponsored programs in Vietnamese languages. No departments of anthropology supported expeditions to the Montagnard peoples. No programs in comparative literature or philosophy examined Vietnamese sources. The result was less that "the center failed to hold" than that no center focusing and validating arguments ever had an opportunity to form in the context of a war that rapidly became a comprehensive issue of domestic politics and domestic morality rather than a problem restricted to the areas of foreign policy and international relations.

The intellectual pattern that emerged is best described as "ironic confusion." Some of the better grassroots work on Vietnamese village and tribal cultures was produced by Army officers without relevant academic degrees, and to this day remains buried in various official files or among the many thousands of obscure government publications on Vietnam. In contrast, for a broad spectrum of academicians, Vietnam became less a subject of study than a state of mind—a land of Oz, a place of emotional and moral pilgrimage onto which it became not merely possible but legitimate to project dreams and hopes without subjecting one's visions to the tests of critical analysis. A journalistic community initially not merely willing but anxious to "get with the program" articulated by the government faced instead the grim realities of a twilight war, and moved from doubt through confrontation to full-fledged membership in an emerging adversary culture.

Even to its participants, the Vietnam War was a chameleon. The complex terrain and the even more complex social and military conditions in the theater of operations made each tour of duty a unique event, mediate only to itself. Career military men who returned to Vietnam two, three, or four times, faced correspondingly discrete experiences. An officer might begin in 1965 as a lieutenant in a U.S. rifle company, return two years later as a captain assigned to Military Assistance Command, Vietnam (MACV) headquarters in Saigon, then find himself in 1970 as a major assigned to a South Vietnamese division as a senior adviser. Within an individual tour, moreover, two or three different assignments were more the rule than the exception for professional officers and at least the higher noncommissioned grades.

The existence of a limited tour of duty further served to compartmentalize direct understanding and assimilation of the Vietnam experience. Everyone arriving "in-country" knew precisely his or her own date of return to "the world," a date unaffected either by the war's overall progress or by specific individual behavior, such as completing a certain number of missions in the pattern of World War II bomber crews. The result, especially among draftees, was a mind set closely approximating that of a penitentiary, where the ruling atmosphere is "do your own time." One's personal appointment with the "freedom bird" tended to override any general interest or concern for Vietnam as a whole.

A final element exacerbating the process of fragmentation was a selective service process that for most of the war operated to keep "the best and the brightest" of America's younger generation well away from the theater of war, to say nothing of its actual combat zones. The familiar interpretation of Vietnam as a war fought by semiliterate dropouts is significantly exaggerated.[1] Nevertheless, by comparison with their counterparts of 1918, 1944, and even 1951, Vietnam's junior officers and the rank and file were significantly inarticulate outside the scope of their direct experiences, physical and emotional. On the other hand, those able to avoid service directly or through the complex deferment process were equally disinterested in investigating the war they had sidestepped. At the end of the century, Vietnam remains a dividing line and a barrier for a generation of males. On both sides personal memories still tend to shape, when not to overwhelm, the intellectual process.

With the 1980s, as women and minorities began to influence the scholarly community, Vietnam became even more a question relegated to the back burners of curricular debates and university press publishing lists. The war seemed too much an affair of white males, dead or alive, to merit serious attention in an academic climate dominated by feminism, deconstruction, and multiculturalism. At the same time, a paradoxical related factor contributed to Vietnam's difficulties in making a coherent scholarly impact. That factor was its explosion as a teaching field. Despite the continued relative scarcity of specialized academic training in the subject, over four hundred courses are currently being offered on the subject in American colleges and universities. Vietnam is also a burgeoning area of study for secondary schools, in its own right and as a subject for social studies units in larger courses.

A major result has been a proliferation of self-help books and pamphlets offering suggestions on content, approaches, and syllabi. Especially noteworthy is the impact in this field of relatively obscure institutions. Drew University, Southern Illinois, North Carolina at Wilmington, and the University of Guam are hardly competitive with Yale or Berkeley in general terms. But their courses and their faculty have exercised significant influences in structuring academic programs on Vietnam. This grassroots process is enough of a contrast to the normal pattern of academic trends to progress outward from elite institutions that it has arguably contributed not a little to keeping the field in a state of entropy.

The simple passage of time has structured the writing on Vietnam. Works published on the same general subject in 1975, 1983, and 1990 have used significantly different source bases and asked significantly different questions. Vietnam studies, however, remain most influenced by the continued tendency of the soldiers, the scholars, and the popular writers concerned with Vietnam to sustain entropy by presenting their work in the context of limited intellectual and public enclaves. Let us call these enclaves tribes.

The most familiar tribe is the Tribe of the Warriors. These men and women were there, in the front lines. Initially most comfortable with fiction—James Webb's *Fields of Fire* or John Del Vecchio's *The Thirteenth Valley* come readily to mind—the warriors have in recent years created a flourishing subculture of combat memoirs and inspired an impressive number of operational histories. Gen. Hal Moore and Joseph Galloway's *We Were Soldiers Once—And Young,* and Ronald Spector's *After Tet: The Bloodiest Year* are distinguished current examples of a steadily evolving category of history telling the story of the sharp end in a war without front lines.

The Tribe of the Warriors has individual septs as well. The airmen are represented in fiction by Mark Berendt and his series of technothrillers set in the skies over southeast Asia: *Rolling Thunder, Phantom Leader,* and *Steel Tiger.* Jack Broughton's *Thud Ridge* and *Going Downtown* are among the most eloquent American military memoirs in their tight-leashed frustration. The POW/MIA sept has brought forth heroes such as Robinson Risner and James Stockdale, villains and rogues too numerous to mention, and a publication list unlikely to be disturbed by the recent acerbic denials of H. Bruce Franklin, who in *MIA* blames the whole issue on Richard Nixon.

The second major Vietnam collective is best called the Tribe of the Analysts. Its members focus not on combat but on conduct. They concentrate less on how the U.S. armed forces fought than why they fought as they did. A notable characteristic of this tribe is the relative intellectual weakness of its first-person testimonies. Gen. William Westmoreland and Admiral Ulysses Grant Sharp are typical of the major memoirists. Neither set of testimony has made a particular impact, nor have the accounts of lesser figures such as John Singlaub. Special pleading, selective memory, and outright excuse-mongering continue to shape the recollections of most participants above the level of battalion or squadron command.

The most eloquent spokesman for the "military establishment's" view of the Vietnam War is Maj. Gen. Phillip Davidson. His *Vietnam at War* stresses the potentially favorable results of relatively minor adjustments at the levels of planning and operation. Davidson, however, is outnumbered significantly by his tribal brethren who focus on the shortcomings of the U.S. military effort. Harry Summers's *On Strategy* and Dave Richard Palmer's *The 25-Year War* have in common their criticism of a national strategy that left the initiative to the enemy while failing to define its own objectives. Summers's contention that the United States was mistaken in regarding the National Liberation Front (NLF) as its primary enemy, however, is challenged by Andrew Krepinevich, who argues instead for the military establishment's comprehensive failure to understand the nature of revolutionary war as practiced in Vietnam. Mark Clodfelter in *The Limits of Air Power* and Earl Tilford in *Setup* take similar iconoclastic approaches to the air war, making distinct but related cases for the inability of the high-tech, nuclear-tipped air force of the Cold War era to grasp the strategic and intellectual requirements of counterinsurgency in a limited war context.

If the Tribe of the Analysts speaks with many voices, the Tribe of the Statesmen is even more dissonant. This group focuses on Vietnam in its policy-making context. Some of its members treat the war as a case study in modern international relations. Among recent general works, Ralph Smith's *International History of the Vietnam War* sees the conflict as part of a wider Cold War and defends American intervention on the grounds of realpolitik. George Kahin's *Intervention* insists in the Vietnamese origins of the war, and argues that American involvement can be justified on neither moral nor strategic grounds.

Other major studies focus more narrowly on the domestic aspects of the U.S. commitment. Leslie Gelb and Richard Betts argue that successive administrations knew well the risks they were running in deepening their involvement in Vietnam. Nevertheless, the perceived consequences of "losing" Vietnam to communism were great enough to encourage taking increasingly extreme measures to avert that situation. The scholarship of George Herring particularly stresses the solipsism of American policy-makers who consistently underestimated the will, skill, and determination of their Vietnamese antagonists. The result was an ironic inversion of the Japanese-U.S. war of 1941–45, with America seeking to wage an essentially limited war against an adversary willing to stake everything on a total victory. Lyndon Johnson's baffled concept of securing peace by giving North Vietnam its own Tennessee Valley Authority was at one with Robert McNamara's belief in the possibility of opening negotiations by turning the bombing campaign on and off. Both approaches reflected a pattern of mirror-imaging that was itself a product of a thermonuclear Cold War in which the opponents were ideological opposites but pragmatic equivalents.

Another sept of "statesmen" interprets Vietnam in the context of the rapidly polarizing domestic policies of the United States. Kathleen Turner and Larry Berman both emphasize Lyndon Johnson's consistent refusal to choose between reform at home and victory abroad. George Moss makes the same point in a broader context. In *Vietnam: An American Ordeal,* he highlights the war's exacerbating of a broad spectrum of stress points—economic, ethnic, and social—that had their roots in World War II but were sublimated in the "Cold War normalcy" of the 1950s.

Moss's work also can be viewed as a transition between the statesmen and the fourth major category of Vietnam writing, produced by the Tribe of the Metaphorists. These men and women see the Vietnam experience essentially as standing for something else. Frequently that "else" is a loss of American innocence, individual and collective. Philip Caputo and Ron Kovacs have presented familiar and convincing literary expressions. Neil Sheehan's *A Bright Shining Lie* uses the personal character flaws of John Paul Vann to establish the deficiencies of Vann's America. Oliver Stone's films *Platoon* and *JFK* are even more eloquent in their argument that Vietnam is a paradigm for a society that took a fatal turn in a comprehensively wrong direction.

On an academic level, metaphorist Marilyn Young's *The Vietnam War* describes an exercise in what amounts to blind malice generated by the patriarchal values of the United States. Gabriel Kolko's *Anatomy of War* argues for Vietnam as a test between capitalist and Marxist social systems, with the superior system not only triumphing, but also highlighting its adversary's fundamental structural flaws in ways denying the possibility of any but short-term repair. James William Gibson's *The Perfect War* presents the war as a "corporate production system" for imposing American values in Southeast Asia—a real-life reprise of *Teahouse of the August Moon,* with gunships and naplam replacing pentagon-shaped schoolhouses as primary artifacts of imperialism. In *Backfire,* Loren Baritz argues that American culture's most characteristic features—optimism and insensitivity—led us into the war and shaped the way we fought it.

By no means are all the metaphorists identified with the political and cultural left. In *Why We Were in Vietnam,* Norman Podhoretz interprets the war as a triumph of idealism expressed in the realistic policy of containment. Gunter Lewy's *America in Vietnam,* while critical of many specific acts and decisions, concludes that the military conduct of the war was essentially moral: an appropriate application of western values in an imperfect world.

It is possible to extend the number and complexity of these tribal categories of Vietnam writing. One might discuss, for example, the rapidly growing Tribe of Asianists, with its eloquent arguments for presenting the war in Vietnamese and regional contexts. One might suggest another Tribe of Consequences, whose members focus on the conflict's long-term impacts on America, Vietnam, and the world. The basic point, however, remains that the subject of Vietnam continues to encourage entropy rather than synthesis. General historical works acknowledge the importance of comprehensiveness in the introduction. The texts themselves, however, tend to remain faithful to tribal boundaries and tribal mores. Shelby Stanton, a principal shaman of the warriors, barely notices the works of analysts and statesmen in his accounts of units in battle. Warrior reviewer Paul Braim savages Young's *The Vietnam Wars* in the spring 1992 issue of *Parameters* with a vehemence unusual for a subject with a quarter century's perspective. In such a context, the burgeoning number of textbooks on Vietnam, such as James Olson's and Randy Roberts's *Where the Domino Fell* or Gary Hess's *Vietnam and the United States*, have been able to do little more than present and juxtapose arguments that are also value judgments.

The eight essays presented in this volume represent an effort to transcend tribal boundaries and understand the Vietnam War as a whole, instead of a collection of parts. Norman Graebner, a distinguished student of U.S. diplomatic history, is hardly a narrow specialist on Vietnam affairs. His contribution perceptively summarizes a quarter-century's scholarship in the field while offering a brilliant, concise history of U.S. involvement in Vietnam from 1950 to 1975. Vietnam was not an isolated experience, a "business accident" that can be dealt with by encysting it, treating it as a historical exception. Graebner's persuasive arguments for "depoliticizing" the Vietnam experience in favor of understanding it rests on the conviction, formed from a lifetime's study, that a democracy seriously divided against itself cannot sustain a coherent foreign policy over any length of time. The continued existence of the so-called Vietnam Syndrome is for Graebner a warning, a caveat that "failures, like successes, are replete with the materials for instructing."

The military's willingness to utilize the materials of a failure is highlighted in the contribution of Phillip Davidson. The general makes no secret of his continued adherence to the position that Vietnam was not an endeavor doomed from the start. He stresses three fundamental U.S. errors and argues that each was correctable. First came a failure to establish agreement on the war's character. Inability to decide whether we faced "an insurgency, a conventional war, a combination of the two, or none of the above" dissipated American resources and energy to a critical degree. The second critical error was more specific: the Johnson administration's continued failure to establish coherent military and political objectives. The third error, growing out of the first two, involved resigning the war's initiatives to the enemy at all but tactical levels. The result was a growing negative synergy, with the U.S. war effort self-destructing as men of goodwill sought to implement their particular piece of the action in the absence of an overall focus. Unlike Rudyard Kipling's fictional *SS Dimbula*, which eventually emerges as a ship instead of a ship's component parts, America's Vietnam War never "found itself" and ultimately dissolved in chaos.

George Herring, doyen of the war's diplomatic historians, addresses Lyndon Johnson's conduct of the war by insisting on the importance of focusing on what actually happened instead of on what might have happened or should have happened. Herring makes two major points. First, the Johnson administration never discussed the issue of how the war should be fought. This reflected a combination of institutional overconfidence in U.S. power with Johnson's own "insecurity and inferiority" in military matters. The result was a strategic void, negatively complemented by increasingly direct operational control that provided the illusion of mastery for an increasingly divided government.

Herring also stresses the administration's limited and cautious efforts to mobilize public support for the war. For all Johnson's expressed concern for public opinion, his administration maintained a low-key approach in the face of steadily eroding public confidence in what was happening. Johnson sought to wage a war in cold blood, a restricted war avoiding the domestic and international risks of mobilization or of declaring war on North Vietnam. The difficulties inherent in conducting limited war against a determined enemy were thus exacerbated to a critical point by specific decisions that reflected ongoing commitment to crisis management rather than the application of a coherent military strategy.

Crisis management influenced the armed forces as well as the administration. Andrew Krepinevich extends his previous work by describing the ground war from 1965 to 1968 in terms of a U.S. strategy that sought a quick victory by quick fixes, in contrast to the "more flexible and comprehensive" Communist strategy of people's war. North Vietnamese Army (NVA) or NLF defeats were never final. They could always deescalate the war's military aspects while continuing to focus on the political and psychological elements of strategy. This flexible policy struck at their enemy's most vulnerable point: a South Vietnamese government that Krepinevich dismisses as corrupt, incompetent, and illegitimate. It rendered correspondingly ineffective a U.S. strategy based on "deterrence through punishment," as opposed to eliminating the internal threat to South Vietnam.

Air power was viewed throughout the war as a major instrument of punishment, and air power is the subject of a comprehensive and compelling essay by Larry Cable, who describes the Vietnam War as not only "a limited war in support of policy" but also a war whose character repeatedly changed in the crucial years between 1964 and 1969. The Johnson administration, however, viewed the conflict in fixed terms. The Vietcong were seen as both externally controlled and depending on Hanoi for support. Evidence suggesting that North Vietnam was in fact in a period of diplomatic retrenchment during the early 1960s was discounted or disregarded, not least because air power promised a quick, clean, and cheap resolution of what the Johnson administration regarded from start to finish as a minor problem in the context of its global policy of containment.

Cable's research evokes two images. One involves the old joke of a child seeking a lost quarter under the street lamp "because the light is best there." The strategy of the air war over North Vietnam, with its gradual escalations and measured pauses, was not merely "massively irrelevant" to the actual war in South Vietnam but was, Cable argues, counterproductive. The bombing campaign in fact "invited" Hanoi to enter the war on a large scale in pursuit of its own goals.

This introduces a second image, borrowed from C. S. Forester's *The General.*

It involves people who have never seen a screw attempting to remove one from a block of wood by doing the apparently logical thing and increasing the direct force applied. The senior military command, Cable argues, had "limitless faith" in the air war. If bombing neither stopped the war nor produced negotiations, the appropriate response involved not rethinking but expanding existing approaches. This rigidity was exacerbated by a loss rate high enough that abandoning the bombing paradigm increasingly seemed a dismissal of years of heroism and sacrifice. The Johnson administration was trapped politically and morally in its own structures.

Krepinevich and Cable, each in his own way, suggest a point first introduced by Davidson: the Vietnam War was ultimately a Vietnamese war. Whatever its specific combination of invasion and insurgency, the conflict could not be finally won by Americans. This point, obscured by Lyndon Johnson's pursuit of a quick fix, was central to the Nixon administration's policy of "Vietnamization" introduced in April 1969. Jeffrey Clarke describes this as the wrong idea at the wrong time. Vietnamization, he argues, took too little account of the war's essential changes since 1965. By emphasizing the internal security and counterinsurgency missions of the South Vietnamese armed forces, the United States left its so-called ally unprepared for the conventional operations that in fact decided the war in Hanoi's favor. Vietnamization, in short, was not a strategy but a policy that largely reflected Nixon's commitment to disengagement. In turn, this commitment encouraged the same sort of wishful thinking and picture making that had characterized America's Vietnam policy-making for almost twenty years. This time the illusions proved fatal, if only to the Republic of Vietnam.

One of the major myths of "Nixon's war" involves his alleged "unleashing" of air power against Hanoi in December 1972. For airmen, in particular, Operation Linebacker II often represents a last hurrah, a demonstration of what the United States could have done absent the restraint and interference that shaped America's conduct of the war. Mark Clodfelter's model exercise in revisionism demonstrates instead that the results of Linebacker II were "largely fortuitous." The strategic situation, he argues, had changed from 1965 to 1968. By 1972 the North Vietnamese had won many of their principal goals. American forces were going home. Hanoi had secured the right to maintain large forces in South Vietnam after the condition of peace. Time was on the North's side, and it made sense not merely to sign an armistice agreement but to give the United States the kind of face-saving "golden bridge" so eloquently advocated centuries ago by Sun Tzu.

The subjectivism generally characteristic of writing on the Vietnam War is enhanced for the conflict's later years by the presence of Richard Nixon. Perhaps even more than Vietnam the Nixon presidency remains an area where values continue to challenge scholarship. Joan Hoff makes an arguable and provocative case that Nixon's approach to foreign policy eventually shaped his approach to domestic dissent, instead of the other way around. Surveillances and wiretaps grew out of the administration's conduct of the war, specifically out of efforts to neutralize or discredit a protest movement that Nixon regarded as harming his increasingly desperate efforts to negotiate a settlement. Ultimately, Hoff argues, Nixon defused the antiwar movement by ending the draft and concluding the January 1973 peace accords. He never came close, however, to placating his career adversaries in academia and the media, who only found further ammunition for their hostility in Nixon's conduct of "his share of the war."

Major obstacles persist in the path of developing a comprehensive understanding of the Vietnam War. In particular the positions of the North Vietnamese and the Vietcong remain opaque. Evaluating American decision-making without access to the inner councils of the other side gives a very skewed picture of the actual results of American actions. One assumes that American actions were met continuously by opposition actions intended to thwart them, that the other side functioned rationally and consistently. That case seems hardly likely. Bureaucratic politics, indecision, human weakness and misjudgment have all been chronicled in great detail on the American side of the Vietnam equation. Very little is known about the decision-making processes of the opposition. When were they discouraged? When were they surprised? What did they argue about? Without the Communist side of the equation, all analysis of the impact of American behavior must remain tentative. One can only assume the reaction of the other side. Without access to the Communist side of the Vietnam saga, continued development of American sources will only add detail, and some refinement, to arguments that have been made to date.

Even in that context the Vietnam War is too painfully embedded in the American consciousness to be considered purely as an intellectual exercise. More than a decade and a half after North Vietnamese tanks rolled into Saigon, deep divisions persist over the meaning of American involvement in that tragic war. Louis Galambos in particular argues for Vietnam as the most debilitating conflict in the nation's history. His analysis of the war's long-term impact paints a bleak picture, which begins with economics. The years following World War II were years of prosperity. The consumer economy arrived with a vengeance. Multinational corporations were able to occupy solid competitive positions in overseas markets from which American goods and services had heretofore been excluded. As one American businessman put it: "The world was our oyster." So dominant were U.S. corporations that people began to talk about the "American Century," a century in which the United States would reign over the world economy as Great Britain had in the nineteenth century.

Then came Vietnam. In its aftermath, U.S. trade was out of balance; productivity increases dropped toward zero; inflation mounted; interest rates soared to unbelievable levels; and America's standard of living no longer led the industrialized world. Something fundamental had changed. Galambos argues that the war, and the massive government expenditures to finance it, helped launch the great inflation of the late 1960s and the 1970s. That inflation, which did not end until the early 1980s, twisted the U.S. economy out of shape. It contributed to a decline in investment in new plants and in research and development.

This, in turn, left us increasingly and continuously vulnerable to foreign competition. According to Galambos, the managers of America's largest firms were preoccupied from 1965 to 1975 with government contracts, with the internal turmoil generated by the war, and with the ill-advised patterns of investment so popular in those years. Inflation particularly encouraged conglomerate investments as a means of sustaining growth and hedging against price increases. Inflation also worked against the sort of long-term perspectives that U.S. management would need to survive in the late 1970s and 1980s. America had lost ten crucial years, adopting policies that made adapting to increased global competition significantly difficult. As Galambos views it, the American people continue to pay for their country's blunder in Southeast Asia.

America, Galambos also believes, has paid a severe and continuing political price for the war. Its focus has been the steady weakening of public values. American values historically favor the private over the public. The Vietnam War left a substantial number of Americans even more suspicious of their government than they had been before. Now they had good cause to believe that they had been deliberately and systematically misled by their presidents and congressional leaders. Vietnam generated an ongoing distrust of government—in particular of national leaders and many of the most important national institutions. The current fragmentation of American identity can be seen as having its roots in the crippling of the common weal as a consequence of the Vietnam War.

Finally, Galambos argues, the Vietnam War was debilitating to the armed forces. The defeat drastically lowered the status of the military in the United States. The resulting national mood led to poor performance and diminished budgets throughout the armed forces. In turn the perceived weakness of the U.S. military in the late 1970s led to the massive, ill-planned, unfortunate cycle of increased expenditures in the 1980s. The latter cycle, which Galambos considers a product of the war and the attitudes it engendered, created the debt that has limited America's financial flexibility and threatens to do so for years to come. The fundamental nature of the Reagan buildup encouraged a wild service rush to gain relative position over the long term. Expenditures preceded strategy. The procedure was backwards, and the price of this mistake, Galambos contends, continues to be very high.[2]

But is Galambos's position too extreme? William Bundy, who served as assistant secretary of state for Asian affairs during a crucial period of the war, believes that "the degree of blame [Galambos] assigns to the Vietnam War for our economic troubles and loss of competitiveness is quite a bit overdrawn."[3] Military historian and defense analyst Col. Harry Summers sarcastically accuses Galambos of blaming the Vietnam War for all the ills of mankind, stopping just short of attributing to that conflict the heartbreak of psoriasis.[4]

Current events continue to influence our understanding of the Vietnam experience. The symposium at which these essays were initially presented was held in October 1990. Less than three months earlier Saddam Hussein had invaded Kuwait, and the United States found itself involved in its largest military operation since the Vietnam War. Though the outcome of Operation Desert Shield was far from clear in October 1990, participants at the conference were well aware of the heightened relevance their academic deliberations had assumed as a result of events in the Middle East.

Norman Graebner discusses the negative consequences of the Vietnam syndrome on America's ability to conduct its foreign policy. His call for a new attempt to find consensus on the meaning of the Vietnam experience is even more compelling in a post–Cold War world whose traditional verities have been overtaken by events. In a more specific context, Larry Cable's and Mark Clodfelter's essays on the misuse of air power in Vietnam also acquired an unexpected relevance. The successful application of air power against Iraq lay in the future, and these papers offered a cautionary note for those contemplating its use as a general panacea.

The "relevance" of the Vietnam War at the time of Desert Shield/Desert Storm highlights the continuing role of Vietnam as a source of support for preconceptions on the present and future. And this in turn suggests the utility of another concept. Roger Dingman has suggested that the concept of "a dilemma" is the most appropriate epithet to put on America's Vietnam experience. If it is not yet possible to reach consensus on the meaning of the Vietnam experience, it may be feasible to move toward an understanding of different points of view. In this context the concept of a dilemma might at least help to cool some of the ideological heat. In commenting on his own remarks at the symposium, William Bundy said, "I wish I had stressed more the theme of dilemma . . . and the need to think not in terms of scapegoats or flawed processes but of national tragedy, more justified and rightly motivated than critics of the left will admit, but marred at every stage by skewed perceptions, dogmatism, and every ill to which democratic societies are prone."[5] Whether the end of the Cold War and the successful prosecution of the Gulf War will provide an atmosphere in which some consensus can begin to grow about the Vietnam War remains to be seen. In the meantime the concept of dilemma may serve to move the tribes of Vietnam closer together.

Notes

1. Arnold Barnett, Timothy Stanley, and Michael Shore, "America's Vietnam Casualties: Victims of a Class War?" *Operations Research* 40 (1992): 856–66.

2. Louis Galambos, "Paying Up: The Price of the Vietnamese War" (Paper presented at the Fourteenth Military History Symposium, U.S. Air Force Academy, 19 October 1990).

3. Comments of William P. Bundy on the paper by Louis Galambos, presented at the Fourteenth Military History Symposium, U.S. Air Force Academy, 19 October 1990.

4. Col. Harry G. Summers, "Commentary on the Fourteenth Military History Symposium," sent to the editors, 11 March 1991.

5. William P. Bundy, "Reflections on the Vietnam Symposium," sent to the editors, 22 October 1990.

The Scholar's View of Vietnam, 1964–1992

Norman A. Graebner

When Lyndon B. Johnson, in February 1964, launched Operation Plan 34A to inaugurate a campaign of harassment against North Vietnam, it was clear that reactions to the burgeoning American struggle in Southeast Asia would reflect conflicting assumptions regarding the Cold War itself. Official Washington, in its effort to define the Soviet danger and design a proper defense against it, concluded as early as 1948 that the Kremlin's expansionary power, especially outside Europe, rested less on military might than on the Marxist-Leninist advocacy of world revolution. The National Security Council's study, NSC 7, dated 30 March, emphasized the Soviet challenge's ideological-global dimensions: "The ultimate objective of Soviet-directed world communism is the domination of the world."[1] Succeeding NSC documents refined this theme. NSC 68 in April 1950 comprised the final and most elaborate attempt of the Truman leadership to define a national security policy. In a world of polarized power, NSC 68 warned, "the issues that face us are momentous, involving the fulfillment or destruction not only of this Republic but of civilization itself."[2] Thereafter global containment against undifferentiated Communist pressures became the essence of United States policy, accepted by all elements of American society with surprisingly little debate.[3] Thoroughly conditioned members of Congress and the press stood ready to challenge the patriotism of any administration that faltered in its opposition to any perceived Communist-led aggression.

Scholars who have defended the American military involvement in Vietnam accept without question the official rationale of the Truman administration that the fall of Nationalist China to Mao Zedong in 1949 designated Vietnam the key to the containment of Soviet-based Asian communism. An NSC report that summer declared that "it is now clear that southeast Asia is the target of a coordinated offensive directed by the Kremlin. . . . The extension of communist authority in China represents a grievous political defeat for us; if southeast Asia also is swept by communism we shall have suffered a major political rout the repercussions of which will be felt throughout the rest of the world."[4]

By midcentury, Washington had marked Ho Chi Minh, Marxist leader of the anti-French forces in Vietnam, as the special agent of Soviet expansionism in Asia. For Secretary of State Dean Acheson, Moscow's recognition of Ho's Democratic Republic in early 1950 revealed Ho "in his true color as the mortal enemy of national independence in Indochina."[5] After January 1953 the Eisenhower administration continued to support the French armies fighting Ho as a necessary defense against the expansion of Communist power.[6] With France's decision to leave Southeast Asia in the early summer of 1954, the Eisenhower administration moved to build a permanent anti-Communist bastion in South Vietnam under Ngo Dinh Diem. In defending that decision Edwin Brown Firmage, Louis A. Fanning, and other scholars argue that the Geneva accords of 1954 created two nations, thereby denying Ho legal claims to the South and designating the subsequent Communist insurgency an international aggression against a legitimate and widely recognized country.[7]

After 1953 the Eisenhower administration, like that of Harry Truman, cast the danger of Communist expansion in the image of falling dominoes. Dwight Eisenhower himself informed newsmen on 7 April 1954 that the predictable sequence of events, should Saigon fall, could include "the loss of Indochina, of Burma, of Thailand, of the Peninsula, and Indonesia . . . the so-called island defensive chain of Japan, Formosa, of the Philippines and to the southward . . . Australia and New Zealand."[8] Five years later Eisenhower explained to a Gettysburg audience why the defense of South Vietnam was essential. "Strategically," he said, "South Vietnam's capture by the Communists would . . . set in motion a crumbling process that could, as it progressed, have grave consequences for us and for freedom."[9] Accepting such suppositions of danger, a host of writers, including Edwin Firmage, Ralph Smith, Norman Podhoretz, Frank Trager, and Whittle Johnston, have argued the United States, as the chief exponent of global containment, had no choice but to intervene heavily in Vietnam.[10] But policies so easily rationalized and defended should have faced no problem of execution. Indeed, the Eisenhower administration anticipated no major trouble and, thinking it unnecessary, avoided the creation of an American strategy for the region's defense. Something went wrong. The subsequent United States involvement was neither brief nor inexpensive; it turned out to be long, costly, enervating, divisive, and ultimately futile. The rationalizations for greater involvement at every moment of decision failed to achieve the requisite victory in defense of American and world security.

Writers whose analyses of men and events would anticipate failure, if not ultimate disaster, for U.S. policy in Vietnam have challenged directly almost every assumption and decision of the Truman and Eisenhower administrations that led to American involvement. That rejection begins with a total redefinition of the enemy. Students of Indochinese nationalism note that Ho Chi Minh's entire career was devoted to his country's independence. Such writers as former OSS officer Archimedes L. A. Patti, David G. Marr, and Joseph Buttinger agree that Ho's intense nationalism long preceded his interest in Leninism. For Ho, nationalism and communism were harmonious movements and equally anti-imperialist.[11] Bernard Fall, the noted student of Vietnam, observed that Ho, who wanted nothing but independence, was less an ideologue than an activist.[12] Other writers, led by Stanley Karnow, George Kahin, John Lewis, George Herring, Gary Hess, Andrew Rotter, Robert Shaplen, Lloyd Gardner, Chester Cooper, and David Halberstam observe that the American decisions after 1945 to reject Ho's appeal for aid and to support the French ignored the driving force of Indochinese nationalism and, against ubiquitous warnings, doomed American policy to failure.[13] "Surely," Shaplen concluded, "one way *not* to encourage the growth of an anti-Communist nationalist movement in Indochina was to support an outworn and despised French colonial regime."[14] Such critics saw no promise in the Bao Dai solution of 1949, which the French adopted to stop the disintegration of their position in Vietnam.[15] According to Patti, Herring, and others, the burgeoning fears of Communist aggression after 1950 committed the United States ever more deeply to the French effort and thereby rendered Washington hostage to France's failing cause.[16]

Kahin and Lewis, Douglas Pike, Charles Chaumont, and Max Gordon observe that Ho Chi Minh received scant support from Moscow and Beijing at the Geneva Conference of 1954. "Only the Viet Minh, the winners," writes Pike, "lost or were sold out." Such scholars note the Geneva accords did not create two countries, but stipulated specifically that the 17th parallel, separating two military zones, "should not in any way be interpreted as constituting a political or territorial boundary." Gordon asserts that "unification was unconditional, and there was no hint of two states, before or after the scheduled elections, in the Agreements."[17] By avoiding elections, scheduled for 1956, Ngo Dinh Diem established South Vietnam as a permanent, separate political entity. Burgeoning American military, economic, and moral support for the Diem regime underwrote the creation of the Republic of Vietnam, a state never recognized by the leaders of North Vietnam.[18] David Halberstam saw the irony: "The North was led by a man who had expelled the foreigners, the South by a man who had been installed by the foreigners." Whatever his precarious existence, writes Halberstam, Diem met the need of the Eisenhower administration to create an effective barrier capable of preventing Ho from expanding his power in Southeast Asia.[19] Writers note that Eisenhower, by assigning to South Vietnam the burden of containment in Southeast Asia, soon rendered the United States hostage to Diem as Truman had been to France. Washington could never control him although his regime's very survival rested on U.S. support. For Douglas Pike, Jeffery Race, George Kahin, and Bernard Fall, among many others, the Communist-led insurgency against the Diem regime was fundamentally an indigenous movement, only reluctantly and tardily underwritten by North Vietnam.[20]

John F. Kennedy entered office in January 1961 with the option to terminate Eisenhower's commitment to Ngo Dinh Diem and received much advice to do so. In his long essay in the April 1968 issue of the *Atlantic Monthly,* James C. Thomson delineated at length the new Democratic leadership's refusal to consider any serious reevaluation of the policy it had inherited in Southeast Asia.[21] For David Halberstam, Kennedy's decision to avoid retreat in Vietnam reflected his desire to overcome the illusion of weakness occasioned by the abysmal failure of the administration's effort to overthrow Cuba's Fidel Castro at the Bay of Pigs and by Soviet leader Nikita Khrushchev's rhetorical bullying in Vienna. Larry Berman and Loren Baritz agree with Halberstam that Kennedy was troubled less by Communists in Vietnam than by anti-Communists at home. Such writers recall Kennedy's words, as recorded by John Kenneth Galbraith: "There are just so many concessions that one can make to the Communists in one year and survive politically."[22] No longer, Kennedy ruefully told his aides, could he afford to accept a defeat in Southeast Asia as Eisenhower had done in 1954.[23]

Arthur M. Schlesinger, Jr. defends Kennedy's decision. In *The Bitter Heritage,* he argues that Eisenhower had drawn the line in Southeast Asia and thereby created a vital interest where none had existed before. Now that the South Vietnamese had come to rely on the U.S. commitment, the new president had no choice but to honor it.[24] Halberstam recognized the American commitment. The United States had invented South Vietnam, but by 1961, he acknowledged, Americans "believed firmly in Diem, believed in his legitimacy; they saw South Vietnam as a real country, with a real flag."[25] Unfortunately Diem was rapidly losing control of the South Vietnamese countryside as he faced skillful guerrilla warfare and effective Vietcong recruitment. Still Kennedy hesitated to send American forces into the region. When Gen. Maxwell Taylor, Kennedy's personal military adviser, recommended an American force of 10,000 men to secure South Vietnam's northern border, Kennedy complained to Schlesinger that sending troops would resolve nothing: "Then we will be told we have to send more troops. It's like taking a drink. The effect wears off, and you have to take another."[26] Kennedy in time took a small drink himself, with more to come, encouraged by warnings of disaster should Diem fall and promises of success with each new increment of American military advisers.

Kennedy's decision to escalate the U.S. military presence in South Vietnam appeared reasonable enough. The president viewed the Vietnamese Communists as formidable enemies that could be brought to the bargaining table only after Washington had demonstrated its toughness.[27] Confronted with such necessities, but none demanding drastic responses, Kennedy followed the policy of "one more step" to lure the United States deeper into the quagmire. "In retrospect," Schlesinger concluded, "Vietnam is a triumph of the politics of inadvertence. We have achieved our present entanglement, not after due and deliberate consideration, but through a series of small decisions. . . . Each step in the deepening of the American commitment was reasonably regarded at the time as the last that would be necessary."[28]

Schlesinger's concept of inadvertence faced a serious challenge in the writings of Daniel Ellsberg, who understood from the Pentagon Papers what presumptions drove the country's continuing escalation in Vietnam. General Taylor expressed them in his report of 8 November 1961 following his trip to Southeast Asia. The real challenge facing the administration, he wrote, was whether the United States would "commit itself to the clear objective of preventing the fall of South Vietnam to Communism." Defense Secretary Robert S. McNamara and the Joint Chiefs of Staff added the following dire and uncompromisable proposition: "The fall of South Vietnam to Communism would lead to the fairly rapid extension of Communist control . . . in the rest of mainland Southeast Asia. . . . The strategic implications worldwide, particularly in the Orient, would be extremely serious."[29]

In attributing validity to that description of danger the administration left itself no choice but to move forward with a policy of military escalation with troop projections as early as 1961 exceeding 200,000 men. There was no policy of inadvertence, although Kennedy, to maximize his options and encourage the desired Communist response, limited the escalation to small increments. What mattered was not the nature of the escalation but its unending purpose: to protect the Saigon regime and the credibility of U.S. commitments elsewhere.[30] Not in 1961 or later could the administration regard any escalation as the last, but only the next step in the pursuit of the constant goal of denying victory to Vietnam's Communist forces. Leslie H. Gelb, who headed the Pentagon Papers project, and Richard K. Betts, in their book *The System Worked,* argue, like Ellsberg, that American presidents and those who advised them "did not stumble step-by-step into Vietnam, unaware of the quagmire."[31] They knew what they faced and what their uncompromising purpose in Vietnam would require of the country. They always anticipated the next step, knowing that it would come.

Saigon's declining capacity to stabilize the Vietnamese countryside offered Kennedy the choice of defeat, reform, or direct U.S. military involvement in Southeast Asia. Kennedy rejected the first alternative without embracing the third. With good reason he hoped to avoid an American war in Vietnam. McNamara reminded him that no reasonable U.S. involvement would tip the military scales in the region; the United States might become mired in a land war it could not win. Kennedy shared that pessimism and wondered whether the United States would be more successful than the French in winning the support of the villagers, so essential for success against guerrilla forces. The administration required a strategy that would bridge the gap between the goal of victory and the reality of a limited U.S. involvement. Kennedy found it in the political-military program of counterinsurgency. During the spring of 1961, the president prepared to increase the effectiveness of the anti-guerrilla activities in South Vietnam. To meet the guerrilla challenge, he advised Congress in March 1961 that the United States must organize "strong, highly mobile forces trained in this type of warfare, some of which must be deployed in forward areas."[32] Highly skilled and finely trained American units would be more than a match for any competing force, even in the jungles of Asia. Reflecting the activist spirit of Kennedy's Washington, counterinsurgency became fashionable, even faddish. In Vietnam, however, the special forces achieved little; Washington refused to move them against the guerrillas.[33]

In practice counterinsurgency assumed the form of the strategic hamlet program, instituted in March 1962 to insulate the peasants, with their resources, and thereby deprive the Vietcong guerrillas of their necessary base of supplies. Ngo Dinh Nhu, Diem's brother and political adviser, quickly emerged as the director of the strategic hamlet program. In April he adopted the successful Malayan model of counterinsurgency and the advice of Sir Robert Thompson, the British counterinsurgency expert who had devised it. Unfortunately South Vietnam possessed none of the sociological, political, and ethnic factors that had been crucial in Malaya's triumph over its guerrilla movement. Malaya had no common border with another Communist country. Most of its guerrillas were Chinese, and their support came only from a small minority of Chinese squatters who had nothing to lose but their illicitly acquired rice fields. South Vietnam's guerrillas were ethnically indistinguishable from the vast bulk of their country's population. Unlike their counterparts in Malaya, the Vietcong never lacked the demographic support required for survival. (Even without the means to survive, the 8,000 guerrillas in Malaya continued to hold off the more than 400,000 British, Australian, and Malayan forces opposing them.) Vietnamese peasants, closely tied to the land, deeply resented the effort to move them to more secure locations. Whereas strategic hamlets in Malaya often offered improved living conditions, the tight security measures required to render the strategic hamlets effective in South Vietnam managed to turn many of them into squalid prison camps without stopping Vietcong infiltration or preventing their occasional destruction by guerrilla forces. The hamlets were too porous to matter, but their large numbers permitted Saigon officials to boast of their success and thereby sustain Washington's official faith in Ngo Dinh Diem.[34]

Having rejected defeat and direct military action, Kennedy looked to the Saigon government to institute the reforms essential for its political and military success. He soon discovered, as did Eisenhower, that the U.S. objective in Southeast Asia—essentially South Vietnam's survival—granted its government incredible leverage in dealing with the United States. Vice President Lyndon Johnson's trip to South Vietnam in the summer of 1961 exposed Diem's unique control over the U.S. government. Despite Diem's obvious failures, Johnson reminded Kennedy, Washington had no choice but to support him. "The battle against communism," Johnson observed, "must be joined in Southeast Asia with strength and determination to achieve success there."[35] Robert Shaplen noted that by January 1962 the United States had given Diem everything he wanted with no assurance that his government would carry out any reforms.[36] With Washington's encouragement, Gen. Paul Harkins and Ambassador Frederick E. Nolting, Jr. reminded Diem of the American commitment to his success and repressed any official evidence of failure in the performance of South Vietnam's government or armed forces. Visiting spokesmen of the Kennedy administration reflected Saigon's resulting mood of optimism in their official reports.[37] Halberstam regarded McNamara's visits symbolic of Washington's refusal to deal with Saigon realistically. "He epitomized," wrote Halberstam, "booming American technological success, he scurried around Vietnam, looking for what he wanted to see; and he never saw or smelled nor felt what was really there, right in front of him." In a sense, Halberstam concluded, McNamara acted on knowledge which he himself created.[38] Thus he became caught up in the official optimism, promising after each trip the victory that always eluded him and the nation.

This combined effort to sustain a favorable image faced the endless distractions of reality as proclaimed by members of the press. Saigon faced a major challenge in early January 1963 when, at Ap Bac in the Mekong Delta, a contingent of the Army of South Vietnam (ARVN), equipped with armored personnel carriers and artillery, and supported by American planes, helicopters and advisers, surrounded a Vietcong battalion one fourth its size. After Saigon's forces had suffered heavy casualties with five American helicopters shot down and nine more damaged, they withdrew and permitted the Vietcong to escape.[39] Herring notes in *America's Longest War* that such correspondents as Halberstam of the *New York Times* and Neil Sheehan of United Press International, while not questioning American policies of containment, had become convinced that Diem's regime was politically and militarily ineffective.[40] Their reporting had become, by 1962, a matter of deep concern to both Harkins and Diem. Their confidence in Harkins's leadership was not enhanced when the general declared Ap Bac a victory for Saigon.

What occurred during and after the battle dominates Sheehan's noted volume on the war, *A Bright Shining Lie: John Paul Vann and America in Vietnam*. Lieutenant Colonel Vann had observed the battle of Ap Bac from his spotter plane and his taking command prevented a much greater ARVN defeat. After the battle he wrote a scathing report to Harkins on the ARVN's persistent refusal to engage the enemy. Harkins ignored the report, but Kennedy responded by sending a JCS commission under Gen. Victor Krulak to examine the war's status. Although the commission heard the negative evaluations of American field officers, its report praised the ARVN. Krulak accused Vann and his field staff of being unduly harsh. "Victory," said the report, "is now a hopeful prospect." Having failed to counter Harkins's defense of Diem's leadership and performance, Vann now revealed to Halberstam what he knew about the Vietcong—their strength and locations, the refusal of Saigon forces to face them, and Harkins's unwillingness to question Diem on the performance of his army. Early in March 1963 this information began to appear in the *New York Times* and led finally to Halberstam's book, *The Making of a Quagmire,* which won the Pulitzer Prize.[41] For Harkins, McNamara, and Secretary of State Dean Rusk, as Chester Cooper observed, Ap Bac was only an embarrassing trough in an upward-moving curve of progress in Vietnam.[42]

Nothing appeared to challenge Washington's strong ties to Diem until, in the summer of 1963, the South Vietnamese leader, with his brother Ngo Dinh Nhu, began to carry out a drastic repression of the Buddhists.[43] Writers such as Kahin, Sheehan, and Herring have examined American complicity in the overthrow and death of Diem and his brother in early November 1963. Their accounts agree that Henry Cabot Lodge, Jr., who succeeded Nolting as ambassador in August, as well as President Kennedy and much of the White House staff, found Saigon's behavior toward the Buddhists embarrassing and unacceptable. The Buddhists' self-immolation in the streets and Nhu's wife's remark that they were "barbecues" compounded the problem. U.S. policy was fixed, but much of Washington could no longer anticipate its final triumph with Diem. Lodge soon discovered a plot among South Vietnam's leading officers to overthrow the Diem regime. Lodge, supported by

Kennedy and his top advisers, encouraged Diem's opponents by assuring them that the United States would do nothing to prevent the coup, but the coup itself was planned and executed by Vietnamese officers.[44] Nolting, in Washington, defended Diem to the end.[45] Three weeks later Kennedy was also assassinated.

As the American effort in Vietnam continued to falter, Kennedy, according to staffer Kenneth O'Donnell, responded favorably to Senator Mike Mansfield's admonitions that the United States should withdraw from Vietnam's civil conflict. In the spring of 1963, O'Donnell recalled, Kennedy informed Mansfield that after his reelection he would risk attacks on his patriotism and order a complete withdrawal of American forces from Vietnam.[46] Kennedy no less than Eisenhower had learned the painful lesson embodied in Truman's alleged "loss of China." Fighting on the Asian mainland had its political risks, but they were far less consequential than what might ensue from another Communist victory in Asia. For Ellsberg the supposition that it was acceptable to leave Vietnam to its fate in 1965 but not in 1963 suggested that the president regarded Vietnam less important than his own political career.[47] To the end Kennedy's commitment to the defense of South Vietnam remained firm. Herring questioned the president's judgment of that country's importance:

> Kennedy and most of his advisers accepted, without critical analysis, the assumption that a non-Communist Vietnam was vital to America's global interests, and their rhetoric in fact strengthened the hold of that assumption. . . . [Kennedy] reacted to crises and improvised responses on a day-to-day basis, seldom examining the implication of his actions. Nevertheless, his cautious, middle course significantly enlarged the American role and commitment in Vietnam, and with the coup, the United States assumed direct responsibility for the South Vietnamese government.[48]

Sheehan observed that Kennedy, despite the limited number of American servicemen in South Vietnam in November 1963, had created an American war in Asia. The president, he wrote, "had raised the Stars and Stripes and shed blood and enveloped the protection and self-esteem of the United States."[49] Kennedy bequeathed to Lyndon Johnson a commitment to Southeast Asia far more pervading and dangerous than the one he had inherited from Eisenhower.

Johnson entered office confronting a new Vietnam crisis. After Ap Bac the Vietcong had spent ten months preparing for the unremitting offensive they launched in November. Outposts fell by the dozens. The strategic hamlet program, lauded by Harkins and Nolting, as well as Washington officials, as the counterinsurgency program that assured the destruction of South Vietnam's guerrillas, ceased to exist. Saigon's forces entered the countryside only at a heavy price.[50] At a conference on 20 November, McNamara endorsed a program proposed by Krulak designed to control the guerrilla activity in the South by exerting military and psychological pressure on the North. By attacking North Vietnam directly, American officials hoped to frighten Hanoi into abandoning the Vietcong and terminating its infiltration of the South. Johnson shared that aggressive and optimistic mood, no more willing than Kennedy to become the first American president to lose a war.[51] Johnson accepted the recommendation of the 20 November conference to inaugurate a clandestine war against North Vietnam. That program, Operation Plan 34A, went into effect on 1 February 1964 with the bombardment and destruction of radar sites, coastal installations, rail and highway bridges. Many scholars find no justification for the notion that the new offensive would stabilize the Saigon government or increase its prospects for survival.[52] Nor would it, they agree, intimidate the North.

Compelled to pursue U.S. purposes in Vietnam through whatever regime existed in Saigon, American leaders readily accepted the government of Gen. Duong Van Minh as a necessity. In January 1964 a military junta, headed by Gen. Nguyen Khanh, overthrew the Minh government to inaugurate a brief period of even greater optimism for the future of South Vietnam. On 26 March McNamara declared that General Khanh, with his grasp of the problems facing his country, would in time dispose of the Communists. That success, Theodore Draper noted in *The Abuse of Power,* appeared to require no more than a limited U.S. military commitment. Still there existed in Washington a growing conviction that the fundamental challenge facing Saigon lay not in the guerrillas of the South but in the force exerted by Northern infiltration, demanding a response far more effective than Operation Plan 34A.[53] As early as May 1964, Ambassador Lodge, National Security Adviser McGeorge Bundy, and the Joint Chiefs of Staff advocated a major bombing campaign against North Vietnamese targets to strengthen the Saigon government. On 10 June a group of senior advisers, led by McGeorge Bundy and his brother, William, assistant secretary of state for Far Eastern affairs, prepared a draft seeking a congressional resolution in support of an air or ground war in Asia.[54] Operation Plan 34A created the occasion for such a resolution in early August when it provoked the Tonkin Gulf incident. On 4 August the president ordered retaliatory air strikes on North Vietnamese torpedo boat bases and storage tank depots. Three days later, by a vote of 88 to 2, the Senate authorized the president "to take all necessary measures to repel any armed attack against the forces of the United States and to prevent further aggression."[55] The resolution gave the president enormous latitude in responding to enemy action in Southeast Asia.

Meanwhile the presidential campaign brought Lodge back to the United States and permitted the president to send Maxwell Taylor to Saigon as the new ambassador. Whatever the troubling concerns of many citizens regarding American intentions in Southeast Asia, as Draper observes, the president throughout his campaign promised to keep the nation out of an Asian land war. In New York on 12 August, he declared that "some others are eager to enlarge the conflict. They call upon us to supply American boys to do the job that Asian boys should do. They ask us to take reckless action which might risk the lives of millions. . . . [S]uch action would offer no solution at all to the real problem of Vietnam." Furthermore, he assured a Texas audience on 29 August that "I have had advice to load our planes with bombs and to drop them on certain areas that I think would enlarge the war

. . . and result in our committing a good many American boys to fighting a war that I think ought to be fought by the boys of Asia." Still in a major campaign speech in Manchester, New Hampshire, in late September, the president reminded the nation that American goals in Southeast Asia had not changed and the United States could not leave until the North Vietnamese and Chinese had been taught to leave their neighbors alone.[56]

During the summer of 1964, General Khanh, conscious of the dangers his government faced, called for bombing the North. Ambassador Taylor advised him confidentially that the United States could not embrace such a program during the presidential campaign. But on 15 August William Bundy acknowledged the United States might find it necessary to broaden the war if North Vietnam did not stop its attacks on the South.[57] The CIA, as Loren Baritz notes, continued to issue pessimistic reports on the absence of leadership and motivation in the South Vietnamese army, as the pressures for bombing continued to mount.[58] Walt W. Rostow, head of the State Department's Policy Planning Staff, argued that North Vietnam, with its industrial base, was vulnerable to air attacks. Indeed, in late August the president, using the Tonkin Gulf Resolution as a pretext, ordered a series of bombing raids on the North Vietnamese to demonstrate his willingness to escalate the penalties should Hanoi persist in its efforts to undermine the Saigon government. Then on 29 September William Bundy told a Tokyo audience: "Expansion of the war outside South Vietnam, while not a course we want to seek, could be forced upon us by the increased pressures of the Communists, including the rising scale of infiltration." As Draper notes, several days later James Reston of the *New York Times* reported that the administration was merely seeking an excuse to launch a bombing campaign against the North. On 1 December, during one of Taylor's visits to Washington, a top-level meeting at the White House adopted a bombing strategy to persuade Hanoi to stop its support of Saigon's enemies in the South.[59]

Following his inaugural in January 1965, President Johnson faced ever-narrowing choices in Vietnam. Writers such as Under Secretary of State George Ball, Kahin, Baritz, Berman, and others noted the president's continuing reluctance to order bombing.[60] But they agree as well that he was even more reluctant to accept the collapse of the Saigon government. As Johnson himself explained: "There would follow in this country an endless national debate—a mean and destructive debate— that would shatter my Presidency, kill my administration, and damage our democracy."[61] Still it was not clear how the administration could achieve the necessary public support for an escalating intervention on behalf of a government that was not only ineffectual but also increasingly antiwar and anti-American. McNamara and McGeorge Bundy met the challenge by advocating sustained bombing of the North as the necessary prelude to the establishment of a viable government in Saigon. For them the United States required no more than Saigon's armed forces as a base for projecting its power. The political base would emerge as the result of the promising atmosphere created by the bombing. George Ball examined this new rationale for bombing the North:

I have always marveled at the way ingenious men can, when they wish, turn logic upside down, and I was not surprised when my colleagues interpreted the crumbling of the South Vietnamese government, the Viet Cong's increasing success, and a series of defeats of South Vietnamese units not as proving that we should cut our losses and get out, but rather that we must promptly begin bombing to stiffen the resolve of the corrupt South Vietnamese government. It was classic bureaucratic casuistry. A faulty rationalization was improvised to obscure the painful reality that America could arrest the galloping deterioration of its position only by the surgery of extrication.[62]

Armed with a rationale for bombing, the president still hesitated to order it. Rather, he sent McGeorge Bundy on a special mission to Saigon. Both James Thomson and Chester Cooper, as insiders, viewed the mission as evidence of Johnson's doubts regarding the wisdom of a bombing campaign without a strong government in Saigon.[63] Before Bundy could return to Washington, Vietcong soldiers, on 7 February 1965, attacked a U.S. helicopter base at Pleiku in the central highlands, killing 8 Americans and wounding 126. This was, Kahin notes, only one of ten Vietcong attacks that day, and not the largest. The president retaliated immediately with a limited bombing of North Vietnamese targets. At a meeting on 8 February, Bundy presented the final rationale for an air war against the North: "The situation in Vietnam is deteriorating, and without new U.S. action defeat appears inevitable. . . . The stakes in Vietnam are extremely high. The American investment is very large, the American responsibility is a fact of life. . . . The international prestige of the United States, and a substantial part of our influence, are directly at risk in Vietnam." He argued that sustained reprisal through air and naval action would improve the climate in Saigon by effecting "a sharp immediate increase in optimism in the South among all articulate groups. . . . This favorable reaction should offer opportunity for increased American influence in pressing for a more effective government."[64]

On 13 February the president, accepting Bundy's rationale, authorized Rolling Thunder, a program of sustained bombing, and instructed Taylor to seek Saigon's approval. Whether the bombing would strengthen the South Vietnamese government and broaden its political base depended on the nature of that government. Bundy continued to favor the faltering Khanh regime, but Taylor assured Vietnamese officers who favored Rolling Thunder, especially the trio of Nguyen Cao Ky, Nguyen Van Thieu, and Nguyen Bao Tri, that the United States no longer favored Khanh. With the backing of Taylor and Gen. William Westmoreland, who had succeeded Harkins, Ky prevailed upon the Armed Forces Council to remove Khanh as commander in chief. Ky and Thieu now emerged as South Vietnam's most powerful public figures. On 1 March the South Vietnamese government announced its approval of the air war against the North; one day later American planes launched their first sustained attack. In June Thieu and Ky assumed command of Saigon's new military government, with Thieu as chief of state and Ky as prime minister. Senator Mansfield reminded Johnson that the United States no longer dealt in Vietnam "with anyone who represents anybody in a political sense." Ky and Thieu,

Kahin observes, acknowledged their lack of public support and their powerlessness to compete politically with the Communist-led National Liberation Front except under wartime conditions. Within days it became clear that Rolling Thunder, for Thomson an act of desperation, would achieve none of its objectives.[65]

Washington's decision to enter an open war against North Vietnam required a new justification. During the autumn of 1964 spokesmen of the Johnson administration defined the challenge of Southeast Asia, like that of Korea, as one of Northern aggression against an independent South Vietnam. The president himself proclaimed that view in an address on 14 October: "With our help, the people of South Vietnam can defeat Communist aggression."[66] To prove that contention the administration, on 27 February 1965, published a White Paper entitled *Aggression from the North: The Record of North Viet-Nam's Campaign to Conquer South Viet-Nam.* Secretary Rusk took up the theme, asserting before public audiences and congressional committees that "small and large nations have a right to live without being molested by their neighbors." The United States would leave Southeast Asia when North Vietnam stopped its aggression.[67] William J. Duiker and other scholars agree that North Vietnamese units moved into the South in late 1963 and regular units arrived in October 1964. Guenter Lewy asserts that "the initial escalation, through the introduction of North Vietnamese combat forces . . . was carried out by the Communists, well before the American decision to bomb North Vietnam."[68] Whether the presence of North Vietnamese forces in the South constituted international aggression depended on conflicting perceptions of the historic legitimacy of the state of South Vietnam, but for Lewy, Norman Podhoretz, William V. O'Brien, Whittle Johnston, and others North Vietnam had unleashed aggressive war against the independent state of South Vietnam and thereby had provided the United States ample justification to repel the aggression and defend the rule of law.[69] For such critics as Kahin, however, the White Paper was designed less to portray the evidence of Northern aggression than to justify the bombing.[70]

Kahin, Karnow, Herring, Berman, Gelb and Betts dwell at length on Johnson's critical decision to dispatch ground forces to South Vietnam. Even before Rolling Thunder, Westmoreland had sought troops to provide security for all U.S. facilities and installations in South Vietnam. On 8 March two Marine battalions landed at Danang. Convinced now that Rolling Thunder would not cripple North Vietnam's fighting capacity or stop the infiltration into the South, the joint chiefs, supported by Westmoreland, requested two divisions for operations against the Vietcong.[71] Taylor argued for an expanded air war, but no ground forces; CIA Director John McCone warned against any further military escalation. McNamara advocated a greater U.S. military involvement but acknowledged there were risks. Nevertheless, on 1 July he assured the president that the American public would support this course of action because it was "a combined military-political program designed and likely to bring about a favorable solution to the Vietnam problem."[72] On 13 July John T. McNaughton, assistant secretary of defense, reminded the administration, as he had earlier, that the *reputation* of the United States as guarantor was at stake.[73] Johnson, still unconvinced, turned to outside advice, creating a Vietnam panel of Gen. Omar Bradley, Roswell Gilpatric, George Kistiakowsky, Arthur Larson, and John J. McCloy. Bundy overwhelmed the panel. Except for Larson, Bundy wrote, the panel members agreed with him that the stakes were high and Vietnam was a test case for wars of national liberation.[74]

Still troubled by the continuing pleas for escalation, Johnson, in mid-July, sent McNamara to confer with Taylor, Westmoreland, Thieu, and Ky in Saigon. Thieu dwelt on his country's weakness and the need for 200,000 U.S. troops. McNamara, backed by the nation's military leaders in the Pacific theater, now advocated heavy increases in American personnel, helicopters, air squadrons, and advisory units to assure the final success of the Saigon government.[75] Again the president refused to accept such a recommendation. On 21 July, and for the following week, all the president's senior civilian and military advisers met in Washington and Camp David to resolve the issue of military escalation. Ball, who opposed the sending of ground forces, argued that a long, protracted war in Vietnam would demonstrate the weakness, not the strength, of the United States. American prudence, not American power, he said, was being tested in Vietnam. Clark Clifford, noted Democratic adviser to presidents, shared Ball's opposition to an American war in Southeast Asia and later observed that a solid phalanx of advice from the main advisers "accepted the domino theory without question and with it the mission to help the South Vietnamese save themselves from Communist aggression."[76]

At Camp David on 25 July, during the final and most critical meeting of Johnson's top advisers, Clifford again warned against escalation and argued that the administration should be probing for a way to leave Vietnam. The president produced a letter from Mansfield which insisted that Vietnam involved no high principle and that the task of the United States was to avoid being thrown out of Vietnam under fire. Such warnings scarcely influenced the decision of 27 July to send additional forces to Southeast Asia. The real issue, Draper notes, was not northern infiltration but the near-collapse of the Saigon regime.[77] At a news conference on the following day the president announced an immediate increase in U.S. fighting strength in Vietnam from 75,000 to 125,000, with additional forces as required. Should the United States be driven from the field in Vietnam, he warned, no nation again could ever trust American promises. But he added, "We do not want an expanding struggle with consequences that no one can perceive."[78] "The war was now entirely America's war," wrote Baritz, "and the president intended to win it without a general mobilization, and without informing either the Congress or the public." For Berman the troubling question was the process by which the administration reached its decision. "What better way to lead the nation into war," he wrote, "than to let American citizens believe that the experts were carefully deliberating on all available policy options."[79]

Throughout the critical months of decision, George Ball challenged the assumptions of U.S. Vietnam policy, troubled, as was James Thomson, by the persistent refusal of official Washington to reexamine the basis of that policy. Ball, like

Thomson, viewed Rolling Thunder as an act of desperation with no chance of success. He recorded his reactions to that decision: "What we charitably referred to as a government in Saigon was falling apart, yet we had to bomb the North as a form of political therapy. . . . Such a tortuous argument was . . . the last resort of those who believed we could not withdraw from Vietnam without humiliation." It was fear of humiliation that gave Saigon its incredible power over Washington, placing the United States, wrote Ball, on the verge of becoming a "puppet of our puppet." Like his predecessors, Johnson became a hostage to Vietnam. Ball sent a memorandum to the president on 18 June, warning that the United States would lose even if it committed a half million men to Vietnam. Then in another memorandum of 1 July, he summarized his arguments for a negotiated settlement and an American withdrawal:

> The South Vietnamese are losing the war to the Viet Cong. No one can assure you that we can beat the Viet Cong or even force them to the conference table on our terms no matter how many hundred thousand *white foreign* (US) troops we deploy. . . . The decision you face now, therefore, is crucial. Once large numbers of US troops are committed to direct combat they will begin to take heavy casualties in a war they are ill-equipped to fight in a non-cooperative if not downright hostile countryside. Once we suffer large casualties we will have started a well-nigh irreversible process. Our involvement will be so great that we cannot—without national humiliation—stop short of achieving our complete objectives. *Of the two possibilities I think humiliation would be more likely than the achievement of our objectives—even after we had paid terrible costs.*[80]

Washington assumed optimistically that American military escalation would soon compel Hanoi's compliance with U.S. demands. To render a conventional struggle effective, William Kaufman observes, requires the capacity to convince the enemy that war at any level would cost his country far more than it would the United States.[81] After 1960 two authors, Thomas Schelling and Herman Kahn, attempted to refine the theory of deterrence and the effective use of force. For Schelling the distinguishing element in coercive war was "the direct exercise of the power to hurt, applied as coercive pressure, intended to create for the enemy the prospect of cumulative losses that were more than the local war was worth, more unattractive than concession, compromise, or limited capitulation."[82] Wallace J. Thies, in his perceptive book, *When Governments Collide,* observes that the Johnson administration not only embodied these requirements in Rolling Thunder, but also presumed Hanoi understood the essential fact, underscored by Schelling, that the United States possessed unspent capacity to assure ever greater damage in the future.[83] Yet it was apparent that North Vietnam was not being moved by the bombing. In setting its course of escalation, the administration overlooked two inescapable factors—what was it asking of Hanoi and what were the relative economic and strategic interests of the United States and North Vietnam in Southeast Asia?[84]

What the United States demanded of Hanoi was precise and non-negotiable. It rested on deeply held suppositions of danger that conformed to the imagery of falling dominoes, rendering the conflict in Southeast Asia only part of a wider pattern of aggression. The president restated the requirements of containment in Asia in his noted Baltimore address of 7 April 1965: "Our objective is the independence of South Vietnam, and its freedom from attack. We want nothing for ourselves—only that the people of South Vietnam be allowed to guide their country in their own way."[85] The president did not offer negotiations; there was nothing to negotiate. In subsequent statements members of the administration repeated these minimum demands, inviting Hanoi to stop its aggression and accept the independence of South Vietnam.[86] Realist critics inside and outside the administration warned that such inflexible demands would lead to an interminable war. Thomson complained to Bundy on 19 February that the administration had "failed to do any significant exploration of Hanoi's actual private terms for a settlement." Nor had Washington offered any negotiable terms of its own. Ball reminded his colleagues that American success in Vietnam, by their definition, required Hanoi's unconditional surrender. There would be no settlement, he declared, until the administration receded from its publicly stated aims. Ball advised negotiations for a tactical withdrawal, even one that might enable Hanoi to prevail in the end.[87] Any other course, he predicted, would be worse.

Writers whose analyses anticipated the failure of coercion acknowledged the infinite resiliency and determination of North Vietnam's leadership. Those in Hanoi who defined their country's goals, as Thies examines at length, had invested a full quarter-century or more in their struggle for the independence and unification of Vietnam.[88] North Vietnamese Premier Pham Van Dong proclaimed Hanoi's minimum objectives in April 1965: "the peaceful reunification of Vietnam is to be settled by the Vietnamese people in both zones, without any foreign interference."[89] No one in Washington could estimate what level of destruction would prompt Hanoi to accept a settlement that failed to ratify that purpose. Those who had studied North Vietnam reminded the administration that it would always underestimate the strength and staying power of the enemy. Rolling Thunder would never convince Hanoi it faced the choice between surrender and doom; bombing would never seriously impede the Vietcong in the South or infiltration from the North. From the beginning Hanoi recognized its ultimate advantage—the United States, whatever its official rhetoric, had no more than a limited interest in the war.[90] This enabled the North Vietnamese to dwell less on objectives than on the nature and timing of their counterstrategies.

Even as Washington unleashed an American war in Southeast Asia it accepted constraints in the use of force that denied the seriousness of its intentions. From the outset the Johnson administration adopted a strategy, not for military victory, but for the avoidance of defeat—what Berman calls the strategy of stalemate. The president assured his Baltimore audience that the United States would do only what was necessary to sustain South Vietnam's integrity. From the public he wanted ample support to underwrite the war effort, but not enough to endanger his purpose of fighting a limited war. During the spring of 1965, the president achieved an astonishing political triumph as Congress passed measure after measure of his Great Society program. He did not wish to see that program die in the jungles of Southeast Asia. Nor did he desire to press the offensive to the point of inviting direct Soviet or Chinese involvement. Having embarked on an escalating war without a formal declaration, the president had little choice but to curtail the war's expenditures.[91] State Department lawyers perfected their case that the president's wartime powers as commander in chief of the armed forces eliminated the constitutionality of any congressional restraints.[92]

Johnson's domestic strategy worked. His purpose of defending South Vietnam at minimum cost won the support of Congress, which voted the necessary funds, as well as the American public.[93] Washington supplied South Vietnam with men and weapons in abundance, but even with larger American forces in the field it never prepared a strategy to bring Hanoi to terms. Nor did the administration, as Thies, Gelb, and Betts conclude, coordinate the considerable force it expended with any effort to further genuine negotiations.[94] All this mattered little. American bombing was designed to achieve capitulation, not negotiation. Hanoi's resistance continued to puzzle American officials. General Taylor complained, "one likes to feel able to count on the rationality and good sense of a dangerous opponent." The administration assumed that the enemy would capitulate when the destruction reached a reasonable level. To assure that conclusion it fought the air war with gradually diminishing restraint until the total tonnage dropped on Vietnamese targets, North and South, exceeded by 50 percent all the bombs dropped in World War II. The effort failed, writes Thies, because Washington, whatever the damage it inflicted, could not change Hanoi's motives and intentions.[95]

By 1967 Johnson's escalating war in Vietnam collided with an escalating antiwar movement in the United States as students, scholars, journalists, generals of distinction, and key members of Congress became active critics.[96] Like others among the war's opponents, John Kenneth Galbraith and George F. Kennan denied the United States had any vital interests in Southeast Asia and should withdraw as quickly as possible. By the late fall of 1967 the administration faced a press that denied any progress in the war. The president, supported by his advisers and cabinet members, launched a counterattack, not only reexplaining the war but also challenging the argument that the U.S. effort was not succeeding.[97] To discount the evidences of failure pouring out of Saigon, the president called Ambassador Ellsworth Bunker, Taylor's successor in Saigon, and General Westmoreland to Washington to assure the nation that the allied forces in Vietnam were achieving steady progress in the war. Westmoreland noted confidently that "whereas in 1965 the enemy was winning, today he is certainly losing." With U.S. forces standing at a half million, he said, "we have reached the important point where the end begins to come into view."[98]

Official assurances of success no longer impressed Pentagon spokesmen. By late 1967 McNamara himself had become totally disillusioned with the war, convinced that the bombing would not stop Hanoi even while the destruction created lasting enemies for the United States. McNamara's assistant, Townsend Hoopes, in his book, *The Limits of Intervention,* questioned the administration's continued refusal to lower its expectations in a losing cause.[99] Still Washington predicted Hanoi would negotiate when it discovered that it could not win. Halberstam observed that Rostow, now national security adviser, had become the administration's chief dispenser of optimism. In the White House basement his aides pulled the reports from Saigon, segregating the favorable ones to prove that the war was going well—indeed, about to be won.[100] This official optimism mounted until late January 1968 when Rostow informed newsmen in his White House office that captured documents foretold the impending collapse of the enemy in Vietnam.

Suddenly on 31 January the Tet Offensive burst like a bombshell over South Vietnam. American and ARVN casualties were considerable; those of the Vietcong and North Vietnamese forces far more so. Reports of death, chaos, and destruction on television and in the press revealed the horrors of the war and destroyed any illusion the United States had the war well in hand.[101] Many correspondents covering Tet regarded it as a major defeat for the United States and its allies. Walter Cronkite of CBS exemplified this conclusion when he declared: "It is increasingly clear to this reporter that the only rational way out . . . would be to negotiate, not as victors, but as an honorable people."[102] Meanwhile officials and pro-administration members of the press argued that the Communist offensive had been a military disaster. General Westmoreland proclaimed that the enemy had suffered defeat. Don Oberdorfer, in his book *Tet!,* accepted that conclusion: "Tens of thousands of the most dedicated and experienced fighters emerged from the jungles and forests of the countryside only to meet a deadly rain of fire and steel within the cities. The Vietcong lost the best of a generation of resistance fighters." Peter Braestrup's extensive study of media coverage of Tet, *Big Story,* concluded that information available to correspondents demonstrated Tet went badly for the Vietcong, fairly well destroying it as a fighting force. He attributed the continuing misrepresentations in the press to the bias of reporters who had become disillusioned with the war.[103]

If the Tet Offensive, even the adverse reporting of it, brought nothing new to light regarding the war's costs and ineffectiveness, why did it create a crisis in official policy? For Oberdorfer, the administration produced its own dilemma by insisting during previous weeks that the United States stood on the verge of victory. It was the contrast between such promises and the violence of Tet that magnified the public's doubts.[104] Hoopes explained the adverse reaction of many top Pentagon officials: "One thing was clear to us all: the Tet Offensive was the eloquent counterpoint to the effusive optimism of November. It showed conclusively that the U.S. did not in fact control the situation, that it was not in fact winning, that the enemy retained enormous strength and vitality—certainly enough to extinguish the notion of a clear-cut allied victory in the minds of all objective men."[105]

When the president called an advisory group, the "Wise Men," to the White

House for a briefing on Tet, he discovered that a majority, including Dean Acheson, favored disengagement from Vietnam. So did Clark Clifford, his new secretary of defense. For Braestrup, in retrospect, the widespread loss of confidence in the days after Tet focused on the president more than the war. Johnson's popularity continued to disintegrate until, on 31 March, he announced his decision to withdraw from the 1968 presidential race and open truce negotiations with Hanoi.[106] With that decision the United States began its long retreat from Vietnam. Still, for Johnson, even a negotiated escape from the Vietnam War proved elusive. The tedious diplomatic maneuvering of 1968 finally brought all Vietnam contestants to the table in Paris, but it offered no promise of success. Hanoi had demonstrated that four years of bombing had not diminished its confidence or modified its goals.

In January 1969 Richard Nixon inherited a disastrous policy in Vietnam without a guiding strategy for victory or withdrawal. He and his national security adviser, Henry A. Kissinger, understood well the war's death and anguish, as well as the public dismay over an engagement that mocked every effort to end it. No less than others, they regarded the American escalation of the Johnson years a tragic blunder; friends reminded the new president that the war belonged to the Democrats. Still Nixon and Kissinger believed that a great nation had no choice but to maintain even a mistaken commitment. "However we got into Vietnam, whatever the judgment of our actions," Kissinger warned, "ending the war honorably is essential for the peace of the world. Any other solution may unloose forces that would complicate prospects for international order."[107] Kissinger explained further in his memoir, *White House Years,* that "we had to remember that scores of countries and millions of people relied for their security on our willingness to stand by allies." The United States could not morally abandon a small ally merely to obtain respite for itself. "It seemed to me important," he concluded, "for America not to be humiliated, not to be shattered, but to leave [the war] . . . with dignity and self-respect."[108]

Nixon was determined to achieve peace in Vietnam without losing. Kissinger had outlined a plan for disengagement without defeat in the January 1969 issue of *Foreign Affairs.* His proposal began with a two-track formula, one seeking a military truce, the other a political settlement for South Vietnam. The former required success on the battlefield; the second, Saigon's willingness to broaden its base so it might meet the Communist political challenge more effectively.[109] For Kissinger the dual approach presaged a rapid and honorable American withdrawal. "Give us six months," he told a group of Quaker critics, "and if we haven't ended the war by then, you can come back and tear down the White House fence."[110] Why Kissinger's approach to a Vietnam solution would fail was clear as early as January 1969 when Nixon dispatched Henry Cabot Lodge to Paris and instructed him to call for a military withdrawal of all U.S. and North Vietnamese forces from South Vietnam. Washington hoped thereby to enable the Vietnamese to negotiate a political settlement. But Saigon denied that the negotiators in Paris had any right even to discuss

South Vietnam's political future. Unfortunately, if Saigon would concede its enemies no opportunity to gain power by political or diplomatic means, Hanoi and its allies in the South had no choice but to accept a settlement dictated by Saigon or continue the struggle. Hanoi warned Washington that it would never recognize the Saigon government or American military superiority on the battlefield.

During February Kissinger received a massive bureaucratic report on Vietnam revealing almost total disagreement and confusion within the government on every aspect of the American involvement.[111] Still Nixon's Washington, caught in a sinking tragedy, soon proclaimed a new strategy to end the war honorably. It began with plans for a broader, more ruthless bombing of enemy targets. As early as 18 March the president launched Operation Breakfast, a massive secret bombing of North Vietnamese supply lines and sanctuaries in Cambodia.[112] The second innovation in the Nixon strategy took form in March when Defense Secretary Melvin Laird informed Congress that the United States would increase the fighting capacity of the South Vietnamese armed forces beyond the levels contemplated in 1968 by the previous administration. Laird coined the term "Vietnamization." Whereas Johnson had sought to prepare Saigon to cope with internal insurgency after the achievement of peace, Nixon ordered the creation of South Vietnamese combat forces capable of replacing Americans in the continuing war itself.[113] To George Ball, Nixon and Kissinger, apparently unmindful of either the limits of bombing or the nature of the enemy, were doomed to repeat Johnson's mistakes: "Kissinger's initial assessment of our Vietnam prospects sounded as though he had been absent on Mars during the preceding three years. . . . By dealing North Vietnam some 'brutal blows' we could, he was confident, force it to make the kinds of concessions that would secure peace. . . . It was the McNamara quantitative approach all over again."[114]

Nixon's withdrawal policy ruled out any strategy for victory but in no way diminished his confidence that he could, in time, coax Hanoi into an agreement that would protect the interests and survival of South Vietnam. Even his withdrawal policy, he believed, would further successful negotiations by demonstrating to Hanoi that the United States was serious about a diplomatic settlement. At a press conference on 26 September, Nixon advised newsmen: "Once the enemy recognizes that it is not going to win its objectives by waiting us, then the enemy will negotiate and we will end this war before the end of 1970."[115] Kissinger records that he discovered in his first diplomatic initiative of late 1969 that Hanoi would not retreat from its goal of establishing a coalition government in Saigon, one without Thieu and Ky and composed of Communist elements as well as remnants of the old Saigon regime. Hanoi, moreover, demanded the complete withdrawal of all U.S. and allied forces from Vietnam. Kissinger explained his failure, then and later, to come to terms with Xuan Thuy, then North Vietnamese negotiator:

> Hanoi . . . continued to insist that the United States establish a new government under conditions in which the non-Communist side would be made impotent by the withdrawal of the American forces and demoralized by the removal of its

leadership. If the United States had the effrontery to withdraw without bringing about such a political upheaval, the war would go on and our prisoners would remain. Over the years we moved from position to position, from mutual to unilateral withdrawal, from residual forces to complete departure. But Hanoi never budged. We could have neither peace nor our prisoners until we achieved what Hanoi apparently no longer trusted itself to accomplish: the overthrow of our ally. . . . This seemed to us an act of dishonor that would mortgage America's international position for a long time to come. Our refusal to overthrow an allied government remained the single and crucial issue that deadlocked all negotiation until October 8, 1972, when Hanoi withdrew the demand.[116]

Nixon's success in continuing the war could not hide its futility. In launching the Cambodian incursion in May 1970, the president declared the action indispensable for the success of Vietnamization, the achievement of a negotiated peace, and the protection of American prestige. "It is not our power," he said, "but our will and character that is being tested tonight. . . . If we fail to meet this challenge all other nations will be on notice that despite its overwhelming power the United States, when a real crisis comes, will be found wanting."[117] Beyond the destruction of food and munitions, the gains from the Cambodian operation and the subsequent Operation Lam Son 719 in Laos were uncertain. It brought no victories for Vietnamization or negotiation. Nor did it inhibit the expansion of the antiwar movement.[118] Kissinger described the administration's dilemma:

We could not end [the war] on terms acceptable to Hanoi without jeopardizing everything else we were doing abroad; we could not pursue it to a decisive military result without risking all cohesion at home. So we navigated between conflicting necessities: holding out hope to our citizens that there would be an end, but posing sufficient risk to Hanoi to induce a settlement compatible with our international responsibilities and our national honor.[119]

Throughout 1971 administration officials proclaimed the triumphs of American bombing and Vietnamization. In his annual foreign policy report of February 1972, the president boasted, "As our role has diminished, South Vietnam has been able increasingly to meet its own defense needs and provide growing security to its people."[120] Then came the enemy's devastating 1972 Easter Offensive when ARVN troops could only hold against the advancing North Vietnamese with the aid of massive U.S. air strikes.

Suddenly the balancing act seemed to pay off in the long negotiations that followed Linebacker I, the heavy bombing campaign designed to counter the enemy's spring offensive. On 8 October Kissinger presented his final peace plan to North Vietnamese negotiator Le Duc Tho in Paris. The United States would withdraw its ground forces from Vietnam, but would continue to supply the South Vietnamese army. Hanoi, in exchange, would release all American prisoners of war. There would be a National Council of Reconciliation with Communist representation, but the Thieu regime would remain in place. So would the North Vietnamese armed forces. Le Duc Tho accepted the formula; formal signings would come on 31 October. Kissinger claimed a diplomatic victory because Hanoi had apparently dropped its demand for a coalition government. Nixon viewed the terms as "a complete capitulation by the enemy." But Kissinger also had made a major concession. He had failed to secure North Vietnam's military withdrawal from the South. Le Duc Tho argued that South Vietnam was not a foreign country; withdrawal, therefore, would have been synonymous with total surrender.[121]

Thieu had veto power over the settlement and was determined to use it. He saw clearly that the truce agreement threatened his country's very existence. It gave North Vietnam the right to keep 150,000 troops in the South. Communist membership in the National Council of Reconciliation, he predicted, meant a coalition government, the issue on which Washington and Saigon had always stood firm. Thieu demanded the total withdrawal of North Vietnamese forces and the elimination of the national council. Kissinger explained Thieu's disappointing behavior:

> We failed early enough to grasp that Thieu's real objection was not to the terms but to the fact of *any* compromise. Conflict between us and Thieu was built into the termination of the war on any terms less than Hanoi's total surrender. By definition sovereignty cannot be divided. Any outcome that left Thieu in less than total control of his entire territory was therefore for him a setback.[122]

Nixon knew he could not extract the concessions Thieu demanded from Hanoi. Unwilling to reject what Hanoi had accepted, Nixon promised Thieu on 14 November: "You have my absolute assurance that if Hanoi fails to abide by the terms of the agreement, it is my intention to take swift and severe retaliatory action."[123] Still Nixon could not prevent Thieu from demanding so many modifications in the October draft that the North Vietnamese broke off the negotiations. In one final effort to bring Hanoi to terms, Nixon, on 18 December, launched Linebacker II, the most devastating air attack of the war.[124]

Following the bombing halt on 29 December, Kissinger resumed his negotiations with the North Vietnamese while Nixon repeated his earlier guarantees to Thieu. Nixon addressed Thieu on 5 January: "Should you decide, and I trust you will, to go with us, you have my assurance . . . that we will respond with full force should the settlement be violated by North Vietnam."[125] The revised draft of 13 January 1973, granted the United States greater leeway in supporting Saigon, restricted the power of the national council, and reaffirmed the creation of a demilitarized zone. Kissinger believed the changes to be a gain for Saigon. Others wondered why the president would cause so much death and destruction merely to improve some phraseology in an empty document.[126] Nixon warned Thieu that he had no choice but to accept the Kissinger draft; the American war in Vietnam was over. Thieu, still doubtful of his future, accepted Nixon's guarantees and acceded to U.S. pressure but only at the very last moment.[127] On 27 January the four Vietnam belligerents signed the cease-fire agreement for Vietnam. Nixon could scarcely conceal his resentment toward editors and congressmen who refused to praise his "peace with honor." Loren Baritz spoke for many, stating that "the nation could not celebrate the war's end. . . . Too much death, and too much absurdity. Too many lies. Too much hatred on all sides. There was no victory to celebrate."[128] Nor did the cease-fire resolve the great debate within the United States. Unfortunately, writes Walter H. Capps in *The Unfinished War,* "neither side could claim victory or was satisfied, yet neither would acknowledge defeat. Indeed, neither was quite sure what the outcome was."[129]

Scholars have agreed overwhelmingly that the cease-fire of January 1973 left the struggle for Vietnam where Americans had found it twelve years earlier. Again North and South Vietnam faced each other in a conflict that knew no political or territorial bounds. Arnold R. Isaacs concludes in his book, *Without Honor,* that the Paris accords did not stop the struggle for power in Vietnam for a single hour. Kissinger acknowledged in his memoirs that the years of war failed to improved Saigon's power to survive in the continuing conflict. The South Vietnamese, after years of American participation, were not psychologically prepared to confront Hanoi alone.[130] George Ball agreed: "I never had the slightest doubt that the truce agreements reached in January 1973 . . . assured the extinction of a separate South Vietnam. With American troops withdrawn and Hanoi's forces left occupying large areas of the South, there was no way a demoralized South Vietnam could hold out."[131] Whether Thieu possessed the strength and political skill to preserve a divided Vietnam was indeed problematical. Washington retained no authority to govern his decisions; for some scholars this assured his downfall. Maynard Parker, writing in *Foreign Affairs,* argues that Thieu, to exploit his temporary military advantage, followed the truce agreement with an offensive to drive the Communists back to their sanctuaries. Both Isaacs and Vietnamese writer Ngo Vinh Long accept that judgment. Frank Snepp and John McAulif conclude that both sides violated the agreement, but Thieu's violations came first.[132] Norman Podhoretz noted, in defense of Thieu, that South Vietnam's measures were taken in self-defense whereas Hanoi's were aimed at conquest.[133]

For writers such as Louis Fanning, Guenter Lewy, Richard Nixon, and Norman Podhoretz, Thieu might still have saved his regime from the Communist aggression had Congress not stopped the American bombing of Cambodia in August 1973 and thereafter refused to honor Nixon's guarantees to Thieu with adequate aid appropriations. Lewy concluded that by the fall of 1974 "available funds were no longer sufficient to allow the one-for-one replacement of lost aircraft, tanks, or artillery pieces permitted by the Paris agreement."[134] In late April 1975 North Vietnamese forces entered Saigon as U.S. officials escaped by helicopter from the roof of the American embassy.[135] Podhoretz concludes his condemnation of America's failure to save South Vietnam by asserting: "We will never know whether the outcome might have been different if the South Vietnamese . . . had not been so disastrously affected by the sense of abandonment and the defeatism this naturally aroused."[136]

Some scholars, reflecting the growing conservative mood of the late 1970's, rejected the widespread notion that the Vietnam War was a costly mistake and began to defend the conflict as a justifiable use of American power. A 1975 *Wash-*

ington Post editorial set the new tone: "If much of the actual conduct of the Vietnam policy over the years was wrong and misguided—even tragic—it cannot be denied that some part of the purpose of that policy was right and defensible."[137] Whereas the new writings were far from monolithic, they shared a strong conviction that the war merited a more sympathetic treatment than found in the critical studies of the war and postwar years. Despite the war's futility, it composed for many a legitimate use of force on behalf of a small nation's independence. The death and destruction, if extensive, were no greater in magnitude than the damage wrought by the century's other wars. Guenter Lewy, a leader among the revisionists, denies that the United States was guilty of genocide; his figures reveal the populations of both North and South Vietnam increased amid the heavy bombing. For Lewy, moreover, the presence of Vietcong rendered the villages legitimate targets. In addition, he found that the percentage of civilian to total deaths was smaller in Vietnam than in World War II and Korea.[138] Norman Podhoretz, with other writers, notes that the Christmas bombing of December 1972 killed no more than 1,500, a small number compared with the bombing raids on German and Japanese cities in the World War II. For such scholars the horrors of the Vietnam War, especially when measured by the country's laudable intentions, were not excessive.[139]

What underscored this justification of the war was the terror that befell Vietnam and Cambodia in the wake of the Communist triumphs. The tide of misery that swept across Vietnam after Saigon's fall sent perhaps two million refugees out of the country to an uncertain fate. The dismal repression suffered by victors and vanquished alike, observes Douglas Pike, "is traceable to the dozen men of the Hanoi politburo, with their unchallenged monopoly of power."[140] Still the suffering of the Vietnamese people pales when contrasted with the genocide perpetrated against the Cambodian population by the Khmer Rouge. Between 1975 and 1978 an estimated two million Cambodians died, most of them victims of intentional murder. Elizabeth Becker has delineated the disaster in her book, *When the War Was Over: The Voices of Cambodia's Revolution and Its People.* Cambodia's Pol Pot regime portrayed again the human cost of government conducted in behalf of doctrinal rather than political objectives. For some revisionists the record of Communist misgovernment in Southeast Asia proved the essential morality of the American cause.[141] It was proper, writes Podhoretz, that the United States accepted the obligation to save South Vietnam from the known evils of communism. The fact that the effort exceeded America's intellectual and moral capabilities, he concluded, in no way denies what the United States did has been "overwhelmingly vindicated by the hideous consequences of our defeat."[142] If the war was neither ignoble nor immoral, and if successive presidents acted to protect the cause of humanity no less than the security interests of the United States, their sometimes flawed judgment, Lewy suggests, "does not make them villains or fools." Had Hitler conquered Britain, Lewy continues, "this would not have proven wrong Churchill's belief in the possibility and moral worth of resistance to the Nazis."[143]

In time the costs of failure that gave justification to the Vietnam War appeared to extend far beyond the human tragedy of Southeast Asia. For the war's new defenders, Soviet expansionism after 1975 vindicated the globalist assumption that a Communist triumph anywhere was tantamount to the expansion of Soviet power and influence. The domino theory thus proved to be accurate. If the dominoes did not topple throughout South and Southeast Asia, as wartime Washington predicted, the American failure in Vietnam seemed to give encouragement to revolutionary leaders in Africa and Central America as they launched Soviet-supported wars of national liberation. Podhoretz argues:

> No sooner had Vietnam fallen than Soviet proxies in the form of Cuban troops appeared in Angola to help the Communist faction there overwhelm its pro-Western rivals in a civil war. With local variations, the same pattern was repeated over the next few years in Ethiopia, Mozambique, South Yemen, and Afghanistan, all of which were taken over by Communist parties subservient to or allied with the Soviet Union.[144]

Others detected Soviet gains elsewhere. Robert F. Turner assigned the national liberation movements in Nicaragua and El Salvador to the list of Soviet encroachments. Vietnam itself, he notes, emerged from its Communist victory with massive Soviet naval and air bases from which the USSR could threaten Southeast Asia and the western Pacific.[145] For Whittle Johnston the successful Soviet exploitation of the revolutionary situation in Vietnam "paved the way of the unparalleled range of Soviet activities in the 1970s, until now, in the 1980s, the United States is reduced to wringing its hands in indecision over increasing Soviet-backed penetration into regions which since the dawn of the Republic have been seen as vital to its security."[146]

What added to the burden of failure was the assumption, shared by many, that victory was possible. The causes of failure were strategic; their elimination lay within American capabilities. The United States lost, not because the goals were unachievable at reasonable cost, but because of the insufficient and ineffective use of power. In their memoirs General Westmoreland, General Taylor, and Adm. U. S. Grant Sharp defend the war and attribute defeat to Washington's gradualist strategy. Many scholars agree that the restraints on the use of force rendered defeat inevitable. Other strategies could have terminated the war with success and honor.[147] For some writers the United States did not lose the Vietnam War on the battlefield at all; it lost the struggle at home, especially in the press and on the television screen. Writing in *Encounter,* journalist Robert Elegant argued that misreporting by a hostile press undermined a successful military effort. Elegant's judgment was severe:

> For the first time in modern history, the outcome of a war was determined not on the battlefield, but on the printed page and, above all, on the television screen. Looking back coolly, I believe it can be said (surprising as it may still sound) that South Vietnamese and American forces actually won the limited military struggle. They virtually crushed the Viet Cong in the South . . . and thereafter they threw

back the invasion by regular North Vietnamese divisions. None the less, the War was finally lost to the invaders *after* the United States disengagement because the political pressures built up by the media had made it quite impossible for Washington to maintain even the minimal material and moral support that would have enabled the Saigon regime to continue effective resistance.

Assuming that the West, but especially the United States, had been demoralized by the fall of Saigon, Elegant wondered whether, "Angola, Afghanistan, and Iran would have occurred if Saigon had not fallen amid nearly universal odium—that is to say, *if* the 'Viet Nam Syndrome,' for which the press . . . was largely responsible, had not afflicted the Carter Administration and paralyzed American will."[148]

Other scholars find the explanation for the defeat in the American antiwar movement. Lewy's judgment of the war critics is harsh, but typical of those who defend the war: "The opponents of the war had a constitutional right to express their views, but it was folly to ignore the consequences of this protest. American public opinion indeed turned out to be a crucial "domino"; it influenced military morale in the field, the long drawn-out negotiations in Paris, the settlement of 1973, and the cuts in aid to South Vietnam in 1974, a prelude to the final abandonment in 1975."[149] What is troublesome in much of the criticism of the war's opponents is its focus on the movement's more romantic and ideological elements who defied convention and condemned the war as fundamentally immoral. The special objects of that attack were writers such as Susan Sontag, Frances Fitzgerald, and Mary McCarthy who stressed the immortality of the U.S. effort, wrote approvingly of Hanoi's successes, and proclaimed the popularity of the Vietcong.[150] To condemn such judgments and stress the moral superiority of the American and South Vietnamese effort does not answer the central wartime criticism of the U.S. involvement in Southeast Asia. The commentary that mattered emanated not from student and literary extremists, but from the war's conservative critics: generals, public officials, pundits, scholars, and members of Congress.[151] These critics did not attribute any moral superiority to the North Vietnamese enemy or popularity to the Vietcong; indeed, the question of the war's morality rested rather lightly on them. Official definitions of legitimacy and aggression mattered little to them. They saw the war not as an exercise in morality or human rights, but as an exercise of power. They simply wondered what interests in Southeast Asia rendered victory, or even the war itself, essential for the defense of any historic American interest.[152]

Those who place responsibility for the American failure on flawed strategies or the misguided undermining of national will reveal little interest in the nature and resilience of the enemy. If American leaders knew little about Vietnam, it did not matter. They assumed that every society has a breaking point and that North Vietnam was no exception. But as Vietnamese scholar Ngo Vinh Long advised Henry Kissinger in 1967, only the total wrecking of Vietnamese society and culture would have defeated the Vietnamese revolutionaries.[153] Behind that determination, as many historians note, was the two thousand–year Vietnamese struggle to prevent absorption by China and the ninety-year effort to regain independence from

French colonial rule. History and conflict had created a strong sense of national-ism, and although Communist-led, it expressed the most powerful political currents in Vietnamese society. For George Kahin the ultimate incongruity was the Ameri-can determination to keep Vietnam divided against its historic drive for unity and independence.[154] The South Vietnamese regime was thus doomed by its very nature as the creation of a foreign power, with goals that defied the country's history. To the end, wrote Kahin, South Vietnam remained an artificial entity, dependent on U.S. subsidies and corrupted socially and politically by the huge American pres-ence. The war itself destroyed the base of South Vietnamese agriculture and created millions of refugees who crowded into the cities and diminished any chance the Saigon government possessed to establish a popular government.[155]

Gabriel Kolko, in his *Anatomy of a War,* sees the long struggle for Vietnam as ultimately a contest between social systems—between an imperialist America and "the Revolution," embracing both North Vietnam and the National Liberation Front. In Vietnam, Kolko argues, the United States attempted to maintain its global cred-ibility, not to defend its welfare, but to create "a controllable responsive order elsewhere . . . that would permit the political destinies of distant places to evolve in a manner beneficial to American goals and interests."[156] In Vietnam the United States confronted a revolution with a variety of counterrevolutionary policies. To explain their failure, Kolko examines in detail the nature of the South Vietnamese economy, society, and political culture—all of which, he believes, determined the outcome of the war. Unable to comprehend the social forces at work in Vietnam, the United States simply relied on its wealth and resources to compensate for its lack of understanding. For Kolko American power inflicted monumental suffering and economic dislocation across Vietnam, but never enabled the United States to come to terms with the revolution or the weakness of its client state in South Viet-nam and Saigon's profound failures in every aspect of public life.[157] Such a government, divorced politically from its environment, had no chance against Vietnam's revolutionaries, and no administration in Washington would pay the exorbitant price to save it. Yet, as George Herring notes, the Vietnamese triumphed less because of the superiority of their social system than because of their determi-nation, organizational skills, and effective strategies.[158]

Clearly the search for lessons in the Vietnam War, no less than the rationales for the war itself, reflects conflicting notions regarding the Soviet danger in Asia, Africa, and Latin America, and the countering policies it demanded. "As long as the general doctrine of containment of communism remained the consensus," Gelb and Betts have written, "the specific military intervention in Vietnam followed logically. . . . Doctrine dictated containment."[159] For those who saw nationalism, not communism, as the driving force in Third World upheavals, the United States had exaggerated the importance of Vietnam to U.S. and world security and with it the need for global containment. Paul Kattenburg, in *The Vietnam Trauma in Ameri-can Foreign Policy, 1945–1975,* declared that the global, holistic approach to Vietnam created problems, and ultimate failure, by overlooking the war's realities.

Kolko attributed the American defeat in Vietnam to overreaching in the attempt, not merely to contain the Soviet Union, but "to halt and reverse the emergence of states and social systems opposed to the international order Washington sought to establish. . . . Despite America's many real successes in imposing its hegemony elsewhere, Vietnam exposed the ultimate constraints on its power in the modern era."[160] George Herring, in *America's Longest War,* explained his dismissal of global containment:

> The fundamental weakness of the lessons learned thus far is that they assume the continued necessity and practicability of the containment policy. . . . The United States intervened in Vietnam to block the apparent march of a Soviet-directed Communism across Asia, enlarged its commitment to halt a presumably expansionist Communist China, and eventually made Vietnam a test of its determination to uphold world order. By wrongly attributing the Vietnamese conflict to external sources, the United States drastically misjudged its internal dynamics. . . . It elevated into a major international conflict what might have remained a localized struggle. . . . Vietnam made clear the inherent unworkability of a policy of global containment.[161]

Within the context of the new conservatism, many revisionists argue that the United States should not permit the Vietnam experience to become a barrier to the employment of force. For them military power remained an essential element in world stability; Munich had demonstrated the price of failure to confront aggression. Timothy Lomparis warned against drawing the wrong conclusions from Vietnam in his book, *The War Everyone Lost—And Won*: "The American intervention in Viet Nam was one of rich variegation. As in the case of Mark Twain's cat drawing the wrong conclusion from sitting on a hot stove and therefore unquestioningly assumed that stoves are at all times and places hot, the burners of Viet Nam were hot and cold from time to time and place to place."[162] Richard Nixon, in *No More Vietnams,* admonished the American people to learn the correct lesson from the defeat. "In Vietnam," he wrote, "we tried and failed in a just cause. 'No more Vietnams' can mean that we will not *try* again. It *should* mean that we will not fail again." Republican candidate Ronald Reagan, in 1980, accepted the dual proposition that the United States dared not abjure the use of force; neither dared it lose. He asserted in April that "we must rid ourselves of the 'Vietnam Syndrome.' It has dominated our thinking for too long."[163] In keeping with the widespread effort to exorcise Vietnam's constraining influence, the Reagan administration, after January 1981, attempted to recommit the country to a program of global containment.

Certainly the Vietnam War, so divisive and so damaging to the nation's interests at home and abroad, should have furnished ample lessons on which Americans could agree. Tragically, it did not do so. President Reagan's effort to erase the adverse memory of Vietnam, one amply supported by those who defend the long war, eliminated any possibility of a national consensus. This left the country as divided after 1981 on matters of external policy as it had been at the height of the

Vietnam War. Only the absence of fighting clouded the continuing disagreements. Unfortunately, a seriously divided country, as the Vietnam War illustrated, cannot sustain a costly foreign policy over time. In the 1980s few circumstances and few issues around the globe would have permitted the United States to wage war with the full support of the American people. What imaginable crisis would unify rather than further divide the country was not apparent. For many students of foreign affairs, the Vietnam experience should teach some basic truths about proper and promising approaches to external questions; failures, like successes, are replete with the materials for instruction. "To those who insist that we must rid ourselves of the Vietnam syndrome and get about our business," Herring cautioned, "I would respond that understanding of and perspective on the Vietnam experience is an essential basis for shaping a constructive and realistic foreign policy."[164] During the early Reagan years the ongoing Cold War militated against agreement on this central issue facing the nation. Not even the diminution of the Soviet danger after 1989 permitted the forging of some consensus on the Vietnam War and thus on U.S. external policy, although Americans in general favored a cautious response to the multitudinous, largely ethnic, challenges of the post–Cold War world. Nations with the capacity to learn should not repeat the errors of the past. Not even the United States can afford such luxuries.

Notes

For NCS 7, see Thomas H. Etzold and John Lewis Gaddis, eds., *Containment: Documents on American Policy and Strategy, 1945–1950* (New York: Columbia University Press, 1978), 166–67.

2. NSC 68 in ibid., 385–86.

3. David Halberstam discusses this phenomenon at length in *The Best and the Brightest* (New York: Random House, 1969), 134–36.

4. NSC 48/1, 23 December 1949, *The Pentagon Papers: The Defense Department History of United States Decisionmaking on Vietnam,* Senator Gravel, ed., 4 vols. (Boston: Beacon Press, 1971), 1:37–38; quoted in Leslie H. Gelb with Richard K. Betts, *The Irony of Vietnam: The System Worked* (Washington, D.C.: Brookings Institution, 1979), 41. See also *United States–Vietnam Relations, 1945–1967: Study Prepared by the Department of Defense* (The Pentagon Papers), 8 vols. (Washington, D.C.: Government Printing Office, 1971), 1:A-45-46.

5. Acheson's statement of 1 February 1950, Department of State *Bulletin* 22 (13 February 1950): 244. For the Truman administration's decision to support the French in Indochina, see Dean Acheson, *Present at the Creation: My Years in the State Department* (New York: Norton, 1969), 671–77; Andrew J. Rotter, *The Path To Vietnam: Origins of the American Commitment to Southeast Asia* (Ithaca, N.Y.: Cornell University Press, 1987), 5–7. Robert F. Turner emphasizes Ho Chi Minh's ideology and Communist connections in his book, *Vietnamese Communism: Its Origins and Development* (Stanford, Calif.: Hoover Institute Press, 1975), 1–86. Milton Sacks argues that the Communists of Asia were not concerned with independence, but with the expansion of international communism in Asia, thereby threatening the security of the United States and the free world. See Sacks, "The Strategy of Communism in Southeast Asia," *Pacific Affairs* 23 (September 1950): 227–47.

6. Writers see in the period of 1953–54 both Eisenhower's growing commitment to Indochina and his reluctance to engage American fores in another Asian ground war. See George C. Herring and Richard H. Immerman, "'The Day We Didn't Go to War' Revisited," *Journal of American History* 71 (September

1984): 343–63; David H. Petraeus, "Korea, the Never-Again Club, and Indochina," *Parameters* 17 (December 1987): 59–70. On the failure of the Navarre Plan, see Bernard B. Fall, *Viet-Nam Witness, 1953–1966* (New York: Praeger, 1966), 30–40. On the Eisenhower policy leading to the Geneva Conference, see Alexander Kendrick, *The Wound Within: America in the Vietnam Years, 1945–1974* (Boston: Little, Brown, 1974), 60–67; Archimedes L. A. Patti, *Why Viet Nam? Prelude to America's Albatross* (Berkeley, Calif.: University of California Press, 1980), 430–38. For a detailed account of U.S. policy toward Southeast Asia from 1949 to 1954, see Robert M. Blum, *Drawing the Line: The Origins of American Containment Policy in East Asia* (New York: Norton, 1982).

7. For a defense of the American commitment to Ngo Dinh Diem, see Edwin Brown Firmage, "International Law and the Response of the United States to 'Internal War,'" in Richard A. Falk, ed., *The Vietnam War and International Law*, 2 vols. (Princeton: Princeton University Press, 1969), 2:104; Wesley R. Fishel, "One Vietnam or Two? A New Look at an Old Question," *Virginia Quarterly Review* 50 (Summer 1974): 348–67; Louis A. Fanning, *Betrayal in Vietnam* (New Rochelle, N.Y.: Arlington House, 1976), 15; Norman Podhoretz, *Why We Were in Vietnam* (New York: Simon & Schuster, 1982), 39–44.

8. Eisenhower's remarks to the press, 7 April 1954, *United States–Vietnam Relations*, 7:8–11.

9. Eisenhower's Gettysburg speech in Department of State *Bulletin* 40 (27 April 1959): 580–81.

10. Such writers as Norman Podhoretz and Whittle Johnson observe a dangerous process in which the USSR, having been stopped in its effort to expand into Western Europe, backed North Korea's effort to annex South Korea only to face resistance again. It then turned to Indochina to further Communist expansion there. See Podhoretz, *Why We Were in Vietnam*, 11, 26–28; Whittle Johnston, "Containment and Vietnam," in John Norton Moore, ed., *The Vietnam Debate: A Fresh Look at the Arguments* (Lanham, Md.: University Press of America, 1990), 233. Ralph B. Smith, in *An International History of the Vietnam War*, 2 vols. (New York: St. Martins Press, 1983), vol. 1: *Revolution versus Containment, 1955–1961*, sees the struggle for Vietnam as part of a global conflict. Similarly Frank Trager, in *Why Viet Nam?* (New York: Praeger, 1966), accepts the official view of the war.

11. For the view that Ho Chi Minh, although a Communist, was primarily a nationalist, devoted to the independence of Indochina, see Patti, 183–209; David G. Marr, *Vietnamese Anticolonialism, 1885–1925* (Berkeley Calif.: University of California Press, 1971), 249–77; Joseph Buttinger, *Vietnam: The Unforgettable Tragedy* (New York: Horizon, 1977), 17–25; P. J. Honey, *Genesis of a Tragedy: The Historical Background of the Vietnam War* (London: Ernest Benn, 1968), 57–62; Edward R. Drachman, *United States Policy toward Vietnam, 1940–1945* (Rutherford N.J.: Fairleigh Dickinson University Press, 1970), 88–158; Bernard B. Fall, *The Two Vietnams: A Political and Military Analysis* (New York: Praeger, 1967), 81–103; and Jean Lacouture, in *Ho Chi Minh: A Political Biography*, trans. Peter Wiles (New York: Random House, 1968), passim. For the failing effort of the Division of Southeast Asian Affairs to commit the United States to Ho Chi Minh as a nationalist see the May 1972 report of Abbot Low Moffat before the Senate Foreign Relations Committee in Norman A. Graebner, ed., *Nationalism and Communism in Asia: The American Response* (Lexington, Mass.: Heath, 1977), 24–33. Moffat later recalled: "I have never met an American, be he military, O.S.S., diplomat, or journalist, who did not reach the same belief: that Ho Chi Minh was first and foremost a Vietnam nationalist." See George McT. Kahin, *Intervention: How America Became Involved in Vietnam* (New York: Knopf, 1986), 7.

12. Bernard Fall's superb essay on Ho Chi Minh can be found in *Last Reflections On a War* (Garden City, N.Y.: Doubleday, 1967), 59–90, and his statement on Ho's ideology and goal of national independence appears in ibid., 73, 79.

13. Among the major writers on Vietnam who hold this view of Ho's nationalism are Stanley Karnow, *Vietnam: A History* (New York: Viking, 1984), 146–75; Kahin, 3–28; George McTurnan Kahin and John W. Lewis, *The United States in Vietnam*, rev. ed. (New York: Dial Press, 1967), 25–30; Chester Cooper, *The Lost Crusade: America in Vietnam* (New York: Dodd, Mead, 1970), 1–55; Robert Shaplen, *The Lost Revolution: The U.S. in Vietnam, 1946–1966*, rev. ed. (New York: Harper & Row, 1966), 1–54; Halberstam, *Best and Brightest*, 98–108, 149–50; Kendrick, 35–49; Gelb and Betts, 36–40; George C. Herring, *America's Longest War: The United States in Vietnam, 1950–1975* (New York: Wiley, 1979), 1–8. Until 1949, as Herring and others note, the United States maintained a pro-French neutrality, hesitating to be-

come involved in France's colonial war. For criticism of the American decision to support the French see idem, "The Truman Administration and the Restoration of French Sovereignty in Indochina," *Diplomatic History* 1 (Spring 1977): 97–117; Ellen J. Hammer, *The Struggle for Indochina, 1940–1955* (Stanford, Calif.: Stanford University Press, 1954); Lisle A. Rose, *Roots of Tragedy: The United States and the Struggle for Asia, 1943–1953* (Westport, Conn.: Greenwood Press, 1976); Lloyd Gardner, *Approaching Vietnam: From World War II Through Dienbienphu, 1941–1954* (New York: Norton, 1988); Rotter, *Path to Vietnam*; Donald Lancaster, *The Emancipation of French Indochina* (London: Oxford University Press, 1961); Gary Hess, *The U.S.'s Emergence as a Southeast Asian Power, 1940–1950* (New York: Columbia University Press, 1987). Joseph Buttinger stresses the poor choices that the French offered the people of Indochina in *Vietnam: A Dragon Embattled,* 2 vols. (New York: Praeger, 1967), vol. 1: *From Colonialism to the Vietminh,* 209–14.

14. Shaplen, *Lost Revolution,* xxi.

15. Gary R. Hess, "The First American Commitment in Indochina: The Acceptance of the 'Bao Dai Solution,' 1950," *Diplomatic History* 2 (Fall 1978): 331–50. See also Rotter, 91–98; Shaplen, *Lost Revolution,* 59–66; Cooper, 57; Karnow, *Vietnam: A History,* 176–77; Kahin, 32–33; Richard J. Barnet, *Intervention and Revolution: The United States in the Third World,* rev. ed. (New York: New American Library, 1972), 218.

16. Herring, *America's Longest War,* 15–21; Shaplen, *Lost Revolution,* 67–94; Victor Bator, *Vietnam: A Diplomatic Tragedy* (Dobbs Ferry, N.Y.: Oceana Publications, 1965), 2–73; Buttinger, *Vietnam: Unforgettable Tragedy,* 27–30; Gelb and Betts, 42–48; Kahin, 38–52. Patti, 405, concluded that "our consuming fear of the communist specter was our undoing." Robert Blum, head of the American aid program, declared when he left Saigon in late 1951 "that the situation in Indochina is not satisfactory and shows no substantial prospect of improving, that no decisive military victory can be achieved, that the Bao Dai government gives little promise of developing competence and winning the loyalty of the population, that French policy is uncertain and often ill-advised, and that the attainment of American objectives is remote." Blum quoted in Shaplen, *Lost Revolution,* 87.

17. Quotation in Douglas Pike, *Viet Cong* (Cambridge, Mass.: M.I.T. Press, 1966), 52; Charles Chaumont, "A Critical Study of American Intervention in Vietnam," Falk, ed., *Vietnam War,* 2:152; Max Gordon, "Vietnam, the United States, and the United Nations," ibid., 336; Kahin and Lewis, 45–48; Gardner, 248–314; Lancaster, 313–37. For basic studies of the Geneva Conference see Robert F. Randle, *Geneva 1954: The Settlement of the Indochina War* (Princeton, N.J.: Princeton University Press, 1969) and Philippe Devillers and Jean Lacouture, *End of a War: Indochina 1954,* trans. Alexander Lieven and Adam Roberts (New York: Praeger, 1969). Randle notes that the disagreements at Geneva were glossed over as the price of final agreement. Bator, 75–131, stresses the American-British antagonism at Geneva. Cooper, 104–5, notes the absurd behavior of the U.S. delegation acting as if the Chinese delegation did not exist.

18. Douglas Pike notes that Ho and his followers believed they had achieved the right to a united Vietnam because of their victory over the French and had accepted partition at Geneva under Soviet pressure as a temporary arrangement. See Pike, *War, Peace and the Viet Cong* (Cambridge, Mass.: M.I.T. Press, 1969), 32–34. On the efforts of Ngo Dinh Diem, with U.S. support, to build a separate nation see Bator, 149–203; Devillers and Lacouture, 317–98; Kahin, 66–92; Kendrick, 88–114; Kahin and Lewis, 54–63. Loren Baritz, *Backfire: A History of How American Culture Led Us Into Vietnam and Made Us Fight the Way We Did* (New York: Morrow, 1985), sees U.S. intervention in Vietnam, reflecting faith in American institutions and technology, driven not only by security considerations but also by cultural imperialism based on the assumption that South Vietnam was an ideal laboratory for nation-building on the American model. For optimistic reports of American officials and the American press on Diem's success see Clyde Edwin Pettit, *The Experts* (Secaucus, N.J.: Lyle Stuart, 1975), 76–101. As late as August 1958 Wesley Fishel, senior adviser to Diem, could write: "South Vietnam today can be classed as one of the most stable and peaceful countries in Asia today." Ibid., 99. On the "Miracle of Vietnam" see Robert Sheer, *How the United States Got Involved in Vietnam* (Santa Barbara, Calif.: Center for the Study of Democratic Institutions, 1965), 38–61.

19. Halberstam, *Best and Brightest,* 182.

20. For the view that the Southern revolutionaries, the Vietcong, represented a Southern movement, with some variations of interpretation of when and how they received support from North Vietnam, see Pike, *Viet Cong*, Jean Lacouture, *Vietnam: Between Two Truces*, trans. Konrad Kellen and Joel Carmichael (New York: Random House, 1966); Jeffery Race, *War Comes to Long An* (Berkeley: University of California Press, 1972); Kahin, *Intervention;* Bernard B. Fall, "The Theory and Practice of Insurgency and Counterinsurgency," *Naval War College Review* 17 (April 1965): 30–33; William R. Andrews, *The Village War: Vietnamese Communist Revolutionary Activity in Dinh Tuong Province, 1960–1964* (Columbia, Mo.: University of Missouri Press, 1973); P. J. Honey, *Communism in North Vietnam* (Cambridge, Mass.: M.I.T. Press, 1963); Wallace J. Thies, *When Governments Collide: Coercion and Diplomacy in the Vietnam Conflict, 1964–1968* (Berkeley: University of California Press, 1980); Fall, *The Two Vietnams;* Karnow, *Vietnam: A History;* King C. Chen, "Hanoi's Three Decisions and the Escalation of the Vietnam War," *Political Science Quarterly* 90 (Summer 1975): 239–59. For a valuable description of the revolutionary process before 1961 see Fox Butterfield, "Origins of the Insurgency in South Vietnam," *The Pentagon Papers, New York Times* edition (New York: Bantam Books, 1971), 71–81.

21. James C. Thomson, Jr., "How Could Vietnam Happen? An Autopsy," *Atlantic Monthly* 221 (April 1968): 47–53.

22. Halberstam, *Best and Brightest*, 97; Larry Berman, *Planning a Tragedy: The Americanization of the War in Vietnam* (New York: Norton, 1982), 19; Baritz, 112–13; Thomson, 48; Podhoretz, *Why We Were in Vietnam*, 51.

23. Halberstam, *Best and Brightest,* 185.

24. Arthur M. Schlesinger, Jr., *The Bitter Heritage: Vietnam and American Democracy, 1941–1966* (Boston: Houghton Mifflin, 1967), 13.

25. Halberstam, *Best and Brightest,* 185.

26. Schlesinger, 22.

27. On official perceptions of Communist expansionism in Southeast Asia see Halberstam, *Best and Brightest,* 187; Barnet, 245; Podhoretz, *Why We Were in Vietnam,* 52–55.

28. Schlesinger, 31.

29. Daniel Ellsberg, *Papers on the War* (New York: Simon & Schuster, 1972), 59–60. Here McNamara and the joint chiefs, along with the president, adopted the concept of falling dominoes, much as has the Truman and Eisenhower administrations. For the argument that Vietnam comprised a separate episode, not connected to other struggles in the world, see Richard Goodwin in *New Yorker,* 16 April 1966, 72–73.

30. Ellsberg, 67–71; Gelb and Betts, 77; Podhoretz, *Why We Were in Vietnam,* 57–63. Writers are troubled by the Kennedy policies that involved the United States in Southeast Asia without any corresponding strategy to win. Donald Zagoria, in *Vietnam Triangle: Moscow, Peking, Hanoi* (New York: Pegasus, 1968), 29, attributed the escalation to the administration's decision to draw the Cold War line in Asia. What motivated the administration, Ellsberg added, was the supposition that it could not lose to Communists without inviting charges of incompetence and treason. Thus each administration, in turn, made decisions that were inadequate, but always deepened the American commitment. See Ellsberg, 74–82; Cooper, 409.

31. Leslie H. Gelb, "Vietnam: The System Worked," *Foreign Policy* no. 3 (Summer 1971): 140–67; Fall, *Viet-Nam Witness,* 4–5. Fall charges that Washington claimed that each new step was unanticipated and unavoidable, the previous step having failed because of factors beyond U.S. control, but in each case it was deaf to warnings that the process would end in catastrophe. Similarly Theodore Draper, in *Abuse of Power* (New York: Viking Press, 1967), 161, accuses the government of making one miscalculation after another, always increasing the commitment of resources and prestige until the commitment took on a life of its own.

32. Kennedy's special message to Congress, 28 March 1961, *United States–Vietnam Relations,* 7:C7–8. See also Rostow's recommendation for an anti-guerrilla strategy in his address to the U.S. Army Special Warfare School at Fort Bragg, N.C., 28 June 1961, Department of State *Bulletin* 45 (7 August 1961): 237; Barnet, 244.

33. Kennedy placed control of the counterinsurgency program under a special group of State and Defense Department officials, but the special forces, with their anti-guerrilla mission, did not fit the Pentagon's

conception of war and therefore were never accepted. The nation's military leaders never doubted the capacity of American conventional forces, with their superior equipment and firepower, to win the struggle in the jungles or in the cities.

34. Fall, _Two Vietnams_, 340–43, 374–80. For Ambassador Frederick Nolting's claims for success in the strategic hamlet program see Frederick Nolting, _From Trust to Tragedy_ (Westport, Conn.: Greenwood Press, 1988), 54–56.

35. Johnson quoted in Halberstam, _Best and Brightest_, 167–68.

36. Shaplen, _Lost Revolution_, 154; John Mecklin, _Mission in Torment_ (Garden City, N.Y.: Doubleday, 1965), 38–43. Lawrence E. Grinter, "Bargaining between Saigon and Washington: Dilemma of Linkage Politics during War," _Orbis_ 18 (Fall 1974): 837–43, analyzes in depth the inability of the government in Washington to control Diem despite the obvious weakness of the Saigon regime. American influence over Diem almost vanished when Washington made it clear that it would support him whatever the state of reform. This permitted Diem to concentrate on the survivability, not the performance, of his government.

37. For a brief discussion of Washington's official optimism see Norman A. Graebner, _America As a World Power: A Realist Appraisal from Wilson to Reagan_ (Wilmington, Del.: Scholarly Resources, 1984), 233; Pettit, 125–80; Mecklin, 18–19.

38. Halberstam, _Best and Brightest_, 304–6; Neil Sheehan, _A Bright Shining Lie: John Paul Vann and America in Vietnam_ (New York: Random House, 1988), 289.

39. Karnow, _Vietnam: A History_, 259–63; Sheehan, 203–62; Nolting, 97. Nolting regarded Ap Bac as an insignificant affair.

40. On the negative reporting see Herring, _America's Longest War_, 91–92. Malcolm W. Browne, in _The New Face of War_ (Indianapolis, Ind.: Bobs-Merrill, 1965), emphasizes the nature of the war, but also reveals the negative quality of the Saigon regime and its failure to perform. Mecklin, 99–151, dwells on Saigon's break with newsmen, beginning in 1962. Mecklin was the public affairs officer in the U.S. mission.

41. Sheehan, 298–301, 316–17, 328–31.

42. Cooper quoted in Kahin, 142–43.

43. Sheehan, 334–35, 351–58. To counter the critical reporting, following the Buddhist crisis of the summer of 1963, by Halberstam, Sheehan, Browne, as well as Peter Kalischer and Bernard Kalb of CBS, James Robinson of NBC, Stanley Karnow of the _Saturday Evening Post_, and Charles Mohr of _Time_, the Pentagon sent out such noted power journalists as Marguerite Higgins and Joseph Alsop who accepted the Harkins-Krulac line. See ibid., 347–48.

44. Kahin, 146–81; Sheehan, 358–71; Herring, _America's Longest War_, 103–6; Buttinger, _Vietnam: Dragon Embattled_, vol. 2: _Vietnam at War_, 1001–2. For the evolution of the coup itself see Shaplen, _Lost Revolution_, 188–212.

45. Nolting, 124–38.

46. Ellsberg, 97.

47. Ibid., 102.

48. Herring, _America's Longest War_, 107.

49. Sheehan, 375. Kennedy held firm to the conviction that the United States dare not withdraw from Vietnam. See Gelb and Betts, 186.

50. Sheehan, 372–73.

51. Ibid., 374–75.

52. Ibid., 376–79; Baritz, 135–37, argued that the program was based on a complete misunderstanding of the North and had no chance of success.

53. Draper, 61; Gelb and Betts, 98–100; Karnow, _Vietnam: A History_, 336–38. Kahin, 190–99, 203, discusses the strong movement toward neutralism in the Saigon government and the need for new leadership under General Khanh.

54. Karnow, _Vietnam: A History_, 344–45; Baritz, 138; Kahin, 210–11. This argument for air strikes was reinforced at the Honolulu meeting in June. Ibid., 213. Rusk argued that it was more important to strengthen the South first. Ibid., 211–12. For the 10 June meeting see ibid., 218–19.

55. On the Tonkin Gulf Resolution see Draper, 64–66; Kahin, 219–23; Baritz, 140–41; George W. Ball, *The Past Has Another Pattern* (New York: Norton, 1982), 379–80; Karnow, *Vietnam: A History*, 366–76. For critical volumes on the resolution see Joseph C. Goulden, *Truth Is the First Casualty: The Gulf of Tonkin Affair—Illusion and Reality* (Chicago: Rand McNally, 1965); Eugene G. Windchy, *Tonkin Gulf* (Garden City, N.Y.: Doubleday, 1971). John Galloway, *The Gulf of Tonkin Resolution* (Rutherford, N.J.: Fairleigh Dickinson University Press, 1970), is a useful documentary history, including the congressional debates.

56. Draper, 66–67.

57. On Khanh's pressure for a bombing campaign see Kahin, 215; Karnow, *Vietnam: A History*, 378–79; Draper, 68–70.

58. Baritz, 145.

59. Sheehan, 380; Draper, 70–71.

60. Ball, 377; Kahin, 271; Sheehan, 382; Karnow, *Vietnam: A History*, 398–400.

61. Baritz, 145. Johnson expressed his fear of a national debate that would follow an American withdrawal from Vietnam in Lyndon Baines Johnson, *The Vantage Point: Perspectives of the Presidency, 1963–1969* (New York: Holt, Rinehart & Winston, 1971), 151–52.

62. Kahin, 271–75; Berman, *Planning a Tragedy*, 45; Richard Goodwin, *Triumph or Tragedy: Reflections on Vietnam* (New York: Random House, 1966), 31. Taylor was not convinced that bombing would bring a victory, but he believed that the United States had no choice but to try. See Berman, *Planning a Tragedy*, 36–37. For Ball's doubts and his role as a dissenter see Karnow, *Vietnam: A History*, 404–5; Berman, *Planning a Tragedy*, 45–46.

63. Kahin, 276. On the pressures for action, Philip L. Geyelin, *Lyndon B. Johnson and the World* (New York: Praeger, 1966), 216.

64. Kahin, 281–83; Draper, 73. Bundy's statement and Thomson's rebuttal in Berman, *Planning a Tragedy*, 43–45.

65. On changes in Saigon's government see Karnow, *Vietnam: A History*, 382-86; Baritz, 173; Berman, *Planning a Tragedy*, 70; Kahin, 293–305, 344–45; Draper, 85. Doubts regarding the bombing were widespread. See Berman, *Planning a Tragedy*, 47; Baritz, 163–64; Kahin, 314. CIA Director John McCone warned the president that unless the United States bombed every conceivable target in the North it would have little effect on North Vietnam's capacity or determination. McCone cited in Harrison E. Salisbury, ed., *Vietnam Reconsidered: Lessons From a War* (New York: Harper & Row, 1984), 55. For a broad discussion of the growing opposition to the bombing in the press see Kathleen J. Turner, *Lyndon Johnson's Dual War: Vietnam and the Press* (Chicago: University of Chicago Press, 1985), 119–32.

66. Buttinger, *Vietnam: Unforgettable Tragedy*, 77.

67. Adam B. Ulam, in *The Rivals: America and Russia since World War II* (New York: Viking Press, 1976), 385, wondered what Rusk's statements on North Vietnamese aggression had to do with reality. Rusk has restated his defense of the Vietnam War in Dean Rusk as told to Richard Rusk, *As I Saw It*, ed. Daniel S. Papp (New York: Norton, 1990). Rusk based his defense of the war on his belief in collective security and the importance of keeping treaty commitments. For him the American obligation to South Vietnam rested on the SEATO alliance to which he referred repeatedly in his public statements. Rusk acknowledged that he underestimated the persistence of the North Vietnamese and overestimated the staying power of Americans. Goodwin challenged the notion that the United States had a binding commitment to SEATO in *New Yorker*, 16 Apr. 1966, 68–70.

68. William J. Duiker, *The Communist Road to Power in Vietnam* (Boulder, Colo.: Westview Press, 1981), 221–33; Guenter Lewy, *America in Vietnam* (New York: Oxford University Press, 1979), 40; Podhoretz, *Why We Were in Vietnam*, 74–76.

69. For the defense of the White Paper by Podhoretz, Johnston, Lewy, and O'Brien see Moore, 24, 64–67, 89–96, 99–134. These defenses vary in argument but rest on the common assumption of two Vietnams and Northern instigation of revolution in the South.

70. Kahin, 290–91. Writing in the *New York Times Magazine*, 18 Apr. 1965, Hans J. Morgenthau believed that the assertions adduced to support the White Paper bordered on the grotesque. Chester Cooper,

who prepared the White Paper, acknowledged that he was unable to obtain sufficient documentary evidence to convince the nonexpert or the sophisticated skeptic. He failed, he noted, to sway Senator Mansfield and other critics. Cooper, 264–65. Draper, 76–83, is critical of the White Paper and, like Mansfield, believed the problem was not Northern strength but Southern weakness.

71. Ball, 392–93. For the continuing pressure of Westmoreland and the JCS for troops see Berman, *Planning a Tragedy,* 68–71.

72. Kahin, 356.

73. Ibid., 356–57. In a March memorandum prepared for McNamara, McNaughton argued that the country's most important objective in Vietnam was the avoidance of a humiliating defeat and the destruction of the U.S. reputation as a guarantor against Communist aggression. Ibid., 311–13. McNaughton defined that objective further in his noted memorandum of 17 January 1966. Hans Morgenthau, in his January 1968 critique of the war wondered whether the reputation the administration wanted to defend belonged to the country or to those responsible for the war. Jonathan Schell termed McNaughton's rationale for pursuing the war as a "psychological domino theory" that did not reduce the nation's need of victory, but rather increased it by rendering a defeat in Vietnam commensurate with the destruction of the entire global position of the United States. See Hans J. Morgenthau, "U.S. Misadverture in Vietnam," *Current History* 54 (January 1968): 34; Schell quoted in Ball, 386.

74. Kahin, 361.

75. Berman, *Planning a Tragedy,* 100–3; Kahin, 360–65.

76. Kahin, 375, 387. Berman, *Planning a Tragedy,* 109, 121, records the opposition to escalation voiced by Ball, Clifford, and Cooper. Much of the opposition lay within the government itself. Between February and July 1965 the State Department's Bureau of Intelligence Estimates and Special National Intelligence Estimates, warned the administration repeatedly against the use of bombing and ground forces in Vietnam, only to be disregarded. See Thomas L. Hughes, "The Power to Speak and the Power to Listen: Reflections on Bureaucratic Politics and a Recommendation on Information Flows," Thomas M. Franck and Edward Weisband, eds., *Secrecy and Foreign Policy* (New York: Oxford University Press, 1974), 34–38.

77. Karnow, *Vietnam: A History,* 420–26; Kahin, 389; Draper, 85.

78. Kahin, 397–98; White House press conference, 28 July 1965, Department of State *Bulletin* 53 (16 August 1965): 263–64.

79. Baritz, 166; Berman, *Planning a Tragedy,* 128.

80. Ball, 383, 387, 398. Halberstam analyzed McNamara's advantages in confronting Ball with evidence Ball's staff could never find for study and review. Ball thus could not present counterfigures to challenge McNamara's case. See Halberstam, *Best and Brightest,* 705. Halberstam concluded that any dissembling seemed permissible as long as it served a superior. Ibid., 705–6.

81. William Kaufman, "Limited Warfare," in William Kaufman, ed., *Military Policy and National Security* (Princeton, N.J.: Princeton University Press, 1956), 113.

82. Thomas Schelling, *Arms and Influence* (New Haven, Conn.: Yale University Press, 1966), 167, 172–73; Herman Kahn, *On Escalation* (New York: Praeger, 1965).

83. Wallace J. Thies, 1–4, 9–11, on the bombing and the rationale behind it.

84. Alexander George, David Hall, and William Simons, *The Limits of Coercive Diplomacy* (Boston: Little, Brown, 1971), 22, 26.

85. Johnson's speech in *Current,* no 59 (May 1965): 6. On 15 March 1965, seventeen nonaligned countries meeting in Cairo addressed notes to both Washington and Hanoi, asking them to seek peace through negotiations. The administration responded on 8 April that the United States was in Southeast Asia to defend the independence of South Vietnam and would consider peace only when North Vietnam stopped its aggression. *Vietnam Perspective* 1 (November 1965): 42–43, 46–47.

86. U.S. purpose in Vietnam did not change. Gen. Maxwell Taylor described it well in "The Cause in Vietnam Is Being Won," *New York Times Magazine,* 15 Oct. 1967: "When the fighting finally stops, either South Vietnam will be independent and able to choose its own forms of government or it will not. We will either attain this objective or we will fail. Thus the achievement of this objective becomes the true criterion

of victory—it is the accomplishment of what we set out to do in 1954 and what we are still pursuing today."

87. Thomson's view in Kahin, 288–89, 327; Ball's warning in Ball, 391; Berman, *Planning a Tragedy*, 47. Perhaps the most notable warning came from Walter Lippmann who condemned the president's Balitmore speech of 7 April. "It's just a disguised demand for capitulation," he told Bundy. "You've got to give the communists some incentive to negotiate." Ronald Steel, *Walter Lippmann and the American Century* (Boston: Little, Brown, 1980), 562–64.

88. Thies, 262.

89. Kahin, 326. Hanoi responded to the note of the seventeen nonaligned countries on 17 April, proclaiming its goal of self-determination to restore Vietnam's territorial integrity and independence. *Vietnam Perspectives*, 1 (November 1965), 44–45. Hanoi's goals remained as inflexible as those of the United States and, as John M. Gates argues, comprised the removal of any external barriers to a united Vietnam. North Vietnam underwrote that purpose by its willingness to accept horrendous losses in its pursuit of victory. Giap, the famed North Vietnamese military commander, declared that North Vietnam was prepared to fight a hundred years. See John M. Gates, "Vietnam: The Debate Goes On," *Parameters* 14 (Spring 1984); Stanley Karnow, "Giap Remembers," *New York Times Magazine*, 24 June 1990, 36.

90. Thies, 270, 278–81.

91. Karnow, *Vietnam: A History*, 479; Gelb and Betts, 267, 283, 291–93. Karnow notes that by 1967 the Vietnam War was costing only 3 percent of the GNP compared to 12 percent during the Korean War. Karnow, *Vietnam: A History*, 487. Several writers dwell on the question of the Johnson strategy of stalemate. Among them is F. Charles Parker IV, *Vietnam: Strategy of a Stalemate* (New York: Paragon House, 1989). Parker places much of the blame for the American failure on the machinations of Moscow and Beijing and American ignorance in dealing with them. Some writers suggest that Johnson, by avoiding war with China, sought a Korean solution for Vietnam. Vaughn Davis Bornet attributes Johnson's no-win war in Vietnam to domestic constraints in *The Presidency of Lyndon B. Johnson* (Lawrence: University of Kansas Press, 1983), 253–82.

92. Norman A. Graebner, "Presidential Power and Foreign Affairs," in Charles W. Dunn, ed., *The Future of the American Presidency* (Morristown, N.J.: General Learning Press, 1975), 181–83.

93. Gelb and Betts, 353–54. The system worked in that it achieved what it was designed to achieve— a continuing war that avoided defeat. What helped the administration was the refusal of many moderates to accept the demise of the Saigon government. In explaining Johnson's success in sustaining the war, Graebner stresses the Executive control of the public and congressional mind with claims to greater knowledge, the rhetoric of fear, and the advantages derived from the perennial crisis mood. Graebner, "Presidential Power," 183–87.

94. General Taylor, unmindful of the impossibility of achieving the stated goals of American policy except at an unacceptable price, took the negotiating efforts of the administration seriously. See Maxwell D. Taylor, *Swords and Plowshares* (New York: Norton, 1972), 406. Many writers, such as Herring, Ball, Karnow, Kahin, Thies, Gelb and Betts, however, dwell on the futility of the administration's attempts at negotiation. Ball, an insider, notes that Washington was unconcerned with terms other than repeating its inflexible demands for an independent South Vietnam. Ball, 405–6. That the administration did not take the peace efforts seriously is demonstrated by MARIGOLD, the attempt of June 1966 to establish a channel to Hanoi through Polish intermediaries. The effort culminated in preparations for a meeting in Warsaw in early December when American bombers struck sensitive targets around Hanoi and terminated the contacts. For MARIGOLD see David Kraslow and Stuart H. Loory, *The Secret Search for Peace in Vietnam* (New York: Random House, 1968), 5–88; Karnow, *Vietnam: A History*, 492–98; Gelb and Betts, 151–53.

95. Thies, 219, 222. Similarly Franz Schurmann, Peter Dale Scott, and Reginald Zelnik, in their book, *The Politics of Escalation in Vietnam* (Boston: Beacon Press, 1966), conclude that the president, in entrusting American policy in Vietnam to military escalation rather than the search for a political solution, responded to every opening for negotiations with renewed military intervention.

96. For a detailed account of press opposition to the war in 1966 and 1967 see Kathleen Turner, 134–211. During 1967 even such defenders of official policy as *Life* declared that the war was not worth winning. See Karnow, *Vietnam: A History*, 489. Halberstam complained in the *New York Times* that the government,

"paying the price for its management of the news, cannot make a statement about the war—however accurate—that can be accepted without reservation." For Galbraith's criticism see Berman, *Planning a Tragedy*, 152–53; Kennan in the *Atlantic Monthly* 263 (April 1989): 40.

97. Pettit, 305–41; F. M. Kail, *What Washington Said: Administration Rhetoric and the Vietnam War, 1949–1969* (New York: Harper & Row, 1973), 238–41.

98. Ball, 407; for Westmoreland's appearances in Washington see *New York Times,* 30 Apr. 1967; Department of State *Bulletin* 57 (11 December 1967): 788. See also Westmoreland's assurances of victory in the *New York Times,* 9 Sept. 1967.

99. Gelb and Betts, 169–70; Townsend Hoopes, *The Limits of Intervention* (New York: McKay, 1969), 125; Karnow, *Vietnam: A History,* 498–507. Some Pentagon officials were disheartened by the continued efforts of administration spokesmen, such as Rusk, to dwell on Chinese expansionism as the danger in Vietnam. Hoopes, 94.

100. Halberstam, *Best and Brightest,* 701, 773–74; Henry Brandon, *Anatomy of Error: The Inside Story of the Asian War on the Potomac, 1954–1969,* (Boston: Gambit, 1969), 100–17.

101. Gelb and Betts, 171.

102. Cronkite quoted in Podhoretz, *Why We Were in Vietnam,* 125; Baritz, 180–81; Karnow, *Vietnam: A History,* 547–49.

103. Don Oberdorfer, *Tet!* (Garden City, N.Y.: Doubleday, 1971), 329–30; Podhoretz, *Why We Were in Vietnam,* 116–17. For Braestrup's views see Salisbury, ed., *Vietnam Reconsidered,* 168. Joseph Alsop represented those journalists who had no doubt who won: "As the captured documents continue to pour in," he wrote, "it becomes clearer and clearer that the Tet-period attacks on the cities were a major disaster for General Giap." For Alsop the conditions were ideal for increasing the pressure on Hanoi to insure negotiations on American terms. See Hoopes, 149.

104. Braestrup in Salisbury, ed., *Vietnam Reconsidered,* 169; Moore, 277; George C. Herring's essay on Vietnam in Robert A. Divine, ed., *Exploring the Johnson Years* (Austin: University of Texas Press, 1981), 50–52.

105. Hoopes, 146.

106. For the meeting of the advisory group see Brandon, 118–39; Ball, 407–8. On Johnson's decline see Herbert Y. Shandler, *The Unmaking of a President: Lyndon B. Johnson and Vietnam* (Princeton, N.J.: Princeton University Press, 1977); Braestrup in Salisbury, ed., *Vietnam Reconsidered,* 170–71; Moore, 265–66; Gelb and Betts, 170. Many writers have passed critical judgment on the leadership of Johnson and his advisers. Their central criticism focuses on the administration's failure to examine systematically the question of Vietnam's importance to the United States. The debates revolved around how to do things better, not whether they were worth doing. The final judgment of Daniel Ellsberg and David Halberstam is severe. See Ellsberg, 305–9; Halberstam, *Best and Brightest,* 796.

107. Kissinger quoted in Marvin Kalb and Bernard Kalb, *Kissinger* (Boston: Little, Brown, 1974), 123.

108. On the Nixon-Kissinger decision to continue the war see Henry A. Kissinger, *White House Years* (Boston: Little, Brown, 1979), 228–29; Richard Nixon, *RN: The Memoirs of Richard Nixon,* 2 vols. (New York: Grosset & Dunlap, 1979), 1:431–32; Halberstam, *Best and Brightest,* 807; Ball, 409–10.

109. Kalb and Kalb, 121–23.

110. Ibid., 120; Karnow, *Vietnam: A History,* 588.

111. Kalb and Kalb, 125, 129; Karnow, *Vietnam: A History,* 589.

112. For Operation Menu see Nixon, 1:470–72; Kalb and Kalb, 131–32.

113. Kalb and Kalb, 127–28; Karnow, *Vietnam: History,* 588–89; Kissinger, 272, 275; Ball, 414. Kissinger and Ball doubted the efficacy of the withdrawal program. Stephen E. Ambrose questioned Nixon's effort to popularize the war by promising American withdrawals. "The war," he wrote, "had always been a hard sell, once Nixon began to withdraw, it was nearly an impossible one." Ambrose, *Nixon: The Triumph of a Politician, 1962–1972* (New York: Simon and Schuster, 1989), 302.

114. Ball, 410–11.

115. Nixon, 1:482; David Landau, *Kissinger: The Uses of Power* (Boston: Houghton Mifflin, 1972),

228. In this press conference Nixon assured newsmen that he would not be affected by antiwar activity. On 10 October he told Republicans: "I am not going to be the first American President who loses a war." Nixon, 1:493–95; Buttinger, *Vietnam: Unforgettable Tragedy,* 104.

116. Kissinger, 281–82; Nixon, 1:489–90. For the background of Kissinger's meetings with Xuan Thuy and later Le Duc Tho see Kalb and Kalb, 137–39, 149–51.

117. Kalb and Kalb, 164. For a full discussion of the Cambodian episode see ibid., 152–72; Robert Shaplen, *The Road from War: Vietnam, 1965–1970* (New York: Harper & Row, 1970), 348–54; Karnow, *Vietnam: A History,* 610–12. Kissinger defended Nixon's decision: "We had seen enough of Le Duc Tho to know that without a plausible military strategy we could not have an effective diplomacy." Kissinger, 482, 515–17.

118. For the futility of the 1970–71 negotiations see Kalb and Kalb, 172–85.

119. Kissinger, 968. On Nixon's dilemma see also Karnow, *Vietnam: A History,* 626–28. Ambrose summarizes his judgment of the Nixon policy: "In Vietnam, his policy of retreat without surrender, without negotiations, without concessions, was making the remaining American force in South Vietnam ever more vulnerable without satisfying the doves or ending the war. . . . He put himself in the impossible position of fighting a war while retreating from it without attempting to win it but refusing to admit that his country had lost it." Ambrose, 407.

120. Nixon proclaimed the South Vietnamese disaster in Laos during the early weeks of 1971 as a victory. Nixon, 1:617–18; Karnow, *Vietnam: A History,* 629–31. All of Nixon's initiatives of 1971 and 1972, as Ambrose, Landau, Graebner, and others note—the South Vietnamese invasion of Laos, the continued heavy bombing of the North, the interminable assurances of success—were designed to demonstrate the efficacy of Vietnamization. See Landau, 243–46; Norman A. Graebner, *Cold War Diplomacy: American Foreign Policy, 1945–1975,* rev. ed. (New York: Van Nostrand, 1977), 159–60.

121. For the Easter Offensive, the American response, and the beginning of negotiations see Kalb and Kalb, 284–91, 299–309, 336–42, 348–52; Karnow, *Vietnam: A History,* 640–50. On the 8 October agreement see Nixon, 2:189–91; Ambrose, 627; Kissinger, 1354; Karnow, *Vietnam: A History,* 650–51.

122. Kissinger, 1393; Ambrose, 631, 642–43; Nixon, 2:195–96, 199, 223. Nguyen Tien Hung and Jerrold L. Schecter, in *The Palace File* (New York: Harper & Row, 1986), emphasize the consistency of Thieu's assumptions regarding American promises.

123. Kissinger, 1412.

124. On Linebacker II see Karl Eschmann, *Linebacker: The Untold Story of the Air Raids Over North Vietnam* (New York: Ivy Books, 1989); Mark Clodfelter, *The Limits of Air Power: The American Bombings of North Vietnam* (New York: Free Press, 1989).

125. Nixon quoted in Podhoretz, *Why We Were in Vietnam,* 163.

126. Kissinger, 1466–67; Kalb and Kalb, 418–21; Ball, 421; Gareth Porter, *A Peace Denied: The United States, Vietnam, and the Paris Agreement* (Bloomington: Indiana University Press, 1975); Allen E. Goodman, *The Lost Peace: America's Search for a Negotiated Settlement of the Vietnam War* (Stanford, Calif.: Hoover Institute Press, 1978). Hung and Schechter in *The Palace File* argue that Kissinger made it appear North Vietnam had made concessions, whereas the United States had backed down totally. Kissinger himself admitted the gains in the final negotiations were marginal. Kalb and Kalb, 422.

127. Nixon sent another letter to Thieu on 16 January, promising support but demanding that Thieu accept the new draft. Nixon, 2:261. For the pressures on Thieu to accept the truce see Karnow, *Vietnam: A History,* 654. Hung and Schechter, 355, view the Nixon letters as a pledge of honor and regard them binding. Bui Diem, the South Vietnamese ambassador to the United States, passed final judgment on the cease-fire agreement and Nixon's pressure on Thieu to accept it: "Small nations must be wary of the Americans, since U.S. policies shift quickly as domestic politics and public opinion change. The struggle for us was a matter of life or death. But, for the Americans, it was merely an unhappy chapter in their history, and they could turn the page. We were allied, yet we had different interests." Quoted in Stanley Karnow, *Vietnam: The War Nobody Won,* Foreign Policy Association, Headline Series, no. 263 (March/April 1983), 21.

128. Baritz, 230.

129. Walter H. Capps, *The Unfinished War: Vietnam and the American Conscience* (Boston, Mass.: Beacon Press, 1982), 15.

130. Arnold R. Isaacs, *Without Honor: Defeat in Vietnam and Cambodia* (Baltimore, Md.: Johns Hopkins University Press, 1983), 12–13; Kissinger, 1374; Nixon, 2:271; Karnow, *Vietnam: A History,* 654.

131. Ball, 417–18.

132. Maynard Parker, "Vietnam: The War That Won't End," *Foreign Affairs* 53 (January 1975): 362–71; Buttinger, *Vietnam: Unforgettable Tragedy,* 133–36; Isaacs, 101–46; McAulif and Snepp in Salisbury, ed., *Vietnam Reconsidered,* 260.

133. Podhoretz, *Why We Were in Vietnam,* 163.

134. Lewy, 207. On the decision of Congress to stop the air war in Cambodia see Fanning, 159–93; Podhoretz, *Why We Were in Vietnam,* 164–65; Johnston, 245; Graebner, "Presidential Power," 195–98; Earl C. Ravenal, "Consequences of the End Game in Vietnam," *Foreign Affairs* 53 (July 1975): 651–67.

135. On the fall of Saigon see Karnow, *Vietnam: A History,* 660–70; Buttinger, *Vietnam: Unforgettable Tragedy,* 148–52. For the official American reaction to the fall see Norman A. Graebner, "American Foreign Policy After Vietnam," in John Schlight, ed., *The Second Indochina War* (Washington: Center of Military History, 1986), 193–97.

136. Podhoretz, *Why We Were in Vietnam,* 172.

137. *Washington Post* quoted in Marilyn B. Young, "Revisionists Revised: The Case of Vietnam," Society for Historians of American Foreign Relations *Newsletter* 10 (June 1969): 1.

138. Lewy, 232, 301, 303, 451.

139. Podhoretz, *Why We Were in Vietnam,* 121–22. Lewy's *America in Vietnam,* Podhoretz's *Why We Were in Vietnam,* and John Norton Moore's collection of essays in The Vietnam Debate comprise major writings on Vietnam revisionism. Among the critics of revisionist writings are Marilyn Young, 1–10; George C. Herring, "The 'Vietnam Syndrome' and American Foreign Policy," *Virginia Quarterly Review* 57 (Autumn 1981): 594–612; Paul M. Kattenburg, "Reflections on Vietnam: Of Revisionism and Lessons Yet to be Learned," *Parameters* 14 (August 1984): 42–50; and Walter LaFeber, "The Last War, the Next War, and the New Revisionists," *Democracy* 1 (January 1981): 93–103. The great majority of scholars continue to regard the war a mistake. For them the heavy bombing of villages, the killing of countless civilians, the use of chemical defoliants, and, above all, the denial of self-determination to the people of Vietnam, rendered the war pointless, if not immoral. Revisionists, by contrast, begin with the assumption that South Vietnam was a legitimate political entity and that North Vietnam's effort to incorporate it was an external aggression.

140. Douglas Pike, "Vietnam Today," in Salisbury, ed., *Vietnam Reconsidered,* 253. For good descriptions of postwar Vietnam see Karnow, *Vietnam: The War Nobody Won,* 31–53; George C. Carver, Jr., "Interests and Alliances," *Harper's* 261 (July 1986): 18–22; James Fallows, "No Hard Feelings?" *Atlantic Monthly* 262 (December 1988): 71–78.

141. Podhoretz, *Why We Were in Vietnam,* 196–210; Henry Kam, "A Broken Country," *New York Times Magazine,* 20 Sept. 1987, 96–98, 108–10.

142. Podhoretz, *Why We Were in Vietnam,* 173, 210.

143. Lewy, 440.

144. Podhoretz, *Why We Were in Vietnam,* 176–77.

145. Robert Turner, "Myths and Realities in the Vietnam Debate," Moore, ed., *Vietnam Debate,* 51–52.

146. Johnston, 253–54. For a critique of the application of the principle of falling dominoes to the post-Vietnam world see Graebner, "American Foreign Policy," 213–14.

147. Herring, "Vietnam Syndrome," 594–95, citing especially Ronald Reagan and Alexander Haig, Jr.

148. Robert Elegant, "How to Lose a War: Reflections of a Foreign Correspondent," *Encounter* 57 (August 1981): 73. For countering views that wartime reporting was accurate and no cause for the country's failure see statements by Phillip Knightley, David Halberstam, Peter Arnett, George Reedy, Robert Sheer, Morley Safer, Seymour Hersh, Peter Davis, and Harrison Salisbury in Salisbury, ed., *Vietnam Reconsidered,* passim. Halberstam concluded: "I have always been criticized for being too pessimistic. In truth, I

was not pessimistic enough." Ibid., 115.

149. Lewy, 436; Kissinger, 510; Taylor, 401, 408.

150. Podhoretz, *Why We Were in Vietnam,* 85–107, 209–10; Podhoretz, "Questions of Errors of Fact: The Myths and Realities of Vietnam," in Moore, ed., *Vietnam Debate,* 26. Podhoretz criticizes as well the writers of the New Left who insisted that the United States went into Vietnam to protect its economic interests. Ibid., 26–27.

151. For the realist criticism of the war see Steel, 565–66; Ball, 424–33; Porter McKeever, *Adlai Stevenson: His Life and Legacy* (New York: Morrow, 1989), 545–61; Lee Riley Powell, *J. William Fulbright and America's Lost Crusade* (Little Rock, Ark.: Rose Publishing, 1984); William C. Berman, *William Fulbright and the Vietnam War: The Dissent of a Political Realist* (Kent, Ohio: Kent State University Press, 1988); Hans J. Morgenthau, "We Are Deluding Ourselves in Vietnam," *New York Times Magazine,* 18 Apr. 1965; Morgenthau, "Johnson's Dilemma: The Alternatives Now in Vietnam," *New Republic* 154 (28 May 1966): 12–16. For the views of military critics see Bob Buzzanco, "The American Military's Rationale Against the Vietnam War," *Political Science Quarterly* 101 (Winter 1986): 559–76. Charles DeBenedetti, in his massive study of the antiwar movement, *An American Ordeal: The Antiwar Movement of the Vietnam Era* (Syracuse, N.Y.: Syracuse University Press, 1990), doubts that the movement had any major influence on the outcome of the war. For Todd Gitlin the opinion that mattered belonged to such defectors as Dean Acheson, George Ball, Cyrus Vance, C. Douglas Dillon, Clark Clifford, McGeorge Bundy, and Averell Harriman. See Gitlin in Salisbury, ed., *Vietnam Reconsidered,* 73–74.

152. The views of the general such as Ridgway, journalists such as Lippmann, academics such as Morgenthau, and public leaders such as Fulbright are classic arguments that foreign policies should be governed by clearly perceived national interests and a sense of limits. See, for example, Norman A. Graebner, "Matthew B. Ridgway," in Henry S. Bausum, ed., *Military Leadership and Command* (Lexington, Va.: VMI Foundation, 1987), 181–84; Steel, Lippmann, 565–66.

153. Ngo Vinh Long, "The War and the Vietnamese," Salisbury, ed., *Vietnam Reconsidered,* 228.

154. Buttinger, *Vietnam: Unforgettable Tragedy,* 17; Kahin, 249, 323, 399; Herring, "Vietnam Syndrome," 596–98; Shaplen, *Lost Revolution,* 352–53, referring especially to the views of J. William Fulbright; Walter LaFeber in William Appleman Williams, Thomas McCormick, Lloyd Gardner, and Walter LaFeber, eds., *America in Vietnam: A Documentary History* (Garden City, N.Y.: Anchor Press/Doubleday, 1985), 233. This volume contains many key documents regarding the long American involvement in Vietnam.

155. Karnow, *Vietnam: A History,* 436–41; Baritz, 176–77. Note especially the report of Brian Jenkins on the impact of American military and civilian personnel on Vietnamese society. Ibid., 177. Bui Diem complained of the overbearing presence and demands of Americans in Saigon in Bui Diem and David Chanoff, *In the Jaws of History* (Boston: Houghton Mifflin, 1987). Diem condemned the implementation of U.S. intervention in Vietnam in the *Washington Post,* 30 Aug. 1987. As to the Americans, he wrote: "When they wanted to come, they came. And when they want to leave, they leave. It's as if a neighbor came over and made a shambles of your house, then suddenly decides the whole thing is wrong and calls it quits." William Shawcross agrees that "the consequences of the war for Indochina were appalling. The destruction of the infrastructure and the society was atrocious and any government that would have taken over in 1975 would have faced unbelievable problems." Shawcross, "The Consequences of the War for Indochina," Salisbury, ed., *Vietnam Reconsidered,* 243; McAulif, "Vietnam Today," ibid., 261; Ngo Vinh Long, "The War and the Vietnamese," ibid., 234.

156. Gabriel Kolko, *Anatomy of a War: Vietnam, the United States, and the Modern Historical Experience* (New York: Pantheon, 1985), 72.

157. Ibid., 146–49, 182–87, 200, 296.

158. See Herring's review of Kolko's *Anatomy of a War* in *American Historical Review* 92 (April 1987): 360.

159. Gelb and Betts, 366–69; Herring, *America's Longest War,* 41. Berman, *Planning a Tragedy,* 139–47, discusses at length the suppositions that drove U.S. policy in Vietnam.

160. Paul Kattenburg, *The Vietnam Trauma in American Foreign Policy, 1945–1975* (New Brunswick, N.J.: Transaction Books, 1980), 321; Kolko, 546–48.

161. Herring, *America's Longest War,* 270.

162. Timothy J. Lomparis, *The War Everybody Lost—and Won: America's Intervention in Viet Nam's Twin Struggles* (Baton Rouge: Louisiana State University, 1984), 176.

163. Reagan quoted in Johnston, 238. On the refusal of much of the American foreign policy elite to accept the Vietnam syndrome see Marianna P. Sullivan, "The Foreign Policy Consensus After Vietnam," *Peace and Change* 9 (Summer 1983): 82–95.

164. Herring, "Vietnam Syndrome," 612.

The American Military's Assessment of Vietnam, 1964–1992

Phillip B. Davidson

In all the works by military authors on the Vietnam War there is one—only one—point of unanimity: The United States fought the war incorrectly. The titles of some of their works reflect this frustration: *Strange War, Strange Strategy; Self-Destruction; Peace with Honor?;* and finally Adm. U. S. Grant Sharp's *Strategy for Defeat.*[1] Now the military authors disagree widely on what should have been done, but there is general agreement on what they view as the following fundamental errors of American vision and action in Vietnam.

First, the American leaders, both civilian and military, could never arrive at a general agreement as to the character of the war. Was it an insurgency, a conventional war, a combination of the two, or none of the above? This diversity of perception was critical to U.S. defeat. Old Clausewitz spoke to this failure almost two centuries ago when he wrote: "The first, the supreme, the most far-reaching act of judgment that the statesman and the commander have to make is to establish the kind of war on which they are embarking. . . . This is the first of all strategic questions and the most comprehensive."[2] This vital question was never considered.

Some of the writers point out that this failure of perception as to the character of the war came about and was exacerbated by the changing and "mosaic" nature of the Vietnam War itself.[3] For example, the war grew from an insurgency in South Vietnam in the early 1960s to a full-scale conventional war just before and during Tet 1968, then retrograded in intensity until the conventional offensives of 1972 and 1975. The war was not only a war that changed over time, but a "mosaic" war as well. That is, in one province or corps area a conventional war might be raging while nearby smoldered a minor insurgency. The real problem, of course, was that Americans never understood the nature or strategy of North Vietnamese revolutionary war which they had to combat.[4] Authors such as Stewart Herrington go even a step further by stating that these perceptual problems had cultural roots. Americans never fully understood the North Vietnamese or the South Vietnamese.[5]

To the military authors the second error was that the Johnson administration attempted to fight the Vietnam War without clear, tangible, or measurable objectives, both military and political.[6] Without concrete objectives the war lost all logic and coherence. Strategies could not be developed, nor competing concepts be measured against each other. This lack of clear objectives forced the principal executors of the American effort to formulate their own objectives, and to follow them each in their own way, often nullifying the actions of other operators. Above all, without clear political objectives there was no way the war could be explained to the American people, nor could "victory" itself be defined.

The Nixon administration had a clear objective, if not a noble one: get the United States out of the war without abandoning South Vietnam to an *imminent* Communist annexation. The camouflage for this action was Vietnamization. But Vietnamization itself never had concrete objectives. It was never formalized by agreement or treaty; it had no timetable; it had no measurable goals; and its intent confused both the South Vietnamese and the Americans.[7]

The third failure, as viewed by the military writers, was surrendering the strategic initiative to the enemy.[8] The United States yielded it in the South by the restrictions which prevented its ground forces from severing the Ho Chi Minh Trail or attacking enemy sanctuaries and troops in North Vietnam, the Demilitarized Zone (DMZ), Laos, or Cambodia. These restraints forced the American ground troops into a strategy of attrition within Vietnam. Such a strategy could not prevail because the enemy could control the duration and intensity of the ground combat by retreating into the border sanctuaries. By this maneuver he was able to hold his casualties to an acceptable level.

This loss of the strategic initiative had an even more debilitating consequence. By controlling the tempo and intensity of ground combat, North Vietnam forced the United States into the kind of conflict the Communists wanted—a protracted war. If there is one point of total unanimity among the military authors it is that the United States cannot sustain a prolonged, bloody, ambiguous, and limited war. Yet, its loss of the strategic initiative forced the United States into fighting this type of conflict.

Fourth, while theoretically the United States had the initiative in the North by its air attack, nicknamed Rolling Thunder, it was in reality a fumbling, timid, off-again on-again effort which military writers view as a failure.[9] They advance several reasons for the campaign's downfall. First, since the civilians and the military leaders could not agree as to the character of the war, nor as to Rolling Thunder's objectives, the air offensive floundered about with changing and confused goals. Second, from President Lyndon Johnson down, the civilians controlled the targeting, the armament, the intensity, and even the tactics of the campaign, and yet they were almost totally ignorant of what air power could or should do. The civilians— reversing Clausewitz's famous dictum that "war is a continuation of politics by other means"—believed that war was like domestic politics and could be conducted as such, with empty gestures, consensus, and compromise. Third, the air program was conducted timidly, fearful of involving the Soviets or the Chinese Communists, dismayed by the possibilities of enemy civilian casualties, and intimidated by the adverse opinions of the Third World, European allies, and the antiwar dissenters at home. Finally, the policy of "gradualism" robbed air power of its decisive capability which can be attained only when aerial force is used with mass, surprise, and continuity. Gradualism permitted the North Vietnamese to counter the air offensive by passive measures and by the development of probably the most potent air defense in history.

There were other restraints on Rolling Thunder imposed by the enemy and by the military themselves. For moral reasons, U.S. air chiefs opposed attacks on locks, dams, and dikes, the targets that might have been decisive in gaining an acceptable conclusion to the war. There was a debilitating disunity of effort in the direction and use of air power. Finally, the enemy's air defense array plus geography and weather severely inhibited the program.

The military authors see as a fifth reason for American defeat, a disunity of effort in conducting the war.[10] At the highest level, the alliance of the United States, South Vietnam, South Korea, and the other allies depended for unity of effort not on a combined command with a single commander but on the much less effective device of "cooperation." In reality, each nation's forces largely fought its own war without regard for the others. The U.S. effort in Washington was fragmented and diluted among many agencies and bureaucracies without coordination or command. Military Assistance Command, Vietnam (MACV) ran the American ground war in South Vietnam while the Commander in Chief, Pacific Command (CINCPAC) ran the air war against the North. Ambassador Robert Komer conducted the pacification effort, titularly under Gen. William Westmoreland, but actually as a separate fiefdom. The State Department conducted negotiations with the North Vietnamese, but saw several of its diplomatic initiatives unwittingly nullified by uncoordinated air strikes. Harold Brown, one-time secretary of the air force and later secretary of defense once proclaimed, "Certainly the command chain in Vietnam was the most fouled up thing in recent history."[11] The military authors say, "Amen!"

There is a sixth area where the military writers believe that the United States went wrong. They maintain that President Johnson and his civilian advisers held an unwarranted fear of Soviet and Chinese intervention, particularly the latter.[12] The Soviets' prime concern, according to the military, was to prevent World War III. As for the Chinese, the military writers assert that any close analysis (which, incidentally, was never made at the presidential level) would have revealed convincing reasons why China would stay out of the war. First, it would be operating in Vietnam at the end of a long, tenuous, and vulnerable supply line. Second, if China involved itself deeply in Vietnam, the Soviets might attack it in the rear. Third, the Chinese lost about 800,000 dead in the Korean War, and they had a morbid respect for U.S. killing power. Fourth, the military men maintain that certainly after the advent of the Cultural Revolution, which reduced China to chaos starting in November 1965, there should have been little fear of Chinese intervention. Finally, they point out that the North Vietnamese themselves did not want the Chinese in the war. They hate and fear the Chinese who occupied their territory (particularly the North) for centuries. Only *in extremis* would Ho have allowed large forces of Chinese into Vietnam.

The consensus among military authors as to American errors in Vietnam fragments on what they think should have been done. On this focal point, the military writers split into three broad conceptual groups, which may be called: the counterinsurgents, the conventional warriors, and the air power enthusiasts.

The counterinsurgents hold that the conflict in Vietnam from the start was an insurgency, and that the United States failed to adapt to this mode of warfare.[13] They maintain that the allegiance of the South Vietnamese people to their government was the basic objective of the conflict, not the defeat of North Vietnam's large forces. The proponents of this concept stress the need to protect the population, to build democratic political institutions, and to initiate social justice, such as land reform, rural development, and anticorruption measures.

The champions of the counterinsurgency concept maintain that the war had to be won or lost in South Vietnam. They hold that neither the strategic air offensive in the North, nor the conceptual invasions of the DMZ, Laos, and Cambodia, nor even cutting the Ho Chi Minh Trail, would have brought an acceptable end to the guerrilla insurgency in the South.

In broad military strategy this group advocates the "clear-and-hold" operations as practiced by the United States Marines, the enclave strategy, and the "Demographic Frontier" concept. All of these concepts envision American and South Vietnamese forces garrisoning and defending centers of population and agriculture. Troops would stay in the enclaves and would sally out only to meet enemy units moving toward the defended areas. The "Demographic Frontier" concept, a proposal by a group of civilians working for the secretary of defense which was never adopted, visualized a line running down the spine of the Annamite mountain chain in South Vietnam, thence west to the Cambodian-Vietnamese border around An Loc. The territory to the east and south of this "frontier" (in effect, a huge enclave) would be defended by American and South Vietnamese troops. The remainder of South Vietnam would be surrendered to the enemy.[14]

Tactically, the counterinsurgency concept would require American and allied forces to operate by squads and platoons largely at night and on foot. They would use little helicopter or other air mobility, and would almost completely give up the firepower advantages inherent in the use of tactical air support and artillery. In effect, this concept would require American troops to "out-guerrilla" the guerrilla.

Would this counterinsurgency concept have brought the war to an acceptable conclusion? Nobody knows. Detractors of the counterinsurgency strategy among the military authors point out that it is the nature of revolutionary (or people's) war to progress from an insurgency guerrilla war to a conventional one. They argue that when the latter stage arrives such a conventional enemy force must be opposed, not by small, anti-guerrilla units, but by large regular units organized and equipped to fight a conventional war. These critics further point out that the indigenous insurgency in South Vietnam, the Vietcong, had been almost completely eradicated by 1971. In spite of this counterinsurgency victory, South Vietnam was conquered in 1975, not by guerrillas, but by twenty-two North Vietnamese divisions with hundreds of tanks, artillery pieces, and even a tactical air force. The radically changed nature of the war following the Paris Peace Accords leads Col.

William Le Gro to blame Congress for abandoning South Vietnam by not providing the necessary aid to thwart this conventional attack.[15]

On the other end of the strategic spectrum from the counterinsurgents are the "conventional warriors." This group believes that even as far back as the early 1960s the conflict in Vietnam was, or soon would be, a conventional war.[16] They maintain that the Vietcong were not a true indigenous insurgency, since from 1954 on they were supported, staffed, and controlled by the North Vietnamese politburo. With this belief they insist that the U.S. effort, militarily, politically, and diplomatically, should have been directed primarily against North Vietnam.

Since this school views the conflict in Vietnam as a conventional war, they wanted to use the traditional military response—strike North Vietnam as hard as possible, as soon as possible, and keep striking until the will of the North Vietnamese to resist was shattered, and they abandoned their surrogates in South Vietnam. Buttressing this concept of a quick, hard strike, the conventional warriors argue that if the United States must fight a limited war, it must be concluded quickly. Beyond that, they argue, a short, violent war would be less costly in money, casualties (both friendly and enemy, military and civilian), and national divisiveness than would a long, twilight struggle.

The details of the proposed conventional war strategy vary among authors, but the following actions find general endorsement. First, in 1965 President Johnson should have mobilized American public opinion behind the war. Several authors suggest that he should have asked Congress to declare that a state of war existed between North Vietnam and the United States. This declaration would have committed Congress to the war, and through it, the American people. Second, American sea and air forces should have launched an immediate and intensive air and naval campaign against North Vietnam. This campaign would have mined the ports and severed the land lines of communications from China within North Vietnam, cutting off exterior support of the war. Next, an air offensive would destroy North Vietnam's industry and facilities and finally interdict the battlefield. Third, following the declaration of war the president should have mobilized the required forces from the United States Reserves and the National Guard. Fourth, the United States should have put sizable ground forces into South Vietnam as soon as logistical arrangements permitted. Fifth, with these troops the United States would have cut the Ho Chi Minh Trail and kept it cut, meanwhile cleaning out the sanctuaries in Laos, Cambodia, and the DMZ. Sixth, steps should have been taken to fuse the military and political efforts of the United States, the South Vietnamese, and the other allies while unifying the American effort in Washington and in Vietnam. Last, every effort should have been made to build up the Republic of Vietnam Armed Forces.

Would this strategy have brought the war to an acceptable conclusion? Nobody knows. Detractors of this conventional war concept among the military writers condemn the strategy for conflicting reasons. The counterinsurgents assert that it would have little influence on what they believe was the real war in the South. In

Self-Destruction Cincinnatus claims the Army's bureaucratic inertia and opposition to change prevented adoption of strategies not from the traditional mold.[17] The air power enthusiasts maintain that the huge ground forces required by the conventional concept would be unnecessary. Regardless of the negative appraisal of the counterinsurgents and the air power enthusiasts, the conventional war strategy was a "high-risk, high-cost" concept. It might have brought in the Chinese, and it would have been costly in world opinion. It would certainly have entailed a major disruption of American life.

As one contemplates the differences in perceptions of the war's character between the counterinsurgents and the conventional warriors, a natural question arises. How could the two groups, composed of experienced and intelligent American officers, hold such divergent views as to the character of the war? Some of the authors suggest that the changing and mosaic character of revolutionary (or people's) war is largely responsible for this dichotomy.[18] The proponents of either strategy take a situation in a given area, in a given time period, and extend that observation to cover the entire war.

There is also a semantical reason for this disagreement. The loose use of such terms as "insurgency," "guerrilla war," and even "conventional war" permit the disputants to include within their self-crafted definitions of these words many disparate aspects of combat. The counterinsurgents say that their definition of an insurgency includes elements of conventional war. The conventional warriors maintain that they recognize guerrilla insurgency war as a component of a conventional conflict. Viewed in this light the argument comes down to the allocation of resources, as one perceptive author points out.[19] Should the bulk of the resources be applied to combatting the insurgency or to defeating the North Vietnamese Main Force units? Actually, however, the problem is more complex than the allocation of resources. One's vision of the character of the war determines operational art and tactics, and these fundamentals drag in their train such aspects of combat as organization, training, intelligence-gathering, logistic support, and basing, to name only a few.

There is another point of interest in this controversy about the character of the war. There is a conspicuous "generation gap" in the perception of the conflict's character. By far the greatest number who hold that the war was a conventional one were very senior officers in the Vietnam War, veterans of World War II and Korea. Conversely, the counterinsurgents are mostly young officers still on active duty. There are exceptions on both sides of the debate, but this split between the generations is well defined.

The third concept for winning the war in Vietnam is that of the air power enthusiasts, who argue that a properly conducted air offensive against North Vietnam (coupled with the mining of its ports) could have ended the war satisfactorily at any time after early 1965.[20] This group is composed almost entirely of senior United States Air Force officers, although one of its members is Adm. U. S. Grant Sharp, CINCPAC, from 1964 to 1968, the officer who conducted the air campaign against the North.

For reasons already set forth, the air power enthusiasts bitterly censure Rolling Thunder. Admiral Sharp sums up their view for this futile program when he condemns it as "an example of near-flagrant misuse of air power."[21] The air power enthusiasts base this scathing judgment of Rolling Thunder and their proposed strategy on what to them are the lessons of history. In contrast to the inconclusiveness of Rolling Thunder, they cite the air offensives against Germany and Japan in World War II as primarily responsible for American victory in that great conflict. In further support of their concept, they adduce the success of the air campaigns of 1972 in Vietnam, Linebackers I and II. The first destroyed North Vietnam's Easter Offensive, while the second brought the North Vietnamese scurrying back to the conference table after the Communists had stalled negotiations.

The strategy advocated by the air enthusiasts envisions an intensive, continuous air campaign, focused on the enemy's vital systems. In detail the conceived air offensive would: first, deny North Vietnam assistance from China and Russia; second, destroy in depth those resources already in Vietnam that contribute to the support of aggression; third, destroy all military facilities in North Vietnam; and fourth, harass, disrupt, and impede movement of men and materials from North Vietnam into Laos and South Vietnam. This group believes that such an air offensive carried out by a unified effort under a single air commander, free of debilitating civilian restraints, would have destroyed not only North Vietnam's capability to continue the war but also its will to do so.

Would an all-out air offensive against the North have worked? Nobody knows. There are skeptics, however. The U.S. Army leadership doubted from the start of the war that air power alone could win it. General Westmoreland put it more bluntly when in 1967 he said, "Air power alone didn't do the job. It never has, but we give it a chance in every war."[22]

The doubts of the Army skeptics are echoed by the analyses of, strangely enough, two younger Air Force officers.[23] Note again the generational gap. They assert that the air offensive against North Vietnam envisioned by the air power enthusiasts could only succeed against an industrial nation in an all-out war where air power is inhibited by few restraints. In a limited war against an agrarian country waging or supporting an insurgency, such an air offensive will not bring decisive results. North Vietnam could lose what little industry it had and still carry on the war. Air Force Major Mark Clodfelter perceptively points out a second obstacle to the success of any all-out air offensive against the North in the 1965–68 period. This was President Johnson's sweeping political desire as set forth in National Security Action Memorandum No. 288 on 17 March 1964 for an "independent, non-Communist South Vietnam."[24] The achievement of this objective required nothing less than the total defeat of the North Vietnamese Communists. It was a monumental task, one unattainable by air power alone, particularly under the restraints which are inherent in a limited war.

These officers grant the success of the Linebacker offensives, but they maintain that these aerial victories do not validate the expectations of the air power enthusiasts. These air offensives succeeded primarily because (as they see it) the war itself had changed radically. In the 1972 Easter Offensive, Linebacker I succeeded because the war was no longer an insurgency but a large-scale conventional war in which the enemy had huge logistical requirements that were vulnerable to U.S. air power. Linebacker II succeeded because, in contrast to President Johnson, President Richard Nixon's objective was very limited: to conclude an agreement, whose main points had already been settled with the North Vietnamese, and to do this before Congress legislated to end the war. This narrow objective was obtainable by the brief, all-out offensive launched against North Vietnam.[25]

And so, some twenty years later, the debate simmers on about what the United States did wrong in Vietnam and what it should have done there. By and large the assessments of the military writers on the Vietnam War can be summed up, as two of them actually sum them up, by that haunting phrase from John Greenleaf Whittier's poem, "Maud Muller": "For all sad words of tongue or pen, the saddest are these: 'It might have been!'"[26]

Notes

1. Lew Walt, *Strange War, Strange Strategy: A General's Report on Vietnam* (New York: Funk & Wagnalls, 1970); Cincinnatus, *Self-Destruction: The Disintegration and Decay of the United States Army during the Vietnam Era* (New York: Norton, 1981); Ulysses S. Grant Sharp, *Strategy for Defeat: Vietnam in Retrospect* (San Rafael, Calif.: Presidio, 1978).

2. Karl von Clausewitz, *On War,* Michael Howard and Peter Paret, eds., (Princeton, N.J.: Princeton University Press, 1976), 88–89.

3. David R. Palmer, *Summons of the Trumpet: U.S.-Vietnam in Perspective* (San Rafael, Calif.: Presidio, 1978), 111–12; Donald J. Mrozek, *Air Power and the Ground War in Vietnam* (Maxwell Air Force Base, Ala.: Air University Press, 1988), 69; Donn A. Starry, *Mounted Combat in Vietnam* (Washington, D.C.: Government Printing Office, 1978), 10–16; Dennis M. Drew and Donald M. Snow, *The Eagle's Talons: The American Experience at War* (Maxwell Air Force Base, Ala.: Air University Press, 1988), 287; and Phillip B. Davidson, *Secrets of the Vietnam War* (Novato, Calif.: Presidio, 1990), 20–21.

4. Davidson, *Secrets,* 17–26.

5. Stewart A. Herrington makes the case for not understanding the North Vietnamese in *Silence Was a Weapon* (Novato, Calif.: Presidio, 1982) and for not understanding the South Vietnamese in *Peace with Honor?* (Novato, Calif.: Presidio, 1983), vii.

6. Jeffrey J. Clarke, *Advice and Support: The Final Years, 1965–1973* (Washington, D.C.: U.S. Center of Military History, 1988), 104–337; Mrozek, 174–75, 182; Mark Clodfelter, *The Limits of Air Power: The American Bombing of North Vietnam* (New York: Free Press, 1989), 71–72; Drew and Snow, 281–84; and Harry G. Summers, Jr., *On Strategy: The Vietnam War in Context* (Carlisle Barracks, Pa.: Strategic Studies Institute, U.S. Army War College, 1981), 3, 59–66, 92.

7. See also Jeffrey Clarke, "Vietnamization: The War to Groom an Ally," in this volume.

8. Bruce Palmer, Jr., *The 25-Year War: America's Military Role in Vietnam* (Lexington: University Press of Kentucky, 1984), 57–58, 178; Sharp, 236; and Davidson, *Secrets,* 173.

9. Clodfelter, *Limits,* 44, 117–39, 142; Sharp, xvi, 85, 115, 134; William W. Momyer, *Air Power in Three Wars* (Washington, D.C.: Government Printing Office, 1978), 18–26; Maxwell D. Taylor, *Swords and Plowshares* (New York: Norton, 1972), 350; and David Palmer, 73–79, 122–32.

10. Clarke, *Advice,* 81–82, 84, 87–96; Momyer, 65–109; Taylor, *Swords,* 249; Maxwell Taylor, *Re-*

sponsibility and Response (New York: Harper & Row, 1967), 61–64; William C. Westmoreland, *A Soldier Reports* (Garden City, N.Y.: Doubleday, 1976), 499–500; Clodfelter, *Limits,* 164; Andrew F. Krepinevich, Jr., *The Army and Vietnam* (Baltimore, Md.: John Hopkins University Press, 1986), 195–96; Bruce Palmer, 30, 193–94; and Summers, 92, 101–3.

11. John Morocco and the Editors of the Boston Publishing Co., *The Vietnam Experience: Rain of Fire, Air Wars, 1969–1973* (Boston: Boston Publishing Co., 1985), 183.

12. Phillip B. Davidson, *Vietnam at War: The History 1946–1975* (Novato, Calif.: Presidio, 1988), 389–433; idem, *Secrets,* 132–35; Taylor, *Swords,* 247; idem, *Responsibility,* 33–34; and Clodfelter, *Limits,* 74.

13. Cincinnatus, 9–10, 31–35, 50–52; Krepinevich, 10–11, 164, 215, 262–68; Clodfelter, *Limits,* x, 39; and Taylor, *Swords,* 363. For the genesis of U.S. counterinsurgency doctrine in Vietnam see ibid., 201–3. For counterinsurgency in practice see Walt, 105–12.

14. Krepinevich, 242–44.

15. William E. Le Gro, *Vietnam from Cease-Fire to Capitulation* (Washington, D.C.: U.S. Army Center of Military History, 1981), 2–4.

16. Summers, 47–48, 55; Westmoreland, 174–88; Momyer, 22, 287; Sharp, 52, 166; Taylor, *Swords,* 418.

17. Cincinnatus, 113–16.

18. Davidson, *Secrets,* 23–26; David Palmer, 111–12; Drew and Snow, 287–88; Mrozek, 171–75.

19. Krepinevich, 215.

20. Momyer, 13, 21, 34; Bruce Palmer, 34; David Palmer, 132; Sharp, xvii, 49, 110, 167; Mrozek, 7.

21. Sharp, xvi.

22. David Palmer, 132.

23. Maj. Mark Clodfelter and Col. Donaldson D. Frizzell. Clodfelter, *Limits,* 203–10; W. Scott Thompson and Donaldson D. Frizzell, eds., *The Lessons of Vietnam* (New York: Crane, Russak, 1977), 133, 149–50.

24. Clodfelter, *Limits,* 40–41.

25. See also Mark Clodfelter, "Nixon and the Air Weapon," in this volume.

26. John Greenleaf Whittier, *The Poetical Works of Whittier* (Boston, Mass., Houghton Mifflin, 1975), 48.

"Cold Blood":
LBJ's Conduct of Limited War in Vietnam

George C. Herring

Of the two great questions on American involvement in Vietnam—why did we intervene and why did we fail—the latter has provoked the most emotional controversy. Failure in Vietnam challenged as perhaps nothing else has one of our most fundamental myths—the notion that we can accomplish anything we set our collective minds to—and partisans of many diverse points of view have sought in its aftermath to explain this profoundly traumatic experience.

Much of this discussion ignores basic precepts of historical method. Many of those seeking to explain why we failed are in fact arguing that an alternative approach would have succeeded.[1] Such arguments are at best debatable on their own terms. More important, they are dubious methodologically. As Wayne Cole pointed out many years ago of a strikingly similar debate in the aftermath of World War II, the "most heated controversies . . . do not center on those matters for which the facts and truth can be determined with greatest certainty. The interpretive controversies, on the contrary, rage over questions about which the historian is least able to determine the truth."[2]

Much more might be learned by focusing on how the war was fought and explaining why it was fought as it was, without reference to alternative strategies and without presuming that it could have been won or was inevitably lost. This essay will examine two crucial areas: the formulation of and subsequent nondebate over military strategy and the administration's efforts to manage public opinion. By doing this, much can be learned about why the war was fought the way it was and took the direction it did.

I

Limited war requires the most sophisticated strategy, precisely formulated in terms of ends and means, with particular attention to keeping costs at acceptable levels. What stands out about the Johnson administration's handling of Vietnam is that in what may have been the most complex war ever fought by the United States there was never any systematic discussion at the highest levels of government of the fundamental issue of how the war should be fought. The crucial discussions of June and July 1965 focused on the numbers of troops that would be provided rather than how and for what ends they would be used, and this was the only such discussion until the Communist Tet Offensive forced the issue in March 1968. Strategy, such as it was, emerged from the field, with little or no input from the people at the top.

Why was this the case? Simple overconfidence may be the most obvious explanation. From the commander in chief to the G.I.s in the field, Americans could not conceive that they would be unable to impose their will on what Lyndon Johnson once dismissed as that "raggedy-ass little fourth-rate country." There was no need to think in terms of strategy.

The explanation, however, goes much deeper than that. Although he took quite seriously his role as commander in chief, personally picking bombing targets, agonizing over the fate of U.S. airmen, and building a scale model of Khe Sanh in the White House situation room, Lyndon Johnson, unlike James Polk, Abraham Lincoln, or Franklin Roosevelt, never took control of *his* war. In many ways a great president, Johnson was badly miscast as a war leader. He preoccupied himself with other matters, the Great Society and the legislative process he understood best and so loved. In contrast to Lincoln, Roosevelt, and even Harry Truman, he had little interest in military affairs and no illusions of military expertise. He was fond of quoting his political mentor Sam Rayburn to the effect that "if we start making the military decisions, I wonder why we paid to send them to West Point," probably a rationalization for his own ignorance and insecurity in the military realm.[3] Johnson "failed to do the one thing that the central leadership must do," Stephen Peter Rosen has observed. He did not "define a clear military mission for the military" and did not "establish a clear limit to the resources to be allocated for that mission."[4]

Indeed, at crucial points in the war, the commander in chief gave little hint of his thinking. National Security Adviser McGeorge Bundy literally pleaded with him in November 1965 to make clear his positions on the big issues so that Secretary of Defense Robert McNamara could be certain he was running the war "the right way for the right reasons, in your view."[5] By late 1967 private citizen Bundy's pleading had taken on a tone of urgency, warning Johnson that he must "take command of a contest that is more political in character than any in our history except the Civil War."[6]

McNamara himself might have filled the strategic void left by the president, but he was no more willing to intrude in this area than Johnson. In many ways a superb secretary of defense, he was an ineffectual minister of war. Conceding his ignorance of military matters, he refused to interfere with the formulation of strategy, leaving it to the military to set the strategic agenda. When asked on one occasion why he did not tell his officers what to do and reminded that Churchill had not hesitated to do so, he shot back that he was no Churchill and would not dabble in an area where he had no competence.[7]

Johnson and McNamara saw their principal task as maintaining tight operational control over the military. This tendency must be understood in the context of the larger strains in civil-military relations in the 1950s and 1960s. A powerful peacetime military establishment was something new in postwar American life, and civilian leaders were uncertain how to handle it. They recognized the necessity of military power in an era of global conflict, but they feared the possibility of rising military influence within the government. If it confirmed the tradition of civilian preeminence, Gen. Douglas MacArthur's defiance of civilian authority during the Korean War seemed also to symbolize the dangers. Former general and president Dwight D. Eisenhower waged open warfare with his joint chiefs, and civil-military tension emerged full-blown in the Kennedy years. McNamara's efforts to master the arcane mysteries of the Pentagon budget process set off a near revolt within the military, and civilian and military leaders were sharply divided over the handling of such things as the Bay of Pigs, the Cuban Missile Crisis, and the Nuclear Test Ban Treaty.[8]

Suspicious of the military and operating in an age of profound international tension with weaponry of enormous destructive potential, civilians concentrated on keeping the generals and admirals in check. During the Cuban Missile Crisis, McNamara haunted the Navy's command center and even then had difficulty preventing provocative actions, reinforcing his determination to keep control tightly in his own hands.[9] Johnson brought to the White House the Southern populist's suspicion of the military. Suspecting that the generals and admirals needed war to boost their reputations, he, like McNamara, was determined to keep a close rein on them.[10] The consequence in Vietnam was a day-to-day intrusion into the tactical conduct of the war on a quite unprecedented scale. The larger result, Rosen observes, was an unhappy combination of "high level indecision and micromanagement."[11]

Inasmuch as McNamara and Johnson's civilian advisers thought strategically, they did so in terms of the limited-war theories in vogue at the time. Strategy was primarily a matter of sending signals to foes, of communicating resolve, of using military force in a carefully calibrated way to deter enemies or bargain toward a negotiated settlement. This approach must have appeared expedient to Johnson and his advisers because it seemed to offer a cheap, low-risk answer to a difficult problem. It also appeared to be controllable, thereby reducing the risk of all-out war.[12] The Kennedy administration's successful handling of the Cuban Missile Crisis seems to have reinforced in the minds of U.S. officials the value of such an approach. "There is no longer any such thing as strategy, only crisis management," McNamara exclaimed in the aftermath of Kennedy's victory.[13]

He could not have been more wrong, of course, and the reliance on limited-war theory had unfortunate consequences. It encouraged avoidance of costly and risky decisions. It diverted attention from real strategy and caused the military problem of how to win the war in South Vietnam to be neglected. It led the decision-makers into steps they must have sensed the American people might eventually reject. And when Hanoi refused to respond as bargaining theory said it should, the United States was left without any strategy at all.[14]

Created in World War II to provide military advice to the commander in chief, the Joint Chiefs of Staff (JCS) did not effectively play that role in the Vietnam War.

The National Security Act of 1947 as modified by subsequent legislation left the JCS with no formal position in the chain of command. They were merely advisers, and there was no requirement that they be consulted. More important, perhaps, in the new postwar environment civilians had increasingly invaded a once exclusive preserve and senior military officers had abdicated a good deal of responsibility in the area of strategic thought and planning. Postwar military officers had also been "civilianized" through indoctrination in management techniques and limited-war theory at the expense of their more traditional folkways. Thus the new breed of military managers, the joint chiefs handpicked by McNamara, were by and large staff officers, men in many ways ill-equipped to devise sophisticated strategies for a complex war.[15]

Civil-military tensions further complicated the formulation of strategy. From the start, there were profound differences among the Joint Chiefs of Staff and between them and the civilian leadership as to how, or at least at what level, the war should be fought. Perhaps tragically, these differences were never even addressed, much less resolved. Indeed, the decision-making process seems to have been rigged to produce consensus rather than controversy. As a result, some major issues were raised but not answered; others were not even raised. The sort of full-scale debate that might have led to a reconsideration of the U.S. commitment in Vietnam or to a more precise formulation of strategy did not take place. And the tensions and divisions that were left unresolved would provide the basis for bitter conflict when the steps taken in July 1965 did not produce the desired results.

During the process of escalation in Vietnam, civilian and military leaders approached each other cautiously. The joint chiefs compromised their own sharp differences over how the war should be fought and developed unified proposals to prevent the civilians from exploiting their differences.[16] Johnson feared the implications of the joint chiefs' proposals for escalation. Wary at the same time of provoking a military revolt and sensitive to the military's influence with conservatives in Congress, he was determined, in Jack Valenti's words, to "sign on" his military advisers to his Vietnam policies, thus protecting his right flank. The president repeatedly trimmed the joint chiefs' proposals to expand the bombing of North Vietnam and commit combat troops to South Vietnam, but he refused to impose firm limits and at each step he gave them enough to suggest they might get more later.[17]

During the July 1965 decisions on the major troop commitment, deep divisions over strategy were subordinated to maintaining the appearance of unity. While rejecting without any discussion several of the measures the JCS considered essential for prosecuting the war, most notably mobilization of the reserves, Johnson shrewdly co-opted them into his consensus. The Chiefs did not deliberately mislead the president as to what might be required in Vietnam. On the crucial question of North Vietnamese resistance, they probably miscalculated as badly as he did. Perhaps to prevent him from moving to the position advocated by George Ball, however, they downplayed the difficulties the United States might face, and although bitterly disappointed with his refusal to mobilize the reserves, they quietly acquiesced. They seem to have assumed that once the United States was committed in Vietnam they could maneuver the president into doing what they wanted through what JCS chairman Gen. Earle Wheeler called a "foot-in-the-door" approach.[18]

Thus the July 1965 discussions comprised an elaborate cat-and-mouse game with the nation the ultimate loser. Perhaps if the military had perceived Johnson's steadfast determination to limit U.S. escalation, they might have been less ready to press for war. Though they too miscalculated, the military leaders seem to have perceived more accurately than the civilians what would be required in Vietnam. Perhaps, if Johnson had been more aware of their estimates and reservations, he might have been more cautious.

An equally crippling form of bureaucratic gridlock persisted during the period 1965–67. Far more than has been recognized and than was revealed in the *Pentagon Papers,* no one in the Johnson administration really liked the way the war was being fought or the results that were being obtained. What is even more striking, however, is that despite the rampant dissatisfaction, there was no change in strategy or even any systematic discussion at the highest levels of government of the possibility of a change in strategy. Again, the system seems to have been rigged to prevent debate and adaptation.

From July 1965, there were sharp differences over strategy within the Johnson administration, and these differences became more pronounced as the measures taken failed to produce the desired results. The running battle over the bombing, especially between McNamara and the Joint Chiefs of Staff, is well known.[19] But there was also widespread and steadily growing conflict over Gen. William C. Westmoreland's costly and ineffectual ground strategy. From the outset, the Marine Corps strongly objected to the Army's determination to fight guerrillas by staging decisive battles "along the Tannenberg design."[20] Perhaps more significant, within the Army itself there was great concern about Westmoreland's approach. As early as November 1965, after the bloody battle of the Ia Drang Valley, Army Chief of Staff Harold Johnson had been skeptical of Westmoreland's attrition strategy, and increasingly thereafter he questioned the wastefulness and fruitfulness of search-and-destroy operations. Vice Chief of Staff Creighton Abrams seems to have shared at least some of Johnson's skepticism, as did some top officers in the field in Vietnam.[21]

Divisions within the military paled compared to the growing conflict between military and civilians. On their side, the military bristled at Johnson's refusal to mobilize the reserves and chafed under restrictions on the bombing, troop levels, and the use of troops in Laos, Cambodia, and across the Demilitarized Zone (DMZ). They protested bitterly Washington's micromanagement of the war. "The idea," Marine Gen. Victor Krulak complained in 1967, "is to take more and more items of less and less significance to higher and higher levels so that more and more decisions on smaller and smaller matters may be made by fewer and fewer people."[22]

The civilians, on the other hand, observed with growing alarm military proposals for escalation. When the joint chiefs proposed a huge increase in troops, mining of North Vietnam's major ports, and expansion of the war into Laos and Cambodia in March 1967, civilians in the State and Defense Departments mobilized as they had not before to head off what they viewed as a perilous expansion of the war. They disagreed themselves on what should be done about the bombing, but they generally agreed that henceforth the major effort should be south of the 20th Parallel and there was some sentiment that it might be stopped altogether. By this time, the ground strategy was also under fire. Assistant Secretary of Defense John McNaughton warned of the "fatal flaw" of approving more and more troops "while only *praying* for their proper use." At the very minimum, he added, an upper limit should be imposed on American forces. But he urged McNamara to go further. The "philosophy of the war should be fought out now, so everyone will not be proceeding on their own major premises, and getting us in deeper and deeper."[23]

McNamara himself took the lead against expansion of the war in the spring of 1967. In a draft presidential memorandum of 19 May 1967 the secretary went further than the Pentagon and State Department civilians, advancing positions the authors of the *Pentagon Papers* accurately describe as "radical." Warning that the JCS proposals would not achieve victory, he sketched out a complex politico-military "strategy" that at least hinted at extrication. The bombing should be cut back to the area below the 20th Parallel. A firm ceiling should be placed on ground troops, after which the United States should more actively seek a political settlement. He proposed a scaling down of objectives, affirming that the United States should not be obligated to guarantee an independent, non-Communist South Vietnam. He spoke of compromise, even involving "inter alia, a role in the south for members of the VC," and without naming names proposed "major personnel changes within the government."[24]

Despite this widespread dissatisfaction, there was no change in strategy or even serious discussion of a change in strategy. There are several major reasons for the persistence of this bureaucratic and strategic gridlock. Certainly, the military tradition of autonomy of the field commander inhibited debate on and possible alteration of the ground strategy. Although greatly concerned with the cost and consequences of Westmoreland's excessive use of firepower, Army Chief of Staff Johnson deferred to the field commander. "I would deplore and oppose any intervention from the Washington level to impose limitations on further firepower application," he reassured Westmoreland. He would go no further than suggest that it might be "prudent" to "undertake a very careful examination of the problem."[25]

More important was the leadership style of the Commander in Chief. Lyndon Johnson's entirely political manner of running the war, his consensus-oriented modus operandi, effectively stifled debate. On such issues as bombing targets and bombing pauses, troop levels and troop use, by making concessions to each side without giving any what it wanted, he managed to keep dissent and controversy under control.[26]

The president and his top advisers also imposed rigid standards of loyalty on a bitterly divided administration. Unlike Franklin Roosevelt, Johnson had no tolerance for controversy, and he imposed on his advisers the "Macy's window at high noon" brand of loyalty made legendary by David Halberstam.[27] Unfortunately, the two men who might have influenced him, McNamara and Secretary of State Dean Rusk, shared his perverted notions of team play. "I don't believe the government of a complicated state can operate effectively," McNamara once said, "if those in charge of the departments of the government express disagreement with decisions of the established head of that government." Whenever someone dissented, it made more difficult the attainment of the larger group goals.[28] In-house devil's advocate George Ball later recalled that McNamara treated his dissenting memos rather like "poisonous snakes." He was "absolutely horrified" by them, considered them "next to treason." It is now obvious that when McNamara himself became a dissenter in 1967 it was an excruciating experience for him.[29]

Finally, and perhaps even more important, is what might be called the MacArthur syndrome, the pervasive fear among civilians and military of a repetition of the illustrious general's challenge to civilian authority. Johnson, as noted, lived in terror of a military revolt and did everything in his power to avert it. "General, I have a lot riding on you," he blurted out to Westmoreland in Honolulu in February 1966. "I hope you don't pull a MacArthur on me." At Honolulu, Westmoreland later recalled, Johnson carefully sized him up, eventually satisfying himself that *his* general was "sufficiently understanding" of the constraints imposed on him and was a "reliable" and "straightforward soldier who would not get involved in the politics of war."[30]

An encounter in July 1967 is even more revealing of the delicate game being played between the general and his commander in chief. An increasingly frustrated and restive Westmoreland reminded the president that he had made every effort to "ease his burden by my conduct and demands." But he added an only slightly veiled warning that he must think of his own requirements first. Johnson flattered Westmoreland by expressing great admiration for the way he had handled himself. He cleverly sought to appease the general by hinting that he did not always favor his civilian advisers over his military.[31]

Themselves learning from Korea, the joint chiefs carefully refrained from anything even smacking of a direct challenge to civilian authority. Although they remained deeply divided on the conduct of the war, they continued to present unified proposals to the civilians, thus stifling debate within their own ranks. A sophisticated politician skilled in bureaucratic maneuver, General Wheeler's approach was political rather than confrontational and emphasized short-term acquiescence and silence. Hopeful eventually of getting strategic license by gradually breaking down the restrictions imposed by the White House, he encouraged Westmoreland to continue to push for escalation of the war and to accept less than he wanted in order to get his "foot in the door." Wheeler also implored the field commander to keep his subordinates quiet. If escalation were to occur following reports of military dissatisfaction, he warned, critics would conclude that the military was "riding roughshod" over civilians. Officers must understand the "absolute necessity for every military man to keep his mouth shut and get on with the war."[32] Thus rather than confront their differences directly, the president and his top military leadership dealt with each other by stealth and indirection.

In various ways, between July 1965 and August 1967, debate was stifled and dissent squelched. When Army Chief of Staff Johnson warned in a speech that the war might last ten years, Barry Zorthian later recalled, "he got his ass chewed out. That was denied awfully fast."[33] On the "orders" of Ambassador Henry Cabot Lodge, also a critic of Westmoreland, Marine commandant Gen. Wallace Greene in a "deep backgrounder" in Saigon in August 1966 affirmed that it would take 750,000 men and five years to win the war with the prevailing strategy. The reaction, Greene later recalled, was "immediate, explosive, and remarkable." An "agitated" and "as usual, profane" president demanded to know "What in the God-damned hell" Greene meant by making such a statement. The commandant was forced to issue denials, and the White House denied the existence of studies leading to such conclusions.[34]

Deeply alarmed with the ground strategy by mid-1966, Marine Gen. Victor Krulak sought to change it. Certain that the strategy of attrition played to enemy strengths, he proposed an alternative that would have combined protection of the South Vietnamese population with the slow liberation of Vietcong-controlled villages. Krulak was well connected in Washington, and with the blessings of Greene and Commander in Chief Pacific, Adm. U.S. Grant Sharp, he took his proposals to McNamara, Averell Harriman, and the president himself. As Krulak later recalled it, McNamara made only "brief comment." Harriman expressed interest in his proposals for pacification. But he got nowhere with Johnson. When he mentioned that attacks on North Vietnamese ports might be combined with an altered ground strategy, the president "got to his feet, put his arm around my shoulder, and propelled me firmly toward the door."[35]

Even in the spring of 1967, with the secretary of defense now in open revolt against what had once been called "McNamara's war" and civilians and military deeply divided against each other, there was no change of strategy and indeed no discussion of change at the top levels. Johnson continued to fear that adoption of the military's program might provoke a larger war. On the other hand, like his national security adviser, Walt Rostow, he believed that McNamara's dovish proposals went "a bit too far" to the other extreme. Alarmed by what Rostow called "the dangerously strong feelings in your official family," he sought, like his national security adviser, a "scenario" that could "hold our official family together in ways that look after the nation's interest and make military sense."[36] Characteristically, he avoided a confrontation between the positions of the JCS and McNamara. There was no discussion of the issues at the top levels. He delayed a decision for months, and when he decided he did so on a piecemeal basis, carefully avoiding debate on the larger issues. Thus, according to the authors of the *Pentagon Papers,* the debate (if indeed that word can properly be used) "floundered toward a compromise."[37] The president approved an expansion of the bombing, but stopped well short of mining North Vietnamese ports. He refused to approve expansion of the war into Laos, Cambodia, and North Vietnam. He agreed to deploy only 55,000 additional ground forces, but he refused to set a ceiling and he scrupulously avoided discussion of the larger issue of how and for what purposes the troops would be used.

The debate that could not occur within the administration—curiously—took place in Congress in August 1967 in hearings before Sen. John Stennis's Preparedness Subcommittee. Frustrated from above and under growing pressure from increasingly restive officers below, the JCS in August 1967 mounted a MacArthurstyle challenge to civilian authority, abandoning Wheeler's cautious approach and taking their case to Congress.[38] The original intent of the hearings was to "get McNamara" and force Johnson to escalate the war.[39] Ironically, McNamara came to see hearings designed to "get" him as an opportunity to combat growing military pressures for expanding the war without violating his own rigid standards of loyalty to the president. In a strange, almost surreal way, the Stennis Subcommittee hearings became the forum for the debate that could not take place within the inner councils of the government.

According to one account, the Stennis hearings caused a near-revolt on the part of the joint chiefs. As journalist Mark Perry tells it, McNamara's attack on the bombing in his testimony before the committee on 25 August provoked a special emergency meeting of the joint chiefs at which a decision was reached to resign en masse. That decision was allegedly reversed the following morning after General Wheeler had second thoughts. "It's mutiny," Perry quotes him telling his colleagues. "In any event," he is said to have added, "If we resign they'll just get someone else. And we'll be forgotten." Perry's story has sparked considerable controversy, and has been emphatically denied by the two living members of Johnson's Joint Chiefs of Staff.[40]

Whatever the case, the Stennis hearings represented what Johnson had most feared since the start of the war, division within his administration and the threat of a military revolt backed by right-wingers in Congress. Remarkably, he was able to contain it. He "resolved" the strategic differences between his subordinates as he had resolved them before—without addressing the fundamental issues. He kicked the now obviously dissident McNamara downstairs to the World Bank and tossed the JCS a bone by authorizing a handful of new bombing targets. But he refused to confront head on the larger issues of either the air or ground wars.

Publicly, the president dealt with the problem of divisions within his official family by vehemently denying their existence. There were "no quarrels, no antagonisms within the administration," he said. "I have never known a period when I thought there was more harmony, more general agreement, and a more cooperative attitude."[41] Administration officials followed to the letter the script written by their president. Years later, McNamara admitted that he "went through hell" on the Stennis hearings.[42] Yet at a White House meeting, he praised his adversary General

Wheeler for a "helluva good job" before the Stennis Subcommittee and observed that the small differences between himself and the JCS were "largely worked out."[43] Wheeler publicly dismissed rumors that the JCS had contemplated resignation with a terse: "Bull Shit!"[44]

To the end, Johnson continued to deny that significant differences had existed within his administration, and no one could have written a better epitaph for a hopelessly flawed command system than its architect, the man who had imposed his own peculiar brand of unity on a bitterly divided government. "There have been no divisions in this government," he proudly proclaimed in November 1967. "We may have been wrong, but we have not been divided."[45] It was a strange observation, reflecting a curiously distorted sense of priorities. And of course it was not true. The administration was both wrong and divided, and the fact that the divisions could not be worked out or even addressed may have contributed to the wrongness of the policies, at huge costs to the men themselves—and especially to the nation.

II

By the time the divisions over strategy became acute in late 1967, Johnson's attention was drawn inexorably to the impending collapse of his support at home. Vietnam makes abundantly clear that a—perhaps the—central problem of waging limited war is to *maintain* public support without *arousing* public emotion. One of the most interesting and least studied areas of the war is the Johnson administration's unsuccessful effort to do precisely this. Vietnam was not fundamentally a public relations problem, and a more vigorous and effective public relations campaign would not have changed the outcome. Still, what stands out quite starkly from an examination of this topic is the small, indeed insignificant, role played by public opinion in the decisions for war in July 1965 and the strangely limited and notably cautious efforts made by the Johnson administration between 1965 and 1967 to promote public support for the war.

In examining the extensive White House files for June and July 1965, the researcher is immediately struck by the almost negligible attention given to domestic opinion in the discussions leading to Johnson's decisions for war. At a meeting on 21 July, George Ball, the major opponent of escalation, resorted to the obvious analogy, using charts from the Korean War to warn the president that public support could not be taken for granted. Admonishing that the war would be protracted, Ball reminded the group that as casualties had increased between 1950 and 1952, public support had dropped from 56 percent to 30 percent. A long war, he also predicted, would generate powerful, perhaps irresistible pressures to strike directly at North Vietnam, risking dangerous escalation.[46]

Interestingly, no one responded to Ball's warning, but on those few other occasions when the issue came up the tone was much more optimistic. At another point in the same meeting, McGeorge Bundy observed that the nation "seemed in the mood to accept grim news." In another meeting, Marine Corps Commandant Greene predicted that the nation would support the commitment of as many as 500,000 men for as long as five years.[47]

The issue also received a brief and revealing hearing at a meeting on 27 July. Playing the role of devil's advocate, Johnson asked his advisers if Congress and the public would go along with 600,000 troops and billions of dollars being sent 10,000 miles away. Only Secretary of the Army Stanley Resor responded, laconically observing that the Gallup Poll showed that Americans were "basically behind our commitment." But, Johnson persisted, "if you make a commitment to jump off a building and you find out how high it is, you may want to withdraw that commitment," a remarkably prescient observation. No one responded, however, and nothing more was said. His mind apparently made up, the president dropped a crucial question and went on to something else.[48]

Why this absence of discussion of an issue that turned out to be so important? The answer, in one word, seems to have been complacency. Since World War II, the executive branch had successfully managed public opinion on most major foreign policy issues. It had kept a potentially troublesome press in line by appealing to its patriotic instincts, by making it a partner in the national security state, by flattery and favors, and when these failed, by pressures and reprisals. Government bureaucrats had become increasingly adept at analyzing and manipulating public opinion. Perceiving the growing importance of foreign policy elites, they used various means to sway them, giving interest groups special briefings, appointing them to consultative bodies, or even to high office. The government used agencies such as the CIA-funded citizens groups, and on especially urgent issues, it mobilized ostensibly private groups such as the Committee for the Marshall Plan to conduct private campaigns for its policies. Postwar administrations were never free from criticism, but in no case was a major foreign policy initiative frustrated by lack of public support.[49]

Perhaps because of this record of success, those political scientists who developed the theories of limited war so much in vogue in the 1950s and 1960s all but ignored the problem of public opinion. After considerable discussion, Robert E. Osgood conceded that because of their traditional approach to issues of war and peace, Americans might have difficulty accepting limited war. Without indicating how the problem could be resolved, he went on to assert that limited wars must be fought because they provided the only viable military alternative in the nuclear age.[50]

The complacency of top administration officials was reinforced in the summer of 1965 by what seemed clear signs of public support for U.S. policy in Vietnam. Polls even suggested a hawkish mood, a solid plurality of 47 percent favoring sending more troops to Vietnam.[51] Drawing a sharp distinction between the political liabilities that had bedeviled France in the First Indochina War and the political advantages of the United States in 1965, McGeorge Bundy assured Johnson that the American public, although unenthusiastic, was reconciled to the U.S. role in

Vietnam. "While there is widespread questioning and uneasiness about the way in which we may be playing that role, the public as a whole seems to realize that the role must be played," Bundy concluded.[52]

What about the "lesson" of Korea raised by Ball on 21 July, that public support would erode if the war dragged on and casualties increased? The administration seems to have dismissed the Korean analogy, perhaps because it felt it could get what it wanted in Vietnam without the travail and agony of Korea. Johnson and his advisers acted in the expectation that "reason and mutual concessions" would prevail, Bill Moyers later conceded, that Hanoi could be enticed or intimidated into negotiating and a drawn-out war avoided.[53] Thus a fatal miscalculation about North Vietnam's response to U.S. escalation may have been behind an equally fatal miscalculation about U.S. public opinion.

The administration also misread the significance of the budding peace movement. Rusk compared the campus protest of the spring and early summer of 1965 to the 1938 Oxford Union debate, observing that most of those who "took the pledge" in the 1930s subsequently entered military service without protest.[54] McGeorge Bundy later admitted that "We simply hadn't estimated the kinds of new forces that were loose in the land in the middle 1960s. I don't think anybody foresaw in 1964 and 1965 the overall cresting of feeling which had begun in 1964 at Berkeley."[55]

Equally striking—although perhaps less surprising—is how little the administration did in the first years of the war to mobilize public support. Originally anticipating that the president would at least call up the reserves and declare a national emergency, administration officials in June 1965 had proposed a "full scenario" of actions to prepare the nation for war. A presidential message was to be drafted and plans laid for consultation with Congress. McNamara proposed creating a blue ribbon task force to explain the war and generate public support. Presidential aides even suggested the formation of a citizens' committee like the Committee for the Marshall Plan to build elite support. White House adviser Horace Busby urged Johnson to go out and rally the public in the mode of a Franklin Roosevelt or Winston Churchill.[56]

The president rejected all these proposals. He undoubtedly feared that a public debate on Vietnam at this crucial time might jeopardize major pieces of Great Society legislation then pending in Congress. And he really did not want to risk what he later called "the woman I really loved" [the Great Society] for "that bitch of a war on the other side of the world."[57]

But there were larger and more important reasons intimately connected to prevailing theories of the way limited wars should be fought. Johnson also feared that mobilizing the nation for war would set loose irresistible pressures for escalation and victory that might provoke the larger war with the Soviet Union and China, perhaps even the nuclear confrontation that the commitment in Vietnam had been designed to deter in the first place. The administration thus concluded, as Rusk later put it, "that in a nuclear world it is just too dangerous for an entire people to get too angry and we deliberately . . . tried to do in cold blood what perhaps can only be done in hot blood." "I don't want to be dramatic and cause tension," the president told the National Security Council on 27 July.[58]

Indeed for McNamara, the U.S. official who gave practical application to limited-war theory, Vietnam was the very prototype of the way wars must be fought in the nuclear age. "The greatest contribution Vietnam is making," the secretary of defense observed early in the war, "is developing an ability in the United States to fight a limited war . . . without arousing the public ire," almost a necessity, he added, "since this is the kind of war we'll likely be facing for the next fifty years."[59]

For a variety of reasons then, Johnson gambled that without taking exceptional measures he could hold public support long enough to achieve his goals in Vietnam. "I think we can get our people to support us without having to be provocative," he told his advisers.[60]

The United States therefore went to war in July 1965 in a manner uniquely quiet and underplayed—in "cold blood." The president ordered his July 28 decisions implemented in a "low key" way. He announced the major troop increase at a noon press conference instead of at prime time. It was even lumped in with a number of other items in a way that obscured its significance.[61]

With the exception of several hastily arranged, typically Johnsonian public relations blitzes, the administration persisted in this low-key approach until the late summer of 1967. It created no special machinery to monitor and manipulate public opinion. It took only a few modest steps to promote public support, leaving much of the work to nominally private groups. More often than not, its public relations efforts were reactive and defensive—and as the war wore on increasingly vindictive.

The administration's understanding of its public relations problems at the outset of the war combined naivete and myopia with a good measure of perceptiveness. The problem with the Saigon government, some officials reasoned, was its "mushy" public relations program rather than its chronic instability and palpable incompetence.[62] Popular uneasiness with the war was attributed to misunderstanding. The American people and elites, even editors and publishers, did not comprehend how this limited war differed from earlier wars, officials lamented. "We are still looking for the 'front,' still talking largely in terms of battles, number of casualties, tonnage of bombs."[63]

On the other hand, some of Johnson's advisers clearly perceived that public support, although broad, was fragile. There seemed little understanding of the larger policies upon which intervention in Vietnam was based. The public was "extremely vulnerable to rumor, gossip, and quick reverses," and each new initiative fed exaggerated expectations for a settlement that when not quickly realized led to disillusionment. The administration seemed always on the defensive. "We only plug holes and run as fast as we can to stay even," Assistant Secretary of State James Greenfield conceded. Some lower-level officials also shrewdly perceived that the key to ultimate success was not the skill of their public relations activities but signs of progress in Vietnam. "What we need more than anything else is some

visible evidence of success for our efforts to defeat the Viet Cong, deter Hanoi, and
. . . bring peace to the Vietnamese countryside."[64]

Assuming that education rather than exhortation was the key to public support, administration officials mounted a quiet, behind-the-scenes campaign. No
Office of War Information was created and no dramatic programs were undertaken
to rally the public to the cause. A New York public relations firm was hired to
improve the image of the Saigon government. The booklet *Why Vietnam?* was sent
to every member of Congress and to every major newspaper, and a film by the same
name, originally designed for military recruits, was sent out to nearly 500 high
schools and colleges and shown on a number of commercial television stations.
Administration officials conducted briefings for state governors and put together
packets of materials that could be used to defend the war. They closely monitored
press and Congressional debates, watching for and answering criticisms. The administration dealt with the budding peace movement by ignoring it, going out of
its way to avoid "any impression of an overly worried reaction" to major demonstrations in November 1965.[65]

To a considerable degree, the government privatized its selling of the war.
With administration advice and assistance, the Young Democrats mounted drives
on college campuses in support of U.S. policy. The Junior Chamber of Commerce
arranged half-time ceremonies at local and nationally televised football games to
include salutes to the men fighting in Vietnam. The administration persuaded the
American Friends of Vietnam (AFV), the so-called "Vietnam Lobby," to launch a
multi-faceted program to boost support for the war and helped it secure the funds to
do so. Indeed, in the first six months of the war the AFV spearheaded the
administration's public relations campaign.[66]

While privatizing the propaganda campaign, the president and his advisers
contented themselves with responding to critics in a way that was peculiarly
Johnsonian. To deflect attention from Sen. J. William Fulbright's early 1966 televised hearings on Vietnam, Johnson, amidst great fanfare, hustled off to Honolulu
for a "summit" meeting with South Vietnamese Premier Nguyen Cao Ky. A com-
pulsive reader, viewer, and listener, the president himself seemed at first intent on
and then increasingly obsessed with answering every accusation and responding to
every charge. When Gen. Matthew Ridgway came out against the war, the commander in chief ordered Army Chief of Staff Johnson to get statements of support
from *two* World War II heroes, Gen. Omar Bradley and Gen. J. Lawton Collins.[67]
Much valuable time was consumed preparing a detailed "dossier" on hostile columnist Walter Lippmann to demonstrate that he had opposed earlier Cold War
"successes" such as the Truman Doctrine and the Berlin Airlift. Harried White
House staffers spent hours answering line-for-line criticisms from journalists and
congressmen.[68]

Despite growing concern with the steady erosion of public support, the administration deviated only slightly from its low-key approach in 1966 and early
1967. Before the Congressional elections of 1966, Johnson himself mounted a speak-

ing tour of the Midwest, emphasizing, among other things, that American boys in the field were not being given the support they deserved. To get around the increasingly critical major metropolitan newspapers, he sought to get his message out to middle-America by granting special favors to the editors of local newspapers. Just before the elections, he donned the cap of commander in chief, flying off to preside over a conference at Manila of the seven nations fighting in Vietnam, then visiting each ally separately and using the publicity thereby generated to rally support for his policies.[69]

Such efforts were no more than temporarily and modestly successful, however, and by mid-1967, the administration belatedly realized that its most urgent crisis was at home. The president's job approval rating declined steadily through 1966 and into 1967. More ominous, the number of those who thought sending troops to Vietnam was a mistake increased sharply, raising disturbing parallels to Korea.[70] Still more unnerving was the mood of the nation, anxious, frustrated, increasingly divided. This "pinpoint on the globe [Vietnam]," old New Dealer and Johnson adviser David Lilienthal lamented, was "like an infection, a 'culture' of some horrible disease, a cancer where the wildly growing cells multiply and multiply until the whole body is poisoned."[71]

Signs of waning support left the administration deeply troubled. Johnson complained about his inability to get across his message: "It is hell when a president has to spend half of his time keeping his own people juiced up."[72] He and his advisers particularly worried about public perceptions, fed by the press, that the war had become a stalemate.[73] The president groped for some magic formula to reverse the spread of disillusionment, on one occasion longing for "some colorful general like McArthur [sic] with his shirt neck open" who could dismiss as "pure Communist propaganda" the talk of a stalemate and go to Saigon and do battle with the press.[74] "A miasma of trouble hangs over everything," Lady Bird Johnson confided to her diary. "The temperament of our people seems to be, 'you must get excited, get passionate, fight it and get it over with, or we must pull out.' It is unbearably hard to fight a limited war."[75]

III

Writing to Johnson in late 1967, Undersecretary of State Nicholas Katzenbach raised the perplexing question: "Can the tortoise of progress in Vietnam stay ahead of the hare of dissent at home?"[76] Katzenbach's Aesopian analogy suggests the extent to which by late 1967 the two strands of our story had come together. And it made clear the dilemma faced by Lyndon Johnson. To stave off collapse of the home front, progress must be demonstrated in Vietnam; yet such progress might not be possible without clear signs of firm public support at home.

By late 1967, Katzenbach and numerous other civilian advisers were pressing Johnson to resolve the dilemma by doing what he had thus far adamantly refused to do: address directly the issue of how the war was being fought. A now blatantly dissident McNamara on 1 November warned that stubborn persistence in the present course would not end the war and might bring about dangerous new pressures for drastic escalation or withdrawal. Going beyond his proposals of 19 May, he pressed for an indefinite bombing halt. He further advocated stabilizing the ground war by publicly fixing a ceiling on force levels and by instituting a searching review of ground operations with the object of reducing U.S. casualties and turning over more responsibility to the South Vietnamese.[77]

From inside and outside the government, numerous civilians joined McNamara in urging Johnson to check dissent at home by changing the ground strategy. Katzenbach, Bundy, McNamara's top civilian advisers in the Pentagon, a group of establishment figures meeting under the auspices of the Carnegie Endowment, and the president's own "Wise Men" agreed that Westmoreland's search-and-destroy strategy must be abandoned. Warning, as the Wise Men put it, that "endless, inconclusive fighting" was the "most serious single cause of domestic disquiet," they proposed instead a "clear-and-hold" strategy that would be less expensive in blood and treasure. Such a strategy, they reasoned, might stabilize the war at "a politically tolerable level" and save South Vietnam "without surrender and without risking a wider war." They also suggested an incipient form of what would later be called "Vietnamization," urging that a greater military burden should be gradually shifted to the South Vietnamese.[78]

Speech-writer Harry McPherson and presidential adviser McGeorge Bundy went still further, getting closer to the heart of the flaws of Johnson's exercise of presidential powers in wartime. McPherson gently chided his boss for expanding the bombing to head off military criticism. "You are the Commander in Chief," he affirmed. "If you think a policy is wrong, you should not follow it just to quiet the generals and admirals."[79] Bundy pressed Johnson to take control of the war. He should arrange a "solid internal understanding" between Rusk, McNamara, and the joint chiefs on the bombing, a "basic command decision" to settle the issue once and for all. He should also initiate a careful review of the ground strategy at the "highest military and civilian levels." Conceding that it was a "highly sensitive matter" to question the field commander, Bundy went on to say that if the strategy was not wise, "the plans of the field commander must be questioned." Now that the principal battleground was domestic opinion, the "Commander-in-chief has both the right and duty . . . to visibly take command of a contest that is more political in character than any in our history except the Civil War (where Lincoln interfered *much* more than you have)." It was essential, the former national security adviser warned, to end the confusion and conflict in government and steady the home front.[80]

Johnson was not moved by the urgent appeals of his advisers. He continued to fear the risks of an expanded war, and he was unsympathetic to repeated JCS appeals for expansion of both air and ground operations. But he also doubted that McNamara's proposals would bring results. "How do we get this conclusion?" he scrawled on a memo where the secretary had predicted that a bombing halt would lead to peace talks. "Why believe this?" he noted, where McNamara predicted a "strong possibility" that North Vietnam would stop military activities across the DMZ after a bombing halt.[81]

As before, he refused to make the hard decisions, and he refused to take control of the war. Unwilling to admit that his policy was bankrupt, he continued to delude himself into believing that he could find a solution along the middle route. He continued to take recommendations from each side without giving in to either. He rejected the JCS proposals for expanding the air war, agreeing only to follow through with bombing targets already approved and then stabilize the war at that level. But he flatly rejected McNamara's most radical proposal, a bombing halt. In regard to ground operations, he would go no further than privately commit himself to review Westmoreland's search-and-destroy strategy at some undetermined point in the future.[82]

To resolve the dilemma posed by Katzenbach, Johnson attempted to slow down the runaway rabbit of dissent at home rather than speed up or shift the direction of the turtle of progress in Vietnam. In the late summer and early fall of 1967, he did what he had previously refused to do: he mounted a large-scale, many-faceted public relations campaign to rally support for the war. From behind the scenes, administration officials helped to organize the Committee for Peace with Freedom in Vietnam, an ostensibly private organization headed by former Illinois Senator Paul Douglas, the principal aim of which was to mobilize the "silent center."[83] A Vietnam Information Group was established in the White House to monitor public reactions to the war and deal with problems as they surfaced.[84] Johnson's advisers supplied to friendly senators, including some Republicans, information to help answer the charges of Congressional doves.

Believing that his major problem was a widespread perception that the war was a stalemate, the president designed much of his public relations campaign to persuade a skeptical public that the United States was in fact winning. He ordered the embassy and military command to "search urgently for occasions to present sound evidence of progress in Viet Nam." U.S. officials dutifully responded, producing reams of statistics to show a steady rise in enemy body counts and the number of villages pacified, and publishing captured documents to support such claims. The White House even arranged for influential citizens to go to Vietnam and observe the progress firsthand.[85] As part of the public relations offensive, Westmoreland was brought home in November, ostensibly for top-level consultations, in fact to reassure a troubled nation. In a series of public statements he affirmed that "we have reached an important point where the end begins to come into view."[86]

The Communist Tet Offensive of 1968 cut the base from under the administration's public relations campaign. On 31 January 1968, the North Vietnamese launched a series of massive, closely coordinated attacks throughout the cities and towns of South Vietnam. As perhaps nothing else could have, the Tet Offensive put the lie to the administration's year-end claims of progress. Polls taken in late 1967 had shown a slight upswing in popular support for the war and even in the president's approval rating, but in the aftermath of Tet, support for the war and especially for the president plummeted and popular convictions of a stalemate became deeply imbedded.

Tet also forced Johnson to confront his strategic failure. After nearly two months of high-level deliberations focusing for the first time on crucial issues of how the war was being fought, he rejected new JCS proposals to expand the war and instituted some of the measures proposed by his civilian advisers in late 1967. He stopped the bombing beneath the 20th Parallel and launched major new initiatives to open peace negotiations. He placed a firm upper limit on the numbers of ground troops and removed Westmoreland from command in Vietnam, kicking him upstairs to the Joint Chiefs of Staff. He and his top advisers agreed that to ease pressures at home responsibility for the ground war should be shifted as rapidly as possible to the Vietnamese. Johnson's belated intervention came too late and did not go far enough to end the war, however, and he passed on to his successor a far more complex and intractable problem than he had inherited.

IV

To return to the question we began with: Why was the Vietnam War fought as it was? Certainly, Johnson's own highly personal style indelibly stamped the conduct of the war. The reluctance to provide precise direction and define a mission and explicit limits; the unwillingness to tolerate any form of intergovernmental dissent or permit a much-needed debate on strategic issues; the highly politicized approach that gave everybody something and nobody what they wanted and that emphasized consensus more than success on the battlefield or in the diplomatic councils; all these were products of a thoroughly political and profoundly insecure man, a man especially ill at ease among military issues and military people. The determination to dupe or co-opt advisers and the public rather than confront them candidly and forcefully also was a clear manifestation of the Johnson style, as was the tendency toward personalization of the domestic debate. Johnson repeatedly denied that Vietnam was his war. It was "America's war," he insisted, and "If I drop dead tomorrow, this war will still be with you."[87] In one sense, of course, he was right. But in terms of the way the war was fought, Vietnam was far more his than he was prepared to admit or even recognize.

Limited-war theory also significantly influenced the way the war was fought. Korea and especially the Truman-MacArthur controversy stimulated a veritable cult of limited war in the 1950s and 1960s, the major conclusion of which was that in a nuclear age where total war was unthinkable, limited war was essential. Robert McNamara, McGeorge Bundy, William Bundy, and Dean Rusk were deeply imbued with limited-war theory, and it determined in many crucial ways their handling of Vietnam. Coming of age in World War II, they were convinced of the essentiality of deterring aggression to avoid a major war. Veterans of the Cuban Missile Crisis, they lived with the awesome responsibility of preventing nuclear conflagration and they were thus committed to fighting the war in "cold blood" and maintaining tight operational control over the military. They also operated under the mistaken assumption that limited war was more an exercise in crisis management than the application of strategy, and they were persuaded that gradual escalation offered the means to achieve their limited goals without provoking the larger war they so feared. Many of their notions turned out to be badly flawed.

It would be a serious mistake, however, to attribute American failure in Vietnam solely or even largely to the eccentricities of Johnson's personal style or the false dogmas of limited-war theory. A considerable part of the problem lies in the inherent difficulty of limited war. Limited wars, as Stephen Peter Rosen has noted, are by their very nature *"strange* wars."[88] They combine political, military, and diplomatic dimensions in the most complicated way. Conducting them effectively requires rare intellectual ability, political acumen, and moral courage. Johnson and his advisers went into the conflict confident—probably overconfident—that they knew how to wage limited war, and only when the strategy of escalation proved bankrupt and the American people unwilling or unable to fight in cold blood did they confront their tragic and costly failure. Deeply entangled in a war they did not understand and could find no way to win, they struggled merely to put a label on the conflict. "All-out limited war," William Bundy called it, "a war that is not a war" some military officers complained.[89] McPherson phrased it in the form of a question. "What the hell do you say? How do you half-lead a country into war?"[90]

The search for labels suggests the fundamental difficulties of limited war, and we must recognize in retrospect that there are no easy answers to the problems Johnson and his advisers confronted. They key military problem, Rosen contends, is "how to adapt, quickly and successfully, to the peculiar and unfamiliar *battlefield* conditions in which our armed forces are fighting."[91] That this was not done in Vietnam may reflect the limited vision of the political and military leaders, but it will not be easily done elsewhere. Nor is there any clear-cut answer to the dilemma of domestic opinion. Fighting in cold blood seemed not to work in Vietnam. But there is no assurance that a declaration of war or partial mobilization was the answer. Johnson's and Rusk's reservations about the dangers of a declaration of war were well taken, and congressional sanction in the War of 1812 and the Mexican War did nothing to stop rampant and at times crippling domestic opposition. However much we might deplore the limitations of Johnson's leadership and the folly of limited-war theory, they are not alone responsible for failure in Vietnam. Even in the post–Cold War world, we would be wise to accept Lady Bird Johnson's 1967 lament as a caveat: "It is unbearably hard to fight a limited war."

Notes

1. See for example, Guenter Lewy, *America in Vietnam* (New York: Oxford University Press, 1978); Harry G. Summers, Jr., *On Strategy: The Vietnam War in Context* (Carlisle Barracks, Pa.: Strategic Studies Institute, U.S. Army War College, 1981); and Andrew Krepinevich, *The Army and Vietnam* (Baltimore, Md.: Johns Hopkins University Press, 1986).

2. Wayne S. Cole, "American Entry into World War II: A Historiographical Appraisal," *Mississippi Historical Review* 43 (March 1957): 615.

3. Andrew Goodpaster oral history interview, Lyndon Baines Johnson Library (LBJ Library), Austin, TX.

4. Stephen Peter Rosen, "Vietnam and the American Theory of Limited War," *International Security* 7 (Fall 1982): 96.

5. Bundy to Johnson, 5 November 1965, Box 5, Bundy Memoranda, National Security File, Lyndon Baines Johnson Papers (hereafter cited as Johnson Papers), LBJ Library.

6. Bundy to Johnson, 10 November 1967, Box 81, Diary Backup, ibid.

7. Henry Brandon, *Anatomy of Error: The Inside Story of the Asian War on the Potomac, 1954–1969* (Boston: Gambit, 1969), 164; David Halberstam, *The Best and the Brightest* (New York: Random House, 1972), 248, 633.

8. There is no good study of the civil-military conflict of the 1960s. For examples of the growing hostility, see Hanson Baldwin, "The McNamara Monarchy," *Saturday Evening Post*, 9 Mar. 1963, 8–9; Burke to McCain, 18 March 1963, Box 9, Hanson Baldwin Papers (hereafter cited as Baldwin Papers), Yale University Library, New Haven, Conn.; for civilian hostility toward the military, see James G. Nathan, "The Tragic Enshrinement of Toughness," in Thomas G. Paterson, ed., *Major Problems in American Foreign Policy, Vol. 2, Since 1914,* 2d ed. (New York: Heath, 1984), 577–78.

9. Nathan, "Tragic Enshrinement," 570–71.

10. For Johnson's populist observations on the military, see Doris Kearns, *Lyndon Johnson and the American Dream* (New York: Harper & Row, 1976), 262.

11. Rosen, "Vietnam," 96.

12. Ibid., 90–99.

13. Quoted in Nathan, "Tragic Enshrinement," 569.

14. Rosen, "Vietnam," 93–96.

15. Michael Davidson, "Senior Officers and Vietnam Policymaking," *Parameters* 16 (Spring 1986): 55–57. See also "The Management Team," *Time,* 5 Feb. 1965, 22–23; "Joint Chiefs Wear a Different Hat," *Business Week,* 30 July 1966, 68–72.

16. Lawrence J. Korb, *The Joint Chiefs of Staff: The First Twenty-Five Years* (Bloomington: Indiana University Press, 1976), 160.

17. Valenti's admonition is in Valenti to Johnson, 14 November 1964, cited in Brian Van De Mark, *Into the Quagmire: Lyndon Johnson and the Escalation of the Vietnam War* (New York: Oxford University Press, 1990), 260n.

18. Some of the joint chiefs later claimed that they gave Johnson accurate estimates of what would be required. See Hanson Baldwin oral history interview, U.S. Naval Institute Library, Annapolis, Md., 710–11; Wallace Greene to Baldwin, 25 September 1975, ibid.; and Greene handwritten notes, Wallace M. Greene Papers, Marine Corps Historical Center, Washington, D.C. For JCS disappointment at Johnson's refusal to mobilize the reserves, see Hanson Baldwin, "Military Disappointed," *New York Times,* 29 July 1965. For JCS minimizing of the difficulties, see Record of LBJ meeting with JCS, 22 July 1965, and record of meeting in cabinet room, 22 July 1965, both in Meeting Notes File, Box 1, Johnson Papers. Wheeler's "foot-in-the-door" strategy is articulated in Wheeler to Westmoreland, 2 June 1966, Box 20, Westmoreland/CBS Litigation Files, Backchannel Messages, RG 407, Federal Records Center (hereafter cited as FRC), Suitland, Md.

19. See especially Mark Clodfelter, *The Limits of Air Power: The American Bombing of North Vietnam* (New York: Free Press, 1989), esp. chaps. 3 and 4.

20. Krulak to Greene, 19 July 1965, Box 1, Victor Krulak Papers (hereafter cited as Krulak Papers), Marine Corps Historical Center, Washington, D.C.

21. Mark Perry, *Four Stars* (Boston: Houghton Mifflin, 1989), 156–58. Charles F. Brower IV, "The Westmoreland 'Alternate Strategy' of 1967–1968," unpublished paper in possession of author, argues that as early as March 1967, Westmoreland himself was profoundly dissatisfied with the attrition strategy and "proposed an alternate strategy for Vietnam which implicitly recognized the weaknesses of attrition."

22. Krulak to Cushman, 25 May 1967, Box 1, Krulak Papers.

23. McNaughton to McNamara, 6 May 1967, cited in Neil Sheehan et al., *The Pentagon Papers as Published by the New York Times* (New York: Bantam Books, 1971), 534.

24. McNamara draft presidential memorandum, "Future Actions in Vietnam," 19 May 1967, Box 74–75, Country File: Vietnam, National Security File, Johnson Papers.

25. Johnson to Westmoreland, 29 October 1967, Box 20, Westmoreland/CBS Litigation Files, Backchannel Messages, RG 407, FRC.

26. Johnson developed this technique into a fine art, of course, and it was his primary modus operandi in dealing with his various advisers, but the tendency itself is all too common in Vietnam policy-making and indeed in the American political system. For the way in which Richard Nixon operated in similar fashion, see George C. Herring, "The Nixon Strategy in Vietnam," in Peter Braestrup, ed., *Vietnam as History: Ten Years After the Paris Peace Accords* (Washington, D.C.: University Press of America, 1984), 51–58.

27. "I don't want loyalty. I want loyalty," Halberstam reports him saying. "I want him to kiss my ass in Macy's window at high noon and tell me it smells like roses." Halberstam, *Best and the Brightest,* 434.

28. Quoted in Henry Trewhitt, *McNamara* (New York: Harper & Row, 1971), 237.

29. George Ball oral history interview, LBJ Library. McNamara's disillusionment with the war seems to have begun much earlier and to have run much deeper than most scholars have assumed. See, for example, Harriman memoranda of conversations with McNamara, 14, 28, 30 May, 22, 31 August, and 26 November 1966, Box 486, W. Averell Harriman Papers, Manuscript Division, Library of Congress, Washington, D.C., and Harriman memorandum of conversation with McNamara, 10 October 1966, Box 520, ibid. See also Paul Hendrickson, "Divided Against Himself," *Washington Post Magazine,* 12 June 1988, 20–31.

30. Miles interview with Westmoreland, 7 January 1971, Paul Miles Papers, U.S. Military History Institute, Carlisle Barracks, Pa.

31. Westmoreland historical briefing, 12 July 1967, Box 29, William C. Westmoreland Papers, U.S. Army Military History Institute, Carlisle Barracks, Pa.

32. Wheeler to Westmoreland, 2 June 1966, to Westmoreland and Sharp, 13 February 1967, to Sharp and Westmoreland, 6 March 1967, Boxes 15–17, Westmoreland/CBS Litigation Files, Backchannel Messages, RG 407, FRC.

33. Barry Zorthian oral history interview, LBJ Library.

34. Leonard Chapman oral history interview, Marine Corps Historical Center, Washington, D.C.; *New York Herald-Tribune,* 22 and 23 August 1966; Greene to author, 9 May 1988.

35. Krulak to Greene, 1 February 1967, Box 1, Krulak Papers; Victor Krulak, "A Conflict of Strategies," *U.S. Naval Institute Proceedings,* November 1984:85–87.

36. Rostow memoranda, 19 and 20 May 1967, Boxes 74–75, Country File: Vietnam, National Security File, Johnson Papers.

37. Sheehan et al., *Pentagon Papers,* 539.

38. As early as 1966, Hanson Baldwin had detected among some Army officers growing criticism of the military leadership in Washington. By 1967, some military dissidents contemptuously dismissed the joint chiefs as the "five silent men" and ridiculed their "Charlie McCarthy answers" to LBJ's questions. See Baldwin to Peeke, 6 September 1966, Box 13, Baldwin Papers, and unpublished article, Box 29, ibid.; also, *New York Times,* 13 and 24 July 1967.

39. Ginsburgh memorandum, 14 August 1967, Box 3, Name File: Col. Ginsburgh, National Security File, Johnson Papers.

40. Perry, *Four Stars,* 163–64. Perry's source for the story is an unnamed "former JCS flag rank officer." His account has been confirmed by a senior officer close to one of the deceased members of the JCS, but denied by Gen. Wallace Greene and Adm. Thomas Moorer. Actually, rumors of a possible resignation en masse first surfaced at the time McNamara's departure was announced in late 1967 and were heatedly denied by administration officials. See *New York Times,* 29 November, 2 and 4 December 1967.

41. *Public Papers of the Presidents of the United States: Lyndon Baines Johnson, 1967,* 2 vols. (Washington, D.C.: Government Printing Office, 1968), 2:816–17.

42. McNamara deposition for Westmoreland Trial (pp. 113, 176, 322), copy in LBJ Library.

43. Record of meeting, LBJ, McNamara, Wheeler, Rusk, and Rostow, 19 August 1967, Box 1, Meeting Notes File, Johnson Papers.

44. *Washington Post,* 29 Dec. 1967.

45. Tom Johnson notes on NSC meetings, 29 November 1967, Box 1, Tom Johnson Notes on Meetings, Johnson Papers.

46. George W. Ball, *The Past Has Another Pattern* (New York: Norton, 1982), 400; Larry Berman, *Planning a Tragedy: The Americanization of the War in Vietnam* (New York: Norton, 1982), 109; Notes on meeting, 21 July 1965, Meeting Notes File, Box 1, Johnson Papers.

47. Notes on meeting, 21 July 1965, Meeting Notes File, Box 1, Johnson Papers.

48. Berman, *Planning a Tragedy,* 119.

49. See esp. Richard Barnet, *Roots of War* (Baltimore, Md.: Penguin Books, 1973), 266–306, and Michael Leigh, *Mobilizing Consent: Public Opinion and American Foreign Policy* (Westport, Conn.: Greenwood Press, 1976), 99–106.

50. Rosen, "Vietnam," 85–86.

51. Van De Mark, *Into the Quagmire,* 163–64.

52. Bundy memorandum for president, "France in Vietnam, 1954, and the U.S. in Vietnam, 1965—A Useful Analogy," 30 June 1965, Box 43, NSC History: Deployment of Major U.S. Forces to Vietnam, July 1965, National Security File, Johnson Papers.

53. Bill Moyers, "One Thing We Learned," *Foreign Affairs* 46 (July 1968): 662. A number of senior advisers interviewed by a RAND analyst in 1983 could not recall Ball's presentation at the 21 July meeting. Rusk later discounted Ball's estimates of casualties; McNamara claimed not to have seen his charts. David Di Leo, "Rethinking Containment: George Ball's Vietnam Dissent," Unpublished manuscript in possession of author, 275.

54. Memorandum of Rusk-Holt conversation, 28 April 1965, "Asia and the Pacific: National Security Files, 1963–1969," Frame 152, Microfilm Reel 1 (Frederick, Md.: University Publications of America, 1988).

55. Quoted in William Conrad Gibbons, "The 1965 Decision to Send U.S. Ground Forces to Vietnam," paper given at the International Studies Association, 16 April 1987.

56. Record of meeting, 19 July 1965, Johnson Papers, National Security File, Country File, Vietnam, Box 15; Busby to LBJ, 21 July 1965, Johnson Papers, Busby Files, Box 3; Kathleen J. Turner, *Lyndon Johnson's Dual War: Vietnam and the Press* (Chicago: University of Chicago Press, 1985), 149.

57. Kearns, *Johnson and the American Dream,* 251.

58. Rusk's statement is in Michael Charlton and Anthony Moncrief, *Many Reasons Why: The American Involvement in Vietnam,* 2d ed. (New York: Hill and Wang, 1989), 115; Johnson statement in notes on NSC meeting, 27 July 1965, Box 1, Meeting Notes File, Johnson Papers.

59. Quoted in Barbara Tuchman, *The March of Folly* (New York: Random House, 1984), 326.

60. Notes on NSC Meeting, 27 July 1965, Box 1, Meeting Notes File, Johnson Papers.

61. Ibid.; Turner, 149, 151.

62. Memorandum for the record, 4 August 1965, Boxes 196–97, Country File: Vietnam, National Security File, Johnson Papers.

63. Greenfield and Jorden memorandum for Moyers, 13 August 1965, ibid.

64. Memorandum for the record, 4 August 1965, memorandum of discussion in Moyers's office, 10 August 1965, Greenfield and Jorden memorandum for Moyers, 13 August 1965, ibid.; Cooper to Moyers, 13 August 1965, Box 22, ibid.

65. Moyers memorandum, n.d., Box 194, ibid.; Read to Smith, 10 August 1965, Box 21, ibid.; press release, 5 November 1965, Box 13, Richard Dudman Papers, Manuscript Division, Library of Congress, Washington, D.C.

66. Cooper memorandum, 10 September 1965, Box 22, Country File: Vietnam, National Security File, Johnson Papers; Melvin Small, *Johnson, Nixon and the Doves* (New Brunswick, N.J.: Rutgers University Press, 1988), 46–48.

67. Harold Johnson memorandum, 20 July 1966, Box 127, Harold Johnson Papers, U.S. Military History Institute Library, Carlisle Barracks, Pa.

68. Rostow to LBJ, 9 May 1966, vol. 2, Walt Rostow memos, Johnson Papers; Moyers to Krock, 15 September 1966, Moyers Office Files, LBJ Library.

69. Turner, 164–66.

70. Redmon to Moyers, 27 September 1966, Box 12, Moyers Office Files, LBJ Library.

71. David Lilienthal Journal, 4 October 1966, in David Lilienthal, *The Journals of David E. Lilienthal,* 7 vols. (New York: Harper & Row, 1964–1983), 6:296.

72. Notes on meeting with Bob Thompson, 21 August 1967, Box 3, George Christian Files, LBJ Library.

73. Wheeler to Westmoreland, 2 and 30 August 1967, and Westmoreland to Sharp and Wheeler, 3 and 12 August 1967, Box 20, Westmoreland/CBS Litigation Files, Backchannel Messages, RG 407, FRC. Also, Tom Johnson notes on LBJ meeting with Lucas, 14 August 1967, Box 1, Tom Johnson Notes, Johnson Papers.

74. Notes on meeting, 19 August 1967, Box 1, Meeting Notes File, ibid.

75. Lady Bird Johnson diary entry, 5 January 1967, Lady Bird Johnson, *A White House Diary* (New York: Holt, Rinehart & Winston, 1970), 469.

76. Quoted in Larry Berman, *Lyndon Johnson's War: The Road to Stalemate in Vietnam* (New York: Norton, 1989), 106.

77. McNamara to LBJ, 1 November 1967, Box 75, Country File: Vietnam, National Security File, Johnson Papers.

78. Katzenbach to Johnson, 16 November 1967, quoted in Berman, *Lyndon Johnson's War,* 106–7; Jones notes on meeting, 2 November 1967, Box 2, Meeting Notes File, Johnson Papers; Bundy to Johnson, 10 November 1967, Box 81, Diary Backup File, ibid.; Depuy to Westmoreland, 19 October 1967, Folder WXYZ(67), William Depuy Papers, U.S. Army Military History Institute, Carlisle Barracks, Pa.; "Carnegie Endowment Proposals," 5 December 1967, Box 34A, Matthew B. Ridgway Papers, U.S. Army Military History Institute, Carlisle Barracks, Pa.

79. McPherson to Johnson, 27 October 1967, Box 53, Harry McPherson Office Files, LBJ Library.

80. Bundy to LBJ, 10 November 1967, Box 81, Diary Backup, Johnson Papers.

81. Handwritten notes on McNamara memo to LBJ, 1 November 1967, Box 75, Country File: Vietnam, National Security File, ibid.

82. Johnson memorandum, 18 December 1967, in Lyndon B. Johnson, *The Vantage Point: Perspectives of the Presidency, 1963–1969* (New York: Holt, Rinehart & Winston, 1971), 800–801.

83. For the Douglas Committee, see Douglas to Alsop, 22 August 1967, Box 76, Joseph Alsop Papers, Manuscript Division, Library of Congress, Washington, D.C.; Washburn memo, 29 September 1967, Box 7, Name File: Roche, National Security File, Johnson Papers; *Washington Post,* 19 Oct. 1967.

84. For the Vietnam Information Group, see Rostow to LBJ, 15 August 1967, Box 7, Name File, National Security File, Johnson Papers; Christian to LBJ, 22 August 1967, Box 427, Office Files of Fred Panzer, ibid.; Kaplan to Rostow, 9 October 1967, Box 99, Country File: Vietnam, National Security File, ibid.

85. Rostow to Bunker, 27 September 1967, Box 4, Declassified and sanitized Documents from Unprocessed Files, Johnson Papers; Locke to Johnson, 7 October 1967, Box 99, Country File: Vietnam, National Security File, ibid.

86. Cited in Richard P. Stebbins, *The United States in World Affairs, 1967* (New York: Simon & Schuster, 1968), 68.

87. Quoted in Berman, *Lyndon Johnson's War,* i.

88. Rosen, "Vietnam," 83.

89. Bundy is cited in Charlton and Moncrief, 120; the military officers are cited in Hanson Baldwin "magaziner," 16 December 1965, Box 27, Baldwin Papers.

90. McPherson is cited in Walter LaFeber, *America, Russia, and the Cold War,* 5th ed. (New York: Knopf, 1985), 254.

91. Rosen, "Vietnam," 83.

Vietnam: ⚓
Evaluating the Ground War, 1965–1968

Andrew F. Krepinevich

In the course of the two Indochina wars, there was only one period—from 1965 to 1968—in which U.S. ground combat forces attempted to achieve something resembling a military victory against the Communist forces in South Vietnam. From 1950, when the U.S. Military Assistance Advisory Group (MAAG) was established, until 1965, American involvement in the war was characterized by security assistance. The United States provided equipment, training, and advisers to indigenous South Vietnamese forces, but no combat forces.

As late as September 1963, President John F. Kennedy remarked that "it's their war to win. We can help them . . . but in the final analysis, it's their people and their government who have to win or lose this struggle."[1] President Lyndon B. Johnson echoed this belief a year later when he promised, "We are not about to send American boys nine or ten thousand miles from home to do what Asian boys ought to be doing for themselves."[2]

In 1969, after three years of direct intervention in South Vietnam by U.S. ground combat forces, President Richard M. Nixon adopted a policy similar to that espoused by his two predecessors. In announcing the Guam Doctrine, he stated that the United States would provide advice, training, and material assistance to friendly nations threatened by violent Communist takeovers, but they and their neighbors would have to provide the combat forces to win the victory. After 1968 the U.S. policy in Indochina became "Vietnamization," withdrawing American troops from the conflict and turning the fighting over to the South Vietnamese.

Thus, the period 1965–68 stands alone as the only time in the United States' twenty-five-year involvement in the war when it departed from its primary role as adviser and attempted to win the war by deploying its own ground combat forces. This essay examines the ground war in South Vietnam during this unique period. It addresses the question of why the U.S. Army and Marines, in combination with the armed forces of several Pacific allies and the South Vietnamese, made so little progress in defeating the Vietcong and their North Vietnamese sponsors, that American civilian leadership lost faith in the military's strategy and searched for a way to remove U.S. combat forces.

Nature of the Conflict

To understand the ground war during the 1965–68 period of intervention, one has to appreciate the conflict environment, which differed dramatically from the major wars that the U.S. Army and Marines had fought over the previous half century. The Vietcong and North Vietnamese Army (NVA) forces arrayed against the Saigon regime followed a revolutionary war—or, more precisely, a people's war—strategy that had proved successful in the First Indochina War against another Western power, France.

At the grand strategic level, people's war blends the political, social, and military dimensions of strategy into a mutually supporting whole. Political struggle is designed to operate in close conjunction with military struggle. The military dimension itself reflects Maoist revolutionary warfare principles.[3] The people's war strategy recognized the Vietnamese Communists' inability to unseat the Saigon regime quickly or through "traditional" conventional warfare. Recognizing their inferiority in the conventional measures of military effectiveness against the French and the Americans, the Vietnamese Communists sought to involve their enemies in a protracted struggle conducted methodically, step by step, obtaining a series of intermediate objectives that, cumulatively, would lead to the overthrow of the Saigon regime.

In general terms, the strategy's military dimension has three phases. During the first phase of contention, the insurgents build their political infrastructure, espouse a popular cause to recruit followers, and perhaps conduct selected acts of terrorism against the regime. When the insurgents accumulate sufficient strength, they move to the second phase, that of overt violence. This phase continues all operations initiated in the first phase, but also is characterized by guerrilla operations against the government. These operations are designed to gain resources for the insurgent while denying them to the government. They also are designed to reduce popular confidence in, and support of, the regime. The third phase, the counteroffensive, occurs when the military balance has finally tipped in the insurgents' favor as a consequence of successes realized in the two earlier phases of their strategy. In this phase the insurgent guerrilla forces are combined into large formations to contest openly the regime's military forces. The third phase is characterized by conventional or quasi-conventional military operations, as well as by the operations conducted in the earlier two phases.

Thus people's war seeks to weaken its opponents politically, economically, and socially, as well as militarily. It does so by combining political and military struggle into two mutually supporting elements of a comprehensive strategy for victory.

Allied Ground Forces

Just as the Vietcong and their North Vietnamese sponsors continued the method of war that had proven successful against the French, so the United States Army and, to a somewhat lesser extent, the Marines followed, as closely as circumstances permitted, the prescription for success they had employed in earlier wars of this century—the two world wars and the Korean War. This led the U.S. Military Assistance Command, Vietnam (MACV) to take a conventional approach toward defeating a very unconventional enemy.

The Marines adapted better than the Army to the "new" conflict environment in Vietnam, owing to three interrelating factors. First, the Corps retained more of its earlier experiences in unconventional warfare than did the Army. The Marines' involvement in several U.S. interventions in Latin America early in this century had a lasting impression on that service's organizational culture, as can be seen in its manual on small wars issued in 1940.[4] The Army, on the other hand, retained few of the lessons learned in its turn-of-the-century experience battling insurgents in the Philippines.[5] Ironically, the Army's postwar experiences advising friendly governments in Greece and the Philippines in combatting insurgents seemed to perpetuate the service's conventional approach to warfare, rather than give it an appreciation of counterinsurgency requirements.[6]

Second, the Marines' force structure was better suited than the Army's for adapting to the revolutionary warfare conflict environment in Vietnam. Marine divisions were structured to operate along the coast, not to project combat power deep into a country's interior. Army divisions, on the other hand, especially those with organic or detailed helicopter support, were far more comfortable with—and capable of—conducting operations deep into the country's interior. Thus the Marines naturally gravitated toward force deployment along South Vietnam's densely populated coastal region. The Army saw this deployment posture as throwing away its perceived advantages in firepower and mobility. In summary, the Army had both the desire and the wherewithal to attempt to execute the traditional mission of conventional warfare: closing with and destroying enemy military forces. The Marines were more inclined to accept novel approaches to combatting the practitioners of people's war, as exemplified in their Combined Action Platoon (CAP) program.

Thus, the Army and the Marine Corps differed significantly in their views on how to best prosecute the war. The Marines were the first U.S. combat forces to arrive in Vietnam, landing on the beaches around Da Nang in March 1965. They constituted a relatively small percentage of the overall American commitment, however, contributing only two of roughly eleven divisions deployed by the United States at the peak of its involvement. The preponderance of Army ground forces put the Army in overall charge of the ground war. The Marine effort was subsumed by the overall effort pursued by the Army and the Army of the Republic of Vietnam (ARVN) they advised.

By the time U.S. ground combat forces began arriving on the scene in the spring of 1965, their ARVN counterparts had already been fighting the Communists, whom they greatly outnumbered, for nearly ten years with a singular lack of success. One measure of the ARVN's lack of proficiency was their failure to smother the Communist threat in its infancy, when Saigon faced only small, ill-equipped bands of Vietcong guerrillas. The ARVN's poor showing against the Vietcong was a function of several factors, principal among them being the corrupt and inefficient South Vietnamese officers corps in which political loyalty was a commodity accorded far greater value in Saigon than combat leadership.

The ARVN was also hampered by the MAAG. After the 1954 Geneva Accords the MAAG chief, Lt. Gen. Sam Williams, was instructed by the Joint Chiefs of Staff (JCS) to assist the new Republic of Vietnam in organizing and training their armed forces. Fresh from their experience in the Korean War, the American military leadership employed that model of Asian warfare as a template of sorts for the ARVN. Williams set as his goal the creation of an ARVN that could successfully resist an overt North Vietnamese invasion until U.S. (and, it was hoped, other SEATO nations') forces could arrive on the scene and turn the tide of battle.[7] Thus the MAAG set about establishing an ARVN that could conduct corps-size conventional operations. Hanoi, however, had little interest in emulating the North Koreans, and chose to continue the people's war strategy that had proven successful in the First Indochina War.

The ARVN, malstructured and poorly led, proved incapable of containing the rapidly expanding Communist insurgent movement. To cover up their deficiencies, the South Vietnamese forces became increasingly dependent upon American combat advisers, whose numbers expanded rapidly beginning in 1962, and upon American firepower and mobility. These infusions of American support proved unable to offset the ARVN's significant shortcomings. When U.S. ground combat forces arrived in 1965, the ARVN found itself quickly reduced to a subordinate role. It would remain the victim of American benign neglect until Washington decided to withdraw U.S. forces and turn the war back over to Saigon through "Vietnamization."

MACV's Concept of Operations

After his landslide election victory in November 1964, President Lyndon Johnson believed that he could no longer postpone major policy decisions on the U.S. role in the Vietnam War. The U.S. position in South Vietnam had been deteriorating since the late 1950s. The failure of land reform, the corruption and inefficiency of successive Saigon regimes, the Buddhist crisis, the "turnstile governments" following the assassination of President Ngo Dinh Diem, and the growing effectiveness of the Vietcong insurgents could not be offset by 16,000 American advisers supported by what the U.S. military leadership considered the essential elements of modern warfare: firepower and mobility.

Nevertheless, President Johnson was not willing to cede defeat and the loss of South Vietnam to the Communists. By December 1964 he was promoting the use of American ground combat forces to shore up the South Vietnamese. Johnson's attitude was reflected in his 30 December telegram to U.S. Ambassador Maxwell Taylor during the ARVN defeat at Bin Ghia. Discounting Taylor's support for an aerial bombing campaign against North Vietnam, the president felt that "what is much more needed and would be more effective is a larger and stronger use of rangers and special forces and marines. . . . I am ready to look with great favor on that kind of increased American military effort, directed at the guerrillas and aimed to stiffen the aggressiveness of Vietnamese military units up and down the line."[8]

By March 1965 the president crossed his own personal Rubicon and decided to do whatever was necessary to hold the line in South Vietnam. As Secretary of Defense Robert McNamara informed Army Chief of Staff General Harold K. Johnson, the "[U.S.] policy is: anything that will strengthen the GVN [Government of Vietnam] will be sent."[9] That month General Johnson himself told Westmoreland and his fellow generals at MACV that the president was giving the military a blank check. Westmoreland was to tell the president what he needed to win the war.[10]

On 7 June, General Westmoreland requested 44 combat maneuver battalions be deployed from the United States and other free world countries to stem the rising Vietcong tide against the rapidly eroding ARVN.[11] MACV observed the Vietcong as increasingly willing to conduct battalion and regimental size operations, directly challenging the ARVN in open combat. Furthermore, there were reports of NVA forces in the central highlands of South Vietnam and in Laos. It appeared to Westmoreland the enemy was moving into Phase III revolutionary warfare operations. To oppose the Communists, Westmoreland felt he needed "a substantial and hard-hitting offensive capability on the ground to convince the VC that they cannot win."[12] The general proposed to "forget the enclaves" the Marines had established along the coast of Vietnam and "take the war to the enemy."[13]

Westmoreland quickly found himself being asked: How long will it take to complete the job? How will U.S. forces be employed in Vietnam? and How many American troops will be required to accomplish the mission? In response, he outlined a three-phase approach that would culminate in the destruction of all Communist forces and base areas by the end of 1967.[14] Phase I would see the situation stabilized in Vietnam by the end of 1965, thanks to the 44-battalion commitment. Phase II, involving the deployment of an additional 24 battalions in 1966, would allow MACV to resume offensive operations against the enemy. During Phase III, beginning in 1968, mop-up operations would eliminate remaining insurgent forces. MACV's timetable was predicated on nonintervention by the Communist Chinese. Left unaddressed was the effect on the length of U.S. commitment if NVA infiltration increased, as well as the possible changes required in MACV's concept of operations if the enemy reverted to Phase II insurgent operations.

MACV exhibited little appreciation for the multidimensional nature of people's war. Military operations alone could not legitimize the Saigon regime in the eyes of its people. Nor could MACV compel Saigon to make reforms to satisfy the legitimate needs of its people and eliminate the corruption and inefficiency that crippled its attempts to combat the Communists.

Furthermore, the American military leadership did not appreciate the importance of the conflict's social dimension, particularly as it pertained to the American people. Westmoreland claimed maintaining popular support at home for the war effort was "none of my concern."[15] Yet, if the Korean War was any indication, the American people's support for limited war in Vietnam was likely to be a function of the war's duration, the costs involved (in terms of casualties and materiel) and, of course, of the perceived progress toward achieving victory.[16] Recognizing this, and given the protracted nature of people's war and that, in the end, only the South Vietnamese people could win their war, a U.S. strategy for the ground war would logically seek to minimize American casualties and the expenditure of resources to maximize the duration of U.S. support for the GVN. The goal would be to buy the maximum amount of time at the minimum cost to allow the Saigon regime to improve its performance and deal with the internal threat to its security. If the GVN could accomplish that objective, then the prospects for deterring the external threat with U.S. support would be enhanced as well.

To identify the required U.S. troops strength, both MACV and the JCS employed the 3:1 force ratio rule of thumb. It holds that to conduct successful offensive operations in a conventional war, a 3:1 advantage in combat potential is required. By applying a factor to weight U.S. maneuver battalions more heavily than their Communist counterparts, the U.S. military was able to arrive at a favorable ratio of 3.2:1 with the 44 battalions requested by Westmoreland. Accepting the conventional approach, McNamara stated that U.S. forces would "make a significant difference in the kind of war which seems to be evolving in Vietnam—a 'Third Stage' or conventional war in which it is easier to identify, locate and attack the enemy."[17]

However, in the counterguerrilla operations characteristic of Phase II revolutionary warfare, a ratio of 10:1 or better is considered necessary for the government's forces to achieve success. Left unanswered was the question of how MACV would respond if the Communists reverted to Phase II operations to avoid the American advantages in conventional-style combat. McNamara thought the problem would be "manageable," even though he also felt that "the number of US troops is too small to make a significant difference in the traditional 10:1 government government-guerrilla formula."[18]

MACV's Strategic Options

MACV sought to terminate the war by convincing the enemy that a military victory was impossible and, therefore, it was better to cease military operations rather than accept additional punishment.[19] It would have preferred to wage a conventional war, conducting a battle of annihilation against the enemy. American advantages in firepower, mobility, and technology could have been best exploited in this type of war. Operations plans prepared and approved by the Pentagon in the late 1950s and early 1960s emphasized this approach to conflict in Indochina. The plans essentially envisioned a Korean-style conflict initiated by an overt invasion of South Vietnam by the North. The war plans called for a combined allied offensive into North Vietnam, complete with amphibious "hook" operations along the

North Vietnamese coast.[20] According to the Pentagon, such a war would be characterized by a strategic bombing campaign against North Vietnam and by mobile tank warfare on the region's "savannah grasslands and open plains, just like in Europe or west Texas."[21]

Two factors precluded this approach to the conflict. First, the Johnson administration feared following the Korean model—that is, invading the North—would precipitate military intervention by the Chinese Communists, as had occurred in Korea. Thus it was decided that allied ground operations would be limited almost exclusively to South Vietnam. Second, the Communists had no intention of playing to the American military's strong suit: forces equipped and trained for conventional military operations, with a strong emphasis on firepower. Rather than attempting to refight the Korean War, the Vietnamese Communists would stick with the people's war strategy.

Aware of the administration's reservations concerning ground operations in North Vietnam, MACV still hoped to win approval to conduct conventional operations somewhat reminiscent of the U.S. military's Korean War experience. This strategic variant, however, focused primarily on the period of stalemate from 1951 to 1953 in Korea. MACV hoped to isolate North Vietnam, considered to be the source of the problem, from South Vietnam by deploying a blocking force of Army and Marine divisions along the 17th Parallel separating the two Vietnams, through the Laotian panhandle to the town of Savannakhet along the Mekong River.[22]

Despite persuasive evidence to the contrary, MACV believed if external support for the Vietcong from North Vietnam could be cut off, the insurgency would wither on the vine. This Laotian incursion option would be returned to again and again during the period of greatest U.S. involvement in the war. The Pentagon seriously studied the idea in 1964 and 1965; Westmoreland proposed it in 1966 and 1967, and drew up plans to execute it. His request for 206,000 troops in the wake of the Tet Offensive in 1968 was intended, in part, to support the incursion, if only he could win the president's approval.[23]

Discussion of the Laotian incursion option did not die with the war's end, but has persisted in the writings of several soldier-scholars as the strategic alternative that, had it been followed, could have won the war.[24] The persistence of this strategic option is a reflection of the deep, almost desperate, desire on the part of the U.S. military—and the Army, in particular—to try and turn the conflict into a conventional war, to make the war "fit" what U.S. ground forces were organized and trained for. As Lt. Gen. Harry W. O. Kinnard, commander of the Army's elite First Cavalry Division (Airmobile), put it, "I wanted to make them fight our kind of war. I wanted to turn it into a conventional war—boundaries—and here we go, and what are you going to do to stop us?"[25]

Alongside these more conventional strategic options focused primarily on the external threat to South Vietnam's security was another option oriented more on the internal threat and predicated on a more classical counterinsurgency role for U.S. military forces. This was the enclave strategy. It argued that since the war had to be won by the South Vietnamese, the most effective role for American troops would be to assist the ARVN by controlling a number of the densely populated coastal regions, while protecting U.S. bases in those areas. The ARVN would combat guerrilla forces further inland and would receive support from U.S. ground forces only when the Communists deployed in large numbers and offered to fight a pitched battle.

Proponents of the enclave strategy argued that since the Communists were not likely to change their people's war strategy and mass their forces to increase their vulnerability to American firepower, and since the Communists could not drive the American forces out of South Vietnam, MACV should recognize the stalemate and act accordingly.[26] Specifically, it should accept the stalemate at the lowest cost to the United States in casualties and resources and avoid assuming the primary burden for fighting a war that, in the end, the ARVN would have to win. Again, the idea was to buy additional time for the GVN and the ARVN at a relatively low price to the United States.[27]

The Army took a dim view of enclaves, arguing they failed to exploit the service's comparative advantage in firepower and mobility. They represented an affront to the Army's self-image as a hard-hitting offensive force fully capable of performing its traditional mission of closing with and destroying the enemy. According to a Westmoreland staff study, Army forces deployed in enclaves would constitute "an inglorious, static use of American forces."[28]

Precluded from expanding the war beyond South Vietnam's borders, MACV reluctantly abandoned its established war plans and opted for a strategy of attrition. As General Westmoreland put it, he "came up with the concept of leveling off our buildup to achieve a well-balanced, hard-hitting force designed to fight in sustained combat and just grind away against the enemy on a sustained basis—something [the enemy] was not capable of doing, since he didn't have the logistics."[29] As JCS Chairman Gen. Earle Wheeler saw it, U.S. combat power and mobility "will enable us to find the enemy more often, fix him more firmly when we find him, and defeat him when we fight him . . . our objective will be to keep the combat tempo at such a rate that the Viet Cong will be unable to take time to recuperate or regain their balance."[30] This "find 'em, fix 'em, fight 'em, finish 'em" approach, which is a colorful restatement of the combat arms' traditional, conventional mission of "closing with and destroying the enemy," was to find its expression in Vietnam through search-and-destroy operations.

Reduced to its simplest terms, MACV intended to exploit U.S. advantages in technology, mobility, materiel, and firepower to destroy enemy forces more rapidly than the Communists could replace them. Once the "crossover point" had been reached and sustained, MACV believed the Communists would realize they could not win and give up. Maj. Gen. William DePuy, who is sometimes referred to as the architect of the attrition strategy, felt the constant pounding by American forces "would have caused them to perhaps knock off the war for awhile, as a minimum, or even give up and go back north."[31]

While conceding the pacification campaign—the offensive campaign for countering the internal insurgency—was important, General Westmoreland argued that he did not have sufficient forces available for both pacification and search and destroy. When it was pointed out that 90 percent of South Vietnam's population lived along the narrow coastal plain and in the Mekong Delta, and Communist battalions in the remote, sparsely populated areas of the country would be isolated from the people, Westmoreland demurred, contending that "it was not enough to contain the big enemy units. They had to be pounded with artillery and bombs and eventually brought to battle on the ground if they were not forever to remain a threat."[32]

In combatting an enemy waging people's war, there is more than one way of depleting his forces. Insurgents sustain their forces by maintaining access to the population, as well as through external support. From 1965 to 1968 the vast majority of support for the Communist troops in the field came from *within* South Vietnam.[33] MACV could have pursued its attrition strategy by conducting operations designed to separate the Communists from the population or, in Mao Zedong's words, to separate the insurgent "fish" from the "sea" of people.

South Vietnam's highly concentrated population facilitated security and pacification operations. By focusing on pacification—the offensive campaign in a counterinsurgency war—the allies could have denied the Communists access to the manpower needed to replace troop losses and flesh out new units. Food and medicines, and intelligence on allied troop movements, would have been denied to the Communists. At the same time, the government would gain or preserve access to these same resources.

Properly executed, a pacification campaign would have forced the Communists to adopt one of three unpalatable alternatives. First, they could have scaled down their war effort, accepting a reduction in forces due to fewer available recruits and insufficient food. Second, the Communists could have adjusted the mix of external support coming from the North, increasing foodstuffs and manpower, while decreasing ammunition and weapons. However, since the great majority of supplies came from within South Vietnam, this option would have had the same consequences as the first. Third, the Communists could openly contest the allies for control of the population through military operations against the populated areas. This would have played right into MACV's hands, as the allies would be fighting pitched battles on terrain familiar to them. Thus pacification offered General Westmoreland the prospect of a relatively low-cost, low-risk strategy for depleting enemy forces through an "indirect approach."

General Westmoreland's claim that he lacked sufficient troops for both pacification and search-and-destroy operations is not persuasive, unless one posits the simultaneous pacification of the entire country.[34] MACV did not exploit the opportunities of pacification's indirect approach to attriting enemy forces because such operations were not seen as part of what Morton Halperin has termed the Army's "organizational essence."[35] The Army looked for the most "familiar" way to fight the war, not the most effective. Its field commanders had no pacification plans, they simply maneuvered their forces in search of battlefields in which they could execute Westmoreland's guidance to keep pounding the Vietcong and NVA through "spoiling attacks." Asked if he realized that U.S. forces were not achieving anything permanent through these operations, that the Communists would only move right back into an area and dominate the population once the allies had departed, U.S. field force (corps) commander Lt. Gen. Stanley Larsen replied, "Then we'll go back in and kill more of the sons of bitches."[36]

Ground Operations, 1965–1968

For nearly three years, from the early summer of 1965 through the Tet Offensive in 1968, U.S. and allied ground forces pursued MACV's strategy of attrition against Vietcong and NVA forces. Reflecting its conventional mindset, MACV accepted information supporting its concept of operations while discounting or challenging information contradicting its approach to waging the war.

For example, General Westmoreland and other senior Army commanders accepted the successful debut of the First Cavalry Division (Airmobile) in the Ia Drang Valley campaign as validating airmobile and search-and-destroy operations as effective for prosecuting the war. In the Ia Drang Valley, located in the central highlands region, elements of two NVA divisions chose to stand and fight regular U.S. Army forces in November 1965. The battle saw the North Vietnamese sustain heavy losses—over 1,200 killed by MACV's estimate. Since MACV's attrition strategy was designed to generate enemy casualties, these types of engagements were exactly what the Americans were hoping for.

Unfortunately, General Westmoreland and the MACV staff overlooked three important facts. First, it was the NVA that initiated the battle, not the First Cavalry Division. Second, the Communists had chosen to operate in large units on this occasion. As subsequent events over the next three years proved, the Americans could neither force the Communists to fight, nor force them to operate in large formations vulnerable to U.S. firepower. MACV soon discovered that the Communists—as prescribed by their strategy of people's war—quickly reverted from large-unit confrontations with U.S. forces to guerrilla operations.

Third, MACV ignored unpleasant facts regarding the success of other search-and-destroy operations. The Americans might have recognized the reversion of the enemy to lower-level operations if they had been less enamored with the First Cavalry's success in the Ia Drang Valley and focused more attention on operations like those conducted by Brig. Gen. Ellis W. Williamson's 173rd Airborne Brigade in War Zone D, a large expanse of territory to the north of Saigon that had long been a Vietcong stronghold. Between June and November of 1965, the 173rd made *five* separate incursions into War Zone D on search-and-destroy missions against enemy forces. But the Vietcong refused to fight on the Americans' terms. Few of the enemy were killed and little of lasting value was accomplished.[37]

Nevertheless, these types of operations grew in number and magnitude for nearly three years as MACV devoted ever more resources toward reaching the crossover point. Operations such as Birmingham, El Paso I and II, Attleboro, Cedar Falls, and Junction City saw U.S. Army and allied forces engage in search-and-destroy operations in the remote enemy strongholds north and west of Saigon: War Zone C, War Zone D, and the Iron Triangle.

For instance, Junction City, conducted from February to May 1967, involved a multi-division U.S. assault into War Zone C. As General Westmoreland observed, "The operation employed for the first time all our different types of combat forces, including paratroopers and large armored and mechanized units."[38] The operation's target, the Ninth Vietcong Division, was not rendered ineffective. With one exception the only significant engagements were those initiated by the Vietcong. Shortly after the operation's completion, the Communists returned to the area. Despite the operation's meager results (MACV claimed only 1,776 enemy killed), and despite that more often than not the Americans found their hard-hitting operations striking at thin air, the Army contended that Junction City "confirmed the Attleboro experience that such multi-division operations have a place in modern counterinsurgency."[39]

These operations were not only unsuccessful in achieving the attrition strategy's objective of driving enemy casualties to unacceptable levels, they also incurred distinct disadvantages for allied forces. First, they drew troops away from the populated areas, facilitating the Vietcong's access to the people and undermining the pacification program. Second, they forced allied soldiers and marines to fight on unfamiliar terrain (which, of course, was quite familiar to the enemy).

Although they learned little from the Army's relative lack of success in search-and-destroy operations, General Westmoreland and his MACV staff might have learned something from the Marine's CAP program. Far from leading to a strategic innovation by MACV, however, the Marine approach to combatting the Communists as reflected in the CAP program led to a serious row between senior Marine generals and their Army counterparts over strategy for ground operations.

Combined Action Platoons comprised some 15 Marines and 34 Popular Force territorial troops who lived in and provided security for a village or hamlet. Their mission gave high priority to traditional counterinsurgency operations: destroying the insurgent infrastructure, protecting the people and the government infrastructure, organizing local intelligence networks, and training local paramilitary forces.[40] CAPs were employed along the coast in I Corps where the population was concentrated. They achieved impressive results in pacifying their area of operation, especially when one considers that the Marines were located in the narrowest section of South Vietnam, which also bordered on the Demilitarized Zone (DMZ). As noted above, for reasons of organizational heritage, force structure, leadership, and luck, the Marines were more successful than the Army in adopting an innovative, unconventional response to people's war.

The Marines' proclivity for hugging the coast and their aversion to conducting search-and-destroy operations in the sparsely populated interior regions of I Corps drew the ire of the Army. Indeed, the grumbling among the Army brass reached all the way to Westmoreland himself. The First Cavalry Division's commander, Maj. Gen. Harry W. O. Kinnard, was "absolutely disgusted" with the Marines. "I did everything I could to drag them out," he said, "and get them to fight. . . . They just wouldn't play. *They just would not play.* They don't know how to fight on land, particularly against guerrillas."[41] Maj. Gen. William DePuy observed sarcastically, "the Marines came in and just sat down and didn't do anything. They were involved in counterinsurgency of the deliberate, mild sort."[42]

By November 1965 General Westmoreland was sufficiently disappointed in the Marines' failure to participate fully in his attrition strategy that he wrote Maj. Gen. Lew Walt, the commander of the III Marine Amphibious Force (MAF), on the subject. Westmoreland admitted that the Marines were conducting "the only serious pacification effort underway in any areas secured by US or Free World Forces." He nevertheless believed "very strongly that we must . . . seek out and destroy larger VC forces" operating in the remote regions of I Corps, even though over 95 percent of the population lived within 25 miles of the coast, on one quarter of the territory in Walt's area of operations.[43]

Both Lt. Gen. Victor Krulak, the Commanding General Fleet Marine Force Pacific (and former Special Assistant to the Chairman, JCS, on Counterinsurgency and Special Activities—SACSA), and Gen. Wallace Greene, Jr., the corps' commandant, strongly opposed MACV's attrition strategy. Arguing that "the Vietnamese people are the prize," not Communist casualties, Krulak maintained that the enemy's main force units "could move to another planet today, and we still would not have won the war."[44] These units would just be regenerated, Krulak stated, by drawing upon the people and the local guerrilla forces for manpower, supplies, and intelligence. The primary effort must not be focused on an attrition strategy and search-and-destroy operations, which were "the route to defeat." Rather, the main weight of the allied effort must rest on pacification and social and economic reform.[45] Westmoreland, however, retained the support of the JCS and the president for his approach to the war. Although the Marines persisted in expanding the CAP program (79 CAPs existed by 1967), their efforts were increasingly devoted to MACV's big-unit war where effectiveness was measured by "battalion days in the field" conducting search-and-destroy operations.

Westmoreland and his staff did recognize the requirement for population security efforts, but preferred to have the South Vietnamese shoulder the burden for its accomplishment. An Army Staff study produced in the Pentagon in the spring of 1966 and titled "Program for the Pacification and Long-Term Development of South Vietnam," or PROVN, argued that pacification be given top priority in the war effort. Although the study accepted that the bulk of U.S. and Free World Military Assistance Forces should continue operating against enemy main forces and their base camps, it recommended U.S. forces participate in revolutionary development (as pacification was referred to) efforts as well. General Westmoreland was briefed on the study in May 1966 while in Honolulu. He contended MACV was already acting on most of PROVN's recommendations; nevertheless, shortly thereafter PROVN was downgraded from a study to a "conceptual document" in no way binding on MACV.[46]

By midsummer, Westmoreland began to revise his position on pacification, at least as far as the ARVN was concerned. In July he persuaded General Cao Van Vien, the chief of South Vietnam's Joint General Staff, to issue a formal directive declaring area security operations equal in importance to conventional operations. Westmoreland also issued guidance to U.S. advisers that at least 50 percent of ARVN operations should be in support of pacification area security missions.[47] As Jeffrey Clarke has observed:

> . . . reserving the attrition mission for American combat units had the effect of relegating almost the entire South Vietnamese armed forces to static security missions. The existence of two military commands, each pursuing different strategies and each with different roles and missions, also made it easier for American military leaders and their superiors to regard both pacification and the advisory effort as secondary activities and the pursuit of the strategy of attrition as the major task.[48]

Although a combined command had existed during the Korean War, MACV did not pursue with any great energy the formation of a similar command when American combat forces were deployed in 1965. Westmoreland argued that a combined command would have dredged up images of Vietnam's colonial past, when Vietnamese troops served under the French. He further asserted to Maxwell Taylor that such an arrangement was unnecessary, since "I can get them [the ARVN] to do anything I tell them to do." Taylor, who had led the combined command in Korea, had a different view of the situation. "We never really paid attention to the ARVN army," he observed, "We didn't give a damn about them." Nor was General Matthew B. Ridgway, who also headed the combined command in the Korean War, persuaded by Westmoreland's rationale.[49]

This separate but unequal relationship produced pernicious effects in addition to those noted above. First, it allowed the ARVN hierarchy to continue its practice of protecting and promoting politically reliable officers, regardless of their unfitness for command or corrupt practices. Second, it resulted in additional U.S. combat forces arriving in South Vietnam *substituting* for Vietnamese combat forces instead of *augmenting* them. Third, it left the ARVN poorly postured for the relatively rapid transition to full responsibility for the war effort that occurred under Vietnamization. Finally, it did not take long for U.S. officers to realize that advising the South Vietnamese armed forces was not a career-enhancing assignment. The key to landing on the "fast track" for promotions was to be found in assignments in the U.S. main force units conducting offensive, search-and-destroy operations.[50] Consequently, the Army's best officers strove to avoid working with the ARVN, the force that, in the long run, would have to prevail.[51]

From the time Americans began arriving in 1965 through the end of 1967, the

Communists reverted to Phase II operations, increasingly emphasizing guerrilla-style attacks against allied forces and refusing to fight unless the terms of battle were in their favor. Vietcong and NVA battalion-size attacks decreased rapidly, from 9.7 per month in the last quarter of 1965, to only 1.3 per month in the last quarter of 1966. Meanwhile, the number of small-unit Communist attacks increased by roughly 150 percent over the same period.[52] MACV, however, did not adapt to the changing situation. U.S. ground forces remained focused on seeking engagements with large enemy units.

Thus as the Communists moved away from big-unit operations, the Americans emphasized them all the more. As MACV's large-scale operations attempted to create the "body counts" to enable the allies to reach the crossover point, its own data revealed that 88 percent of all engagements were initiated by the enemy.[53] It was the Communists, not the allies, who held the initiative in this war of attrition. They refused or accepted battle on their terms, thus regulating their casualties and frustrating MACV's strategy. Furthermore, because of Westmoreland's insistence on giving battle whenever and wherever the Communists appeared, they controlled *his* rate of loss to a significant degree as well.[54] This was an important consideration, given that the Communist's strategy called for attriting U.S. will to continue the war. Finally, if a stalemate existed, the question must be asked: On whose side is time? Given the three-year timetable initially put forward by Westmoreland in his concept of operations, the growing impatience of the American people, and the Vietnamese Communists' demonstrated ability to engage in protracted conflict, time almost certainly favored the enemies of South Vietnam.

By the autumn of 1966, senior U.S. defense officials were beginning to have serious doubts over Westmoreland's ability to reach the crossover point. It was becoming clear to McNamara and several of his key advisers that MACV's strategy was not succeeding, and filling Westmoreland's continuing requests for additional troops was unlikely to break the stalemate that kept the Communists from expanding to Phase III operations, but which saw them able to persist at lower levels of the conflict almost indefinitely. McNamara, who was now convinced that a strong pacification program was crucial to any chance of success, challenged Westmoreland's attrition strategy and its rationale for search-and-destroy operations in lieu of placing primary emphasis on pacification. He believed that "the large-unit operations war, which we know best how to fight and where we have had our successes, is largely irrelevant to pacification as long as we do not lose it."[55]

Despite the growing reservations of his defense secretary and mounting domestic opposition, President Johnson still hoped to wring success through MACV's attrition-through-firepower approach. However, when General Westmoreland returned to Washington in April 1967 to lobby the president for an additional 4 divisions, he found Johnson unwilling to sign up for this "optimum" force package. (Had the president approved the request, the United States would have had 130 maneuver battalions in South Vietnam by mid-1968, nearly four times the 34 U.S. battalions MACV had requested in June 1965.) Instead, Johnson approved additional forces to bring MACV's strength up to 525,000, with an additional 19 maneuver battalions. The president was forced to hope Westmoreland's claim that "last month we reached the crossover point in areas excluding the two northern provinces" would prove the beginning of the end for the Communists.[56]

Six months later, in November 1967, the president called Westmoreland home to address a joint session of Congress and for a round of media appearances to proclaim the attrition strategy was working. In a speech at the National Press Club, the general declared: "We have reached an important point where the end begins to come into view." Westmoreland indicated that allied forces were on the cusp of the third phase of his concept of operations; indeed, "we have already entered parts of Phase III."[57] In Westmoreland's view his strategy was running right on schedule.

Tet and the Search for a Way Out

For Westmoreland, recent events seemed to confirm his optimistic November assessments. In the second half of 1967, the Communists clashed with allied forces in a series of engagements along the periphery of South Vietnam that became known as the "border battles." For Westmoreland, these battles were an indication that his strategy was working. In the III Corps Tactical Zone, which ran from the Mekong Delta (IV Corps) to the Central Highlands (II Corps), MACV observed with satisfaction that engagements in the four border provinces had increased from 38 in 1966 to 273 in 1967. As Westmoreland saw it, this proved the enemy was being pushed away from populated areas. But this was a chimera. As members of McNamara's staff pointed out, "if allied forces had pushed the enemy to the border provinces, we would expect the attack rates elsewhere in III CTZ to have diminished. They doubled." At the same time the Communists continued their small-unit war: in 1967 over 96 percent of all engagements with the Vietcong and NVA occurred at company level or below.[58]

The Communists' strategy was to draw the allies—the Americans in particular—away from the densely populated regions along the coast to facilitate the infiltration of their forces into those regions. The Hanoi Politburo had decided to alter its defensive posture and reliance on protracted conflict with a massive offensive into the populated areas, the primary objective being to initiate a popular uprising against the Saigon regime. Thus the latter half of 1967 saw the Marines besieged at Con Thien along the DMZ and later at Khe Sanh, an outpost along the juncture of the DMZ and South Vietnam's border with Laos. Further south, Army Special Forces border camps at Loc Ninh and Dak To were attacked, precipitating major engagements between allied and Communist forces.

Despite intelligence indicating that the Communists were planning a general offensive, Westmoreland had "no intention of sitting back to await the enemy's move."[59] A new series of search-and-destroy missions was planned. American forces began preparing for renewed operations in War Zones C and D, while others, like the First Cavalry Division and elements of the 101st Airborne Division, were moved into position to reinforce Khe Sanh which Westmoreland still hoped to use as a jump-off point for an incursion into Laos. Fortunately for MACV, Lt. Gen. Fred C. Weyand, commanding the Army's forces in III Corps, prevailed upon Westmoreland to postpone the forays into the war zones, as well as several operations further north. This facilitated a more rapid allied response to the Communist offensive when it exploded across the entire length of South Vietnam on the night of 30–31 January 1968.

Allied forces initially reeled from the surprising ferocity and scope of the Communist attacks, which saw Saigon and Hue assaulted, along with 36 of the 43 provincial capitals. Although Vietcong sappers penetrated the U.S. embassy compound in Saigon and the battle for Hue raged for over a month, allied forces quickly gained the upper hand. The ARVN did not, as the Communists had hoped, collapse under the shock of the offensive. By 11 February, less than two weeks after it began, the Communist offensive was sputtering to an end.

The Tet Offensive represents the greatest clash between allied and Communist forces during the three-year period under discussion. It also provides the most direct contrast to the two sides' differing approaches to the war. For MACV with its focus on attriting enemy forces, the Tet Offensive could be viewed as a major victory. The enemy had been "forced" to fight and had suffered a grievous defeat, as could be shown from the enormous body count of 37,000 enemy dead claimed by MACV. For Westmoreland, the attack indicated the Communists were on their last legs, just as he had claimed to the American public back in November. There could be no other explanation for the enemy's willingness to challenge the formidable firepower and mobility of the allied forces.

Just as MACV saw the Tet Offensive through the perceptual lens of its attrition strategy, the Communists viewed the outcome through the perspective of their people's war strategy. Ironically, from that perspective the Communists could also claim victory. True, they had not succeeded in achieving their primary objective of instigating a popular uprising to collapse the Saigon regime and force the Americans to leave. They did, however, achieve a number of important secondary objectives. For example, the Communists derailed for months the promising pacification program put in place in 1967 under the name of Civil Operations and Revolutionary Development Support (CORDS). They also increased the refugee population and its burden on the Saigon regime by over 800,000.[60] Equally important, through their atrocities in Hue and their penetration of the U.S. embassy, the Communists showed the South Vietnamese people that no one who openly supported the government was safe from revolutionary "justice." Finally, by killing over 1,000 American troops during the offensive, the Communists felt they were making progress in their own strategy of attrition against U.S. willingness to continue the war.

There is little doubt that the Communists—the Vietcong especially—suffered severe losses. Casualties among the Vietcong infrastructure, whose members had come out into the open to support the offensive, would be especially difficult to replace. But the strategy of people's war had sufficient flexibility to offset these setbacks. As they had in the past, in 1951 after their failed offensive against the French, and in 1965 after the Ia Drang Valley engagement, the Communists could revert back to lower-level operations and continue their protracted struggle against the Saigon regime and its American sponsors. They could take heart in the knowledge that the fundamental conditions for success still existed: a corrupt and inefficient GVN, an ARVN incapable of shouldering the primary burden for the nation's defense, a pacification program yet to prove itself, a flawed American military strategy, and now, rapidly eroding public support in the United States—both among the American people and the civilian leadership—for the military's strategy in Vietnam.

The shock of the Tet Offensive upon the American public led the Johnson administration to review the U.S. war effort. The American public and many of its leaders could not understand how an enemy that had supposedly been pushed back to the borders of South Vietnam and that was reeling from MACV's stunning offensive campaigns could have carried off such a formidable offensive of its own. Concern increased when it was leaked that General Westmoreland was requesting an additional 206,000 troops. If things were going so well, why was an enormous increase in troop strength required?

Clark Clifford, a strong supporter of the president's Vietnam policy, succeeded McNamara as Secretary of Defense at the end of February. General Wheeler had just returned from a trip to South Vietnam and reported that, while the Communists' losses had been heavy, "the judgment is that he has the will and the capability to continue." Wheeler admitted that "there is no doubt that the RD [revolutionary development] program suffered a severe setback. The enemy is operating with relative freedom in the countryside."[61] Wheeler's report reflected the bankruptcy of MACV's strategy. Although the Army had destroyed enemy forces in far greater numbers in the Tet Offensive than in any other period of the war, it had a negligible impact upon U.S. prospects for victory.

Any doubts Clifford might have had on this score were erased when he questioned the JCS several days later. Asked what would be the effect on U.S. prospects for winning the war if the president approved Westmoreland's troop request, the chiefs could not say whether 200,000 more troops could win the war. "Well then," asked Clifford, "can anyone give me an idea when we could bring the war to a conclusion?" The chiefs replied that they did not know when, but if the United States continued grinding down the enemy, the attrition would eventually become unbearable for him.[62]

Clifford's loss of faith in the military's strategy was quickly followed by that of the "Wise Men," President Johnson's distinguished panel of senior foreign policy advisers. After receiving briefings on the war from the Defense and State Departments and the CIA, the group recommended to the president that he begin a program to improve the South Vietnamese armed forces, phase out U.S. combat forces, and seek a negotiated settlement to the war.[63] Within two weeks Lyndon Johnson declared he would not seek reelection in November. Within a month Westmoreland's troop request was disapproved, U.S. troop strength in South Vietnam was frozen, and the initial directives were issued for what later became known as Vietnamization.

Conclusion

After Tet, the U.S. military objective in South Vietnam was no longer victory, but how to extricate American forces while providing the South Vietnamese with the means to ensure their own survival. As Jeffrey Clarke observed, "Vietnamization was not a strategy for fighting or winning the war, or even for achieving America's limited objectives in South Vietnam."[64]

From 1965 to 1968, the ground war in Vietnam pitted an American-dominated allied strategy that sought a quick victory by employing U.S. military strengths for conventional war against the more flexible and comprehensive Communist strategy of people's war. In terms of flexibility, the Communists knew they could never defeat the U.S. armed forces on the battlefield, so they adopted a strategy that did not require a direct confrontation of military forces to achieve victory. Their military defeats were never final, as they showed in 1951, 1965, and 1968, and would demonstrate again after the 1972 Easter Offensive. The Communists could (and did) always drop down to a lower military level of the struggle while continuing the attack on the political front. Their flexible approach to the conflict's military dimension allowed for a protracted war, which supported the political and psychological dimensions of their strategy. As Undersecretary of State Nicholas Katzenbach observed in a memo to President Johnson, "Hanoi uses time the way the Russians used terrain before Napoleon's advance on Moscow, always retreating, losing every battle, but eventually creating the conditions in which the enemy can no longer function."[65] The comprehensive nature of Communists' military strategy considered all the conflict's strategic dimensions—including the political, economic, and social—in its concept and execution.

For the Americans, their fatal misperception was the belief they could win the war by practicing deterrence through punishment; that is, by inflicting pain on the Communists the enemy could be convinced to "knock off the war for awhile, or even give up and go back north," as General DePuy put it. But the Communists proved both willing and able to accept casualties and other forms of punishment that seemed "irrational" to Americans. The allies never reached the crossover point, hence the Communist leadership continued to believe they could win.

Could the allies have won? Given the seemingly congenital incompetence, corruption, and illegitimacy of the South Vietnamese governments during the period, victory was probably beyond the allies' ability. The allies' best chance for success, however, rested not in practicing deterrence through punishment, but deterrence through denial. That is, the allies needed to convince the Communists, not that victory would force them to endure terrible costs, but that victory itself was beyond their means.

A strategy focusing principally on eliminating the *internal* threat to South Vietnam—the threat that was *not* beyond the reach of allied forces—offered the best prospect for success. This strategy would have emphasized counterinsurgency principles (e.g., pacification as the offensive campaign, a combined command, a strategy that actually integrated the multiple dimensions of the struggle) to reduce American casualties and the drain on U.S. material resources, and to exert pressure on the GVN to carry out reforms. This strategic approach would almost certainly have facilitated a longer U.S. presence in South Vietnam, and hopefully convinced the GVN that its allies were not going to shoulder the war's burdens alone. *If* such a strategy could have been executed, the internal threat brought under control, and serious political and economic reforms carried out by the Saigon regime, the Communists in Hanoi might, indeed, have been convinced that at least for the time being, they would have to "knock off" the war and return home.

The strategy of attrition pursued by MACV, however, practically guaranteed failure. It focused primarily on the external threat to South Vietnam's security; yet, for the reasons enumerated above, MACV would never be able to eliminate that threat. Furthermore, MACV's attrition strategy was profligate in its expenditure of material and human resources, undercutting the worthy objective of buying Saigon the maximum amount of time with the minimum expenditure of U.S. resources.

In summary, MACV failed to adopt a strategy to exploit the potential weaknesses of the people's war strategy and instead adopted a strategy congruent with its emphasis on conventional military operations. In so doing, MACV accelerated the dissipation of U.S. public support for the war effort and defeated neither the internal nor the external threats to South Vietnam.

Notes

1. Cited in William Manchester, *One Brief Shining Moment* (Boston, Mass.: Little, Brown, 1983), 224–25.

2. Cited in Stanley Karnow, *Vietnam: A History* (New York: Viking Press, 1983), 395.

3. For a comprehensive analysis of the Communists' strategy in the Indochina Wars, see Douglas Pike, *PAVN: People's Army of Vietnam* (Novato, Calif.: Presidio, 1986), esp. chaps. 9 and 10.

4. Lewis W. Walt, *Strange War, Strange Strategy* (New York: Funk & Wagnalls, 1969), 29.

5. Roy K. Flint, "The United States Army on the Pacific Frontier, 1899–1939," in Joe Dixon, ed., *The American Military and the Far East* (Washington, D.C.: Government Printing Office, 1980).

6. Douglas S. Blaufarb, *The Counterinsurgency Era* (New York: Free Press, 1977).

7. Author's interview with Gen. Maxwell D. Taylor, Washington, D.C., 17 June 1982; Interview with Maj. Gen. Ruggles by the U.S. Army Center for Military History (CMH), Washington, D.C., 27 February 1980.

8. President Johnson to Taylor, 30 December 1964, National Security Files, Lyndon Baines Johnson Library., Austin, Tex.

9. Senator Gravel Edition, *The Pentagon Papers,* 5 vols. (Boston, Mass.: Beacon Press, 1971), 3:474 (hereafter cited as *Papers*).

10. Interview with Maj. Gen. Delk Oden, by Col. Glenn A. Smith and Lt. Gen. August M. Cianciolo, 27 May 1977, U.S. Army Military History Institute, Washington, D.C. (MHI), 18–19.

11. COMUSMACV to CINCPAC, "US Troop Deployment to SVN (S)," 070340Z June 1965, CMH,

1–3. The totals worked out to 34 U.S. battalions and 10 allied (South Korean and Australian) battalions.

12. William C. Westmoreland, *A Soldier Reports* (Garden City, N.Y.: Doubleday, 1976), 169.

13. Ibid.

14. Andrew F. Krepinevich, Jr., *The Army and Vietnam* (Baltimore, Md.: Johns Hopkins University Press, 1986), 165–68.

15. Author's interview with Gen. William C. Westmoreland, New York, 18 May 1982.

16. For an analysis of the relationship between casualties and American public support of the Johnson administration's Vietnam policy, see John E. Mueller, *War, Presidents, and Public Opinion* (New York: Wiley, 1973); and Andrew F. Krepinevich, Jr., "Public Opinion and the Vietnam War" (Cambridge, Mass.: Harvard University, Department of Government, 1979).

17. McNamara to president, "Recommendations of Additional Deployments to Vietnam," 20 July 1965, CMH, 1.

18. Ibid.

19. Krepinevich, *Army and Vietnam,* 164–68.

20. Office of the Deputy Chief of Staff for Operations (ODCSOPS), U.S. Army, "Limited War Capabilities Study—1961" (Draft), 4 August 1961, CMH; and *Papers,* 2:73.

21. Lloyd Norman, "No More Koreas," *Army* 15 (May 1965): 22, 24.

22. For a detailed analysis of the Laotian incursion option, see Krepinevich, *Army and Vietnam,* 261–64.

23. Interview with Gen. Earle Wheeler by Dorothy Pierce McSweeny, 21 August 1969, CMH, II, 5–11; and Westmoreland, *Soldier Reports,* 431–32.

24. Westmoreland, *Soldier Reports;* Bruce Palmer, *The Twenty-Five Year War* (Lexington: University of Kentucky Press, 1984); and Harry G. Summers, *On Strategy: The Vietnam War in Context* (Carlisle Barracks, Pa.: U.S. Army War College, 1981).

25. Interview with Lt. Gen. Harry W. O. Kinnard, by Col. Glenn A. Smith and Lt. Gen. August M. Cianciolo, 31 March 1977, MHI, 36.

26. For an analysis of the enclave strategy, see Krepinevich, *Army and Vietnam,* 141, 153, 264–66.

27. Another counterinsurgency-based strategy, the demographic frontier option, which was not aired until after the Tet Offensive, was a more ambitious version of the enclave strategy. Ibid., 266–68.

28. Westmoreland, *Soldier Reports,* 156.

29. Interview with Gen. William C. Westmoreland (interviewer not cited), 10 April 1971, CMH, 11.

30. Earle Wheeler, "From Marchiennes to Bien Hoa" (Speech delivered to the Annual Reunion of the Second Armored Division, Washington, D.C., 7 August 1965), in *Addresses by General Earle C. Wheeler, Chairman, Joint Chiefs of Staff,* 2 vols. (N.p., n.d.), 2:57.

31. Interview with Gen. William E. DePuy, by Lt. Col. Bill Mullen and Les Brownlee, 26 March 1979, MHI, VI, 21–22.

32. Westmoreland, *Soldier Reports,* 181.

33. Krepinevich, *Army and Vietnam,* 187–88.

34. Ibid., 175–76.

35. Morton H. Halperin, *Bureaucratic Politics and Foreign Policy* (Washington, D.C.: Brookings Institution, 1974).

36. Neil Sheehan, *A Bright Shining Lie* (New York: Random House, 1988), 584.

37. Shelby L. Stanton, *The Rise and Fall of an American Army* (New York: Dell, 1985), 43–50; and Krepinevich, *Army and Vietnam,* 178.

38. Admiral U. S. G. Sharp and General William C. Westmoreland, *Report on the War in Vietnam* (Washington, D.C.: Government Printing Office, 1968), 137.

39. Headquarters, 1st Infantry Division, "After Action Report: Operation Junction City, 22 February 1967—15 April 1967," MHI, 1; John J. Tolson III, *Airmobility, 1961–1971* (Washington, D.C.: Government Printing Office, 1973), 128.

40. Krepinevich, *Army and Vietnam,* 172–77.

41. Author's interview with Lt. Gen. Harry W. O. Kinnard, Washington, D.C., 21 June 1982.

42. Interview with DePuy, 26 March 1979, MHI, V, 26.

43. Westmoreland to Walt, 15 November 1965, CMH.

44. Sheehan, *Bright Shining Lie,* 631.

45. Ibid.

46. Krepinevich, *Army and Vietnam,* 182.

47. Jeffrey J. Clarke, *Advice and Support: The Final Years* (Washington, D.C.: Government Printing Office, 1988), 175.

48. Ibid., 498.

49. Author's interview with Taylor, 17 June 1982; and Thomas C. Thayer, "How to Analyze a War Without Fronts: Vietnam, 1965–1972," *Journal of Defense Research,* ser. B *Tactical Warfare Analysis of Vietnam Data* 7B (1975): 811.

50. MACV, MADJI2 Fact Sheet, "Prestige of Advisors," 9 August 1967, MHI, 1.

51. Krepinevich, *Army and Vietnam,* 207–10.

52. Office of the Secretary of Defense (OSD), Office of Systems Analysis (OSDSA), "Southeast Asia (SEA) Analysis Report," April 1967, 7.

53. OSDSA, memo for secretary of defense, "Force Levels and Enemy Attrition," 4 May 1967, cited in *Papers,* 4:461.

54. Sheehan, *Bright Shining Lie,* 684.

55. OSD, draft presidential memorandum, McNamara to president, "Recommended FY 67 Supplemental Appropriation," 17 November 1966, cited in *Papers,* 4:365.

56. For an excellent study and analysis of the internal debate over MACV requests for force augmentations and the struggle over the Communists' order of battle and the elusive "crossover point," see Larry Berman, *Lyndon Johnson's War: The Road to Stalemate in Vietnam* (New York: Norton, 1989).

57. Ibid., 114–19; see also Sheehan, *Bright Shining Lie,* 698–99.

58. OSDSA, "SEA Report," February 1968, 7, 16–17, and March 1968, 17.

59. Sharp and Westmoreland, *Report,* 136; and Westmoreland, *Soldier Reports,* 381–82, 390.

60. Krepinevich, *Army and Vietnam,* 249–50.

61. *Papers,* 4:546–47.

62. Interview with Clark Clifford by Paige Mulhollen, 2 July 1969, CMH, 16, 26; and Clark Clifford, "A Vietnam Reappraisal," *Foreign Affairs* 47 (July 1969): 601–23.

63. *Papers,* 4:592. For a superb analysis of the events surrounding the post-Tet U.S. strategic reappraisal, see Herbert Y. Schandler, *The Unmaking of a President: Lyndon Johnson and Vietnam* (Princeton, N.J.: Princeton University Press, 1977).

64. Clarke, *Advice and Support,* 498.

65. Cited in Berman, *Lyndon Johnson's War,* 117.

The Operation Was a Success, but the Patient Died: The Air War in Vietnam, 1964–1969

Larry Cable

War exists first as an idea. Before men and materiel are assembled, long before the fear and exhilaration of combat, and very long before the consequences become apparent, war exists as an idea in the minds of policy-makers and military commanders alike. The conceptualizations of war existing in the minds of those who make and execute national security and foreign policy will, in large measure, govern the outcome of war. Negative concepts assure a bad outcome. Neither materiel strength and technological sophistication nor human courage and suffering can redeem a faulty idea.

Policy-makers must conceive of a goal for the war, the political purpose for which it is being fought. Policy-makers and generals must define victory, the reference against which success or failure is gauged. Generals must have a theory of victory, the way in which the war will be fought. These three elements must be internally coherent, consistent over time, consensually accepted and, most important, relevant to the realities that emerge on the ground.

Sometimes, as with the United States in World War II, the fixing of a goal, the defining of victory, and the development and refinement of a theory of victory are accomplished easily and accurately. In other wars, such as the Korean War, the task is made more difficult by the nature of the conflict itself. In the Korean War, unlike World War II, the national survival or core values of the United States were not at risk. There had been no attack on American territory to rally political will. The Korean War, being a limited war in support of policy, made the mobilization of crusading zeal undesirable.

The Vietnam War also was a limited war in support of policy. However, it differed in character from its immediate predecessor by combining aspects of conventional and guerrilla war and by mixing insurgency with partisan conflict. Chameleon-like, it changed character several times between 1964 and 1968. As a result, the formulation of a goal, the definition of victory, and the development of a theory of victory placed difficult demands on the policy-makers and military commanders of the Johnson administration.

The administrations of Presidents John F. Kennedy and Lyndon B. Johnson, as well as the senior American military commanders, viewed the war emerging in South Vietnam between 1961 and 1965 as a partisan conflict between North and South Vietnam. The alternative, that the war in South Vietnam constituted an in-

109

surgency, representing the armed expression of internal political disaffiliation, was discounted. The American view of guerrilla war was simple: all such conflicts were partisan in nature, with the guerrillas operating as auxiliaries to a conventional force across the border. The South Vietnamese picture was confused in the early 1960s, and the war could be seen as either partisan or insurgent. But the American perception of previous guerrilla wars, coupled with the bipolar world view, assured that it would be understood as a partisan conflict.

Accepting the partisan model meant directing the highest priority toward finding and interdicting the avenues by which North Vietnam provided men and materiel to the Vietcong. Curtailing the flow would reduce the guerrillas' morale and combat efficiency and facilitate the creation of political stability in South Vietnam. American air power appeared to be the ideal instrument to accomplish this task. This assessment was not so much an evaluation of what the United States *should* do as a question of what the United States *could* do.

A report by General Maxwell Taylor in November 1961 addressed the interlocking problems of infiltration and interdiction. The report defined the problem as "to establish a force in Vietnam which will deny the northeast frontier bordering Laos to Communist infiltration and which will have the capability of penetrating Communist dominated areas outside South Vietnam to disrupt Communist lines of communication."[1] It assumed infiltrated men and supplies aided the growing combat capacity of the Vietcong. It recommended the creation of a special South Vietnamese ground unit with American advisors which would seek to find and interdict infiltration routes on both sides of the South Vietnamese–Laotian border.[2]

The ability of the North Vietnamese to provide more than rhetorical assistance to the Southern guerrillas was not seriously addressed. There was no inquiry into the motivation of the Vietcong: Were they seeking a unification with North Vietnam, or were they indigenous insurgents seeking revolutionary change in the South with no desire to lose Southern national identity to the Northern outsiders? Unasked questions bring no answers. The assumption that the Vietcong were Hanoi-controlled partisans dependent upon external support underpinned U.S. policy.

The U.S. Military Assistance Advisory Group and its successor, the U.S. Military Assistance Command, Vietnam (MACV), reported upon infiltration from June 1961. For the twelve months concluding in mid-June 1962, the United States estimated that between 5,100 and 8,800 personnel had infiltrated from North to South, primarily through the Laotian Corridor.[3] The argument contained in a widely circulated Rand Corporation report of August 1964 held that the quality of the men and materiel clandestinely sent to the South was far more important than the quantity.[4] The men were experienced, well-trained and highly motivated political-military leaders, while the supplies consisted of critical weapons, sabotage materiel, communications gear, and medical items. Without North Vietnam acting as a secure base of support and the source of trained and able leaders, the Rand analysts contended, the Southern guerrillas would have to fall back upon a smaller and less qualified leadership pool and would lack many of the necessities for war. The report asserted that "by providing material aid, spiritual leadership and moral justification to the insurgent cause, the DRV [Democratic Republic of Vietnam] adds immeasurably to the insurgents' will to fight."[5]

The administration and military commanders accepted this assessment without question because it reflected the American belief that all guerrilla wars were externally sponsored. The partisan model did not depend upon the quantity or even quality of infiltrated support, but upon the very existence of North Vietnam itself. At least implicitly, for interdiction to yield a truly useful result, it must remove Hanoi as a player in the Southern drama.

In spring 1964 there was evidence indicating that North Vietnam, regardless of its rhetoric, was in no position to engage in Southern adventures. The intelligence community believed that Hanoi was in a period of retrenchment and felt no imperative to take action to extend its hegemony over Laos and South Vietnam. Mismanagement, four years of bad weather, and a growing population had created a major agricultural crisis in the North.[6] The North Vietnamese industrial base, although developing rapidly, remained small and concentrated in only four centers, raising concerns in the Hanoi politburo regarding its strategic vulnerability. The North Vietnamese economy was heavily dependent upon aid and trade credits from the People's Republic of China (PRC), and from the Soviet Union and other Warsaw Pact nations, thereby making it liable to outside pressures. There was a danger that these pressures might be exacerbated if the Sino-Soviet split worsened.[7] North Vietnam possessed a large army of 200,000 to 250,000 men with an "experienced and loyal officer corps" and "disciplined and tightly controlled organization."[8] What was known of the deployments of the People's Army of Vietnam (PAVN), however, suggested "a defensive posture."[9] None of these significant structural features gave credence to the belief of significant North Vietnamese sponsorship of the Southern insurgency.

The Central Intelligence Agency (CIA) reported that North Vietnamese assistance to the Vietcong was limited to technicians and political cadre.[10] While the North could increase its presence in the South to the extent of introducing entire PAVN units, this was thought unlikely as it would produce American counterescalation. On balance, the CIA concluded, North Vietnam would pursue a conservative strategy in both South Vietnam and Laos, holding onto its gains in Laos and depending on the Vietcong wearing down the will of the South Vietnamese government and creating a "neutralist" regime. The agency predicted that ultimately the "neutralist" government would be dominated by Hanoi.[11] The Southern insurgency benefited from Northern rhetorical support and some material and manpower assistance. The presence of Northern political cadre polluted the insurgency, but the degree of Northern influence was not sufficient to change the character of the war from insurgent to partisan.

In the summer of 1964 the State Department was frankly skeptical of claims by the South Vietnamese government of Gen. Nguyen Khanh alleging the presence of PAVN formations in the South and of People's Liberation Army troops in North Vietnam.[12] MACV reported only thirty-seven Vietcong infiltrators for the year to date. The State Department cited this and other preliminary reports that a further 180 had entered South Vietnam from Laos after May.

The Johnson administration generally did not accept the State Department's position because of the continued deterioration of the political and military situation within South Vietnam. In January and February 1964, all reports from Saigon had clearly pointed to a continued and dramatic increase in Vietcong-initiated actions,[13] which now had reached their highest level since before the coup against Ngo Dinh Diem. The increase in the scope, frequency, and competence of the Vietcong actions had become obvious. The reasons behind this unpleasant state of affairs were not so apparent. A strong case could be made that pervasive deficiencies within the South Vietnamese army and government had greased the rails upon which the Vietcong were launching their successful efforts. Alternatively, it could be argued that while the Vietcong were taking advantage of the precarious political situation in South Vietnam, Hanoi was providing the directions and the necessities for the guerrillas.

North Vietnamese expansion of their forces and facilities in Laos gave additional credence to the second interpretation. This slow, steady expansion caused concern in the administration.[14] Continued use of Cambodia as a sanctuary by the Vietcong also caused a degree of anxiety. CIA Director John McCone wrote to President Johnson by way of Secretary of Defense Robert McNamara: "The GVN/ US program can never be considered completely satisfactory so long as it permits the Vietcong a sanctuary in Cambodia and a continuing uninterrupted and unmolested source of supply and reinforcement from NVN through Laos."[15]

On 14 March 1964 when the National Security Council (NSC) made the decision to apply "graduated overt military pressure," it accepted the target of this pressure to be North Vietnam.[16] Some anxiety existed that attacking the North directly would carry a risk of Communist Chinese intervention. This possibility exercised a distinctly inhibitory effect upon the administration. As a result, the direct-pressure option would be the last, rather than the first, arrow in the American quiver. The United States would attempt "border control" activities, including the use of American aircraft for interdiction efforts in Laos. In addition, "tit-for-tat" retaliations would be executed against the North in the event of particularly egregious incidents against U.S. installations or personnel.[17] The goal of American air efforts would be interdiction; direct coercion of Hanoi had not yet become a policy aim.

On 17 March 1964 President Johnson signed National Security Action Memorandum (NSAM) No. 288 authorizing planning for actions against the infiltration routes in Laos and Cambodia as well as for the engagement of targets in North Vietnam. The planning efforts led to the development of CINCPAC OPLAN 37-64, which covered air and ground strikes against selected targets in Laos, "hot pursuit" operations into Laotian border areas, tit-for-tat retaliation efforts against

North Vietnam by air strikes, the mining of ports, and amphibious raids. This plan laid the basis for a program of increasingly heavy air attacks to sustain pressure on Hanoi. The United States intended to use strikes against the North Vietnamese as the means of reducing the will and ability of Hanoi to support either the Pathet Lao or the Vietcong and of inhibiting the North Vietnamese from taking direct military actions in either Laos or South Vietnam.[18] This program added coercion to interdiction as a policy goal.

The likelihood of this program accomplishing the coercion objective was dubious, as the CIA reported in a Special National Intelligence Estimate (SNIE) in late May.[19] The only certainty was that the PRC would not become involved directly unless U.S. troops penetrated deeply into North Vietnam.[20]

The first overt use of American aircraft outside of South Vietnam was in a reconnaissance role over the Laotian Corridor. The flights would be at relatively low altitude, thereby supplementing previously authorized U-2 flights that had gone without incident until 5 June 1964 when a Navy RF-8 was shot down by ground fire.[21] The NSC agreed that it was important for the United States to continue the reconnaissance flights, which had detected "a significant increase in night movement on the supply routes from North Vietnam into Laos."[22] There was dissension over the question of attacking the anti-aircraft positions in the area, but a compromise was achieved that allowed future flights to be accompanied by armed escorts with instructions to return fire.

The NSC met in July to review the continued deterioration within South Vietnam. Of particular concern was the great increase in the number of weapons reported lost to the Vietcong by the various components of the South Vietnamese armed forces. The CIA reported that during the first six months of 1964 the South Vietnamese had lost 4,700 weapons, enough to equip ten Vietcong battalions.[23] The weekly intelligence summaries chronicled the continued increase in guerrilla capabilities fueled by local recruiting and training as well as the involuntary quartermaster services provided by South Vietnamese government forces. But this was overshadowed by various North Vietnamese actions, including the renovation of the North-South railroad below Hanoi and the improvement of all-weather roads into the Laotian Corridor which were seen by the administration as increasingly threatening.[24]

The Tonkin Gulf incident triggered the first application of the tit-for-tat response option. The NSC held a meeting on 4 August 1964 to authorize a response to the attack by North Vietnamese patrol boats on two U.S. destroyers. Secretary of State Dean Rusk asserted that "an immediate and direct reaction by us is necessary," for the attack had been "an act of war for all practical purposes."[25] McNamara informed the NSC that a total of four targets would be attacked; a fifth target had been deleted because of its proximity to China. The president then asked if the North Vietnamese wanted war, and McCone replied: "No. The North Vietnamese are reacting defensively to our attacks on their off-shore islands. They are responding out of pride and on the basis of defense considerations. The attack is a signal to us that the North Vietnamese have the will and determination to continue the war. They are raising the ante."[26] McCone also assured the NSC that while the reprisal might cause a "sharp North Vietnamese military reaction," Hanoi would not "deliberately decide to provoke or accept a major escalation of the war."[27] McNamara's target recommendations were approved and the Joint Chiefs of Staff (JCS) issued an execute order to "conduct a one time maximum effort."[28]

The retaliatory attack, code-named Operation Pierce Arrow, was delivered by U.S. Navy fighter-bombers. Following Pierce Arrow, the Johnson administration decided to concentrate on a carefully controlled program of interdiction attacks within the Laotian Corridor under Operations Farmgate and White Star.[29] Authorization was given to U.S. aircraft flying Yankee Team reconnaissance missions over Laos to engage hostile aircraft and to engage in hot pursuit over South Vietnam and Thailand.[30]

In September 1964, Yankee Team missions were flown at the rate of approximately one per day and provided coverage of lines of communication, supply dumps, way stations, troop movements and concentrations, military installations, and infrastructure changes.[31] Despite repeated U.S. diplomatic appeals, the Laotian government was reluctant to allow its small inventory of converted U.S. training aircraft to be employed in attacking targets within the northern panhandle.[32] The American ambassador was informed that the "overall objective of the operation would be to put increasing pressure on Hanoi and clearly indicate that we are serious."[33] Even if the Royal Laotian Airforce (RLAF) threw all its T-28s into the task, it might be doubted that Hanoi would get the message that the United States was serious.

It would take a heavier weight of attack than that which might be delivered by the RLAF or the quite modest American programs either to send signals of American resolve to Hanoi or to interfere with the complex of North Vietnamese facilities and activities within the Laotian Corridor. The North Vietnamese positions in Laos were viewed increasingly by American policy-makers and military commanders as playing a crucial role in the constant improvement of Vietcong combat capabilities. If these facilities presented a major threat to American interests and policy goals in South Vietnam, as so many in the administration believed, then the United States should attack them directly.

The administration was caught between two perceived needs. South Vietnam needed assistance which would have a direct, immediate, and visible effect upon the deteriorating military situation in the country. Political and diplomatic imperatives alike required that the United States present the appearance of being reluctant to use its great military power against a small and relatively weak nation. A third factor entering the calculus was uncertainty about the reactions of Hanoi, Peking, and Moscow to an open employment of American military force on a sustained basis against North Vietnamese targets, even those located in Laos. The administration attempted to balance these various imperatives through creative temporizing. The United States would use only minimal, low signature, and plausibly deniable force within Laos.

There was a fundamental problem with the use of clandestine air power in the Laotian Corridor. If the force employed was small enough to remain clandestine, it was probably too small to be effective. The JCS believed that the only way to move beyond the militarily ineffective covert level of force was to await a major incident by the Vietcong or North Vietnamese. Then, as had been shown by the Tonkin Gulf incident, the United States could respond openly with a level of violence which might have significant military, if not diplomatic, effects upon the Vietcong and their North Vietnamese sponsors.[34]

On 31 October 1964, the Vietcong attacked the air base at Bien Hoa killing four Americans, destroying five Air Force B-57s and damaging thirteen others as well as several South Vietnamese fighters.[35] Local Vietcong forces had used weapons readily available to them. The Johnson administration believed that the mortaring had been ordered by Hanoi and attempted to link the North Vietnamese directly to the attack. More likely, the local Vietcong commander had acted on his own volition to counter a real and immediate threat to him and those under his command.[36]

The psychological effect of the attack was far greater than the material damage done. Gen. William C. Westmoreland and his superiors had comfortably assumed that the enemy would respond in a conventional fashion, with an air attack by North Vietnamese planes upon the bases used by the United States for its tactical efforts. American anti-aircraft batteries with the latest surface-to-air missile, the Hawk, had been sent to protect against just that sort of threat. When the guerrillas attacked a base instead, they simply could not accept that the act had been conceived and executed as a local initiative. The CIA, however, had detected no interest by the North in retaliating for Pierce Arrow or for the use of jet aircraft in operations in the South.[37] Had the presidential election not been so close at hand, there can be little doubt a retaliatory air strike would have been dispatched. The JCS recommended an extremely robust retaliation including a B-52 strike on the major military airfield near Hanoi along with fighter-bomber attacks on other North Vietnamese airfields and oil depots. These attacks would be followed by a sizable program of armed reconnaissance missions directed against Laotian infiltration routes.[38] This package was not approved, but it was a clear indicator of the road ahead.

Assistant Secretary of State William Bundy and Assistant Secretary of Defense John McNaughton served as the principal architects of U.S. policy in the fall of 1964. Their perspective on the situation in South Vietnam and on the relationship between North Vietnam and the Vietcong had a large impact on the decisions made in the winter and spring of escalation. They commented in late November:

> The basic elements of Communist strength in South Vietnam remain indigenous, the North Vietnamese [DRV] contribution is substantial and may now be growing. There appears to be a rising rate of infiltration.
> We believe that any orders from Hanoi would in large measure be obeyed by Communist forces in South Vietnam. The US ability to compel the DRV to end or

reduce the VC [Vietcong] insurrection rests essentially upon the effect of US sanctions on the will of the DRV leadership and to a lesser extent on the effect of such sanctions on DRV capabilities. US-inflicted destruction in North Vietnam and Laos would reduce the elements of DRV support and damage DRV/VC morale.[39]

This assessment directed the Bundy-McNaughton and, subsequently, the administration's theory of victory away from the seemingly intractable problems of South Vietnamese governmental and military competence. Instead, the administration chose to embark on a debatably irrelevant and dangerous policy of coercing the North to end its presumed sponsorship of the Southern war and an interdiction effort to erode the material capacity of the North to provide effective assistance to the Vietcong.

The Bundy-McNaughton thesis received support from an early December CIA assessment of infiltration. Shortly thereafter it became the keystone of American policy. On 7 December 1964, President Johnson approved a position paper on future operations in Southeast Asia.[40] The first phase covering actions to be taken over the next thirty days included "US air protection of Lao aircraft making strikes in the Corridor, US armed reconnaissance and air strikes against infiltration routes in Laos, and GVN and possibly US air strikes against DRV as reprisals against any major or spectacular Vietcong action in the south, whether against US personnel and installations or not."[41] The transition phase, to occur after the initial thirty days, included the option of low-level reconnaissance of infiltration targets in North Vietnam and the "possible initiation of strikes a short distance across the border against infiltration routes from the DRV."[42] After the transition phase:

> If GVN improves its effectiveness to an acceptable degree and Hanoi does not yield on acceptable terms, the United States is prepared—at a time to be determined—to enter into a *second phase* program, in support of the GVN and RLG, of graduated military pressures directed systematically against the DRV. Such a program would consist principally of progressively more serious air strikes, of .weight and tempo adjusted to the situation as it develops (possibly running from two to six months) and of appropriate US deployments to handle any contingency. Targets in the DRV would start with infiltration targets south of the 19th parallel and work up to targets north of that point. This could eventually lead to such measures as air strikes on all major military-related targets, aerial mining of DRV ports and a US naval blockade of the DRV.[43]

The purpose of the proposed phased exercise was to provide Hanoi and all other interested observers the impression of steady, deliberate resolve while maintaining a maximum degree of control from Washington. Air power, it was presumed, could be precisely controlled allowing for fine gradations of weight, tempo, and focus of attack, thus facilitating the use of force in support of policy. The United States would maintain control of the options, to escalate or not, to provide pauses during which talks might be started, to closely monitor enemy actions, and to modify the effort appropriately. It was a policy of extreme rationality, and a theory of victory which played to American strengths very well. It also seemed to have the potential to protect the administration's need to have and effectively exercise political, operational, and even tactical control. Its relevance to the realities on the ground in Southeast Asia was doubtful.

As the position paper made clear, the Laotian Corridor was to be the initial focus of increased American pressure. By early December, it had become obvious that the addition of RLAF T-28 aircraft to the earlier Farmgate and White Star covert attacks had resulted in no diminution of North Vietnamese or Pathet Lao activity in the area. It was time for the first openly American campaign of air attacks in Laos.

A new program, Barrel Roll, was initiated, and the first Barrel Roll strike was delivered on 14 December 1964 with negligible results.[44] Additional missions were flown on 17, 21, and 25 December.[45] The absence of military effect was equalled by the lack of political result. The CIA concluded that Hanoi had missed the fact that Barrel Roll was "the inauguration of a new and different policy."[46] This tracked with what the agency had estimated would be the effect of Barrel Roll a month earlier.[47]

If the intention of the Bundy-McNaughton program was to send messages to a Vietnamese government, neither Saigon nor Hanoi had their receivers turned on. The Barrel Roll sorties and other minor increases in the Laotian interdiction effort had not been noticed by Hanoi.[48] They had not exercised any positive effect upon the continued deterioration of political stability in Saigon. Through January, President Johnson was carefully briefed on political developments in South Vietnam and their baleful influence on the course of the war.[49] There was little doubt that as the center of the South Vietnamese government became less and less coherent, the success of the Vietcong increased. Within the thirty days of phase one, the position of James C. Thompson, a major critic of the escalatory air war, seemed to have been proven correct:

> More fundamentally, I am struck by the basic phoniness of the escalatory options: . . . that high levels of action against the North are an act of desperation bearing little direct relationship to the problems we face in the South.
> . . . our present Vietnam planning seems inordinately focused on how to punish the North, rather than on the intricate priority problem of how to improve our performance—and that of the GVN—in the South. I do not believe that the two problems are in any sense identical.
> This leads to a further and deeply rooted doubt, which I find are shared by most of my friends who are familiar with the post war history of Vietnam: namely, a doubt that any degree of punishment which we care to inflict upon the DRV would induce them to give up their national revolutionary purpose and actions. . . . It is my impression that Hanoi will be able to bear the consequences of our northward push longer than will we.[50]

Thompson's criticisms were trenchant as events through January 1965 demonstrated. The central problem confronting the administration was discriminating between what the United States should do from what it could do to influence the course of events in South Vietnam.

Early on 7 February 1965 the Vietcong, after a week of "virtual standdown" during Tet, attacked the U.S. billeting compound and airstrip at Pleiku, killing eight Americans and destroying five aircraft.[51] A series of urgent NSC meetings held during 6–8 February considered the implications of the Pleiku attack for American policy.

After the first of these Special Assistant for National Security Affairs McGeorge Bundy, in a memorandum to President Johnson, rehearsed all the reasons why the United States must escalate the intensity of its operations over Laos and North Vietnam and provided a dismal but realistic appraisal of the governmental and military situation in South Vietnam. He urgently recommended both a direct tit-for-tat reprisal for the Pleiku attack and its extension into a "policy of sustained reprisal."[52] Bundy was arguing for the immediate application of the phase two actions outlined in the position paper approved two months earlier.

When the final NSC meeting on Pleiku convened on 8 February, Bundy's recommendations had been adopted and it was only necessary to formalize them and to gain the assent of the congressional leadership attending for that purpose. The tit-for-tat retaliatory raid had already occurred. In the strike, code-named Flaming Dart I, U.S. Navy aircraft attacked the North Vietnamese barracks at Dong Hoi.[53] Against this background, discussion of the phase two actions, or to use Bundy's term, "sustained reprisal," began.

> The president summarized the present position:
> 1. Last December we had approved a program of further pressure against North Vietnam but did not initiate actions for the time being, in order to allow Ambassador [Maxwell] Taylor a period of time in which we hoped he would be able to assist the Vietnamese in creating a stable government.
> 2. We are now ready to return to our program of pushing forward in an effort to defeat North Vietnamese aggression without escalating the war.
> 3. We were surprised by the attack on our personnel at Pleiku but we had to respond. If we had failed to respond we would have conveyed to Hanoi, Peking and Moscow our lack of interest in the fate of the South Vietnamese government. In addition, the South Vietnamese would have thought we had abandoned them.
> 4. There is a bad governmental situation in Saigon but it is our hope that current US action may pull together the various forces in Saigon and thus make possible the establishment of a stable government.[54]

There was an evident piece of illogic in a program seeking to defeat the North Vietnamese without escalating the war. There was an obvious irrelevance in the quest to win the war in the South by defeating the North. There was a sense of desperation in the desire that U.S. actions against the North would serve as a stimulus to governmental effectiveness in the South. The president was less than candid in his assertion that the attack at Pleiku caught the United States by surprise; if it had, there had been a breakdown not of intelligence but of command responsibility.[55] He was quite accurate about the poor political situation in Saigon.

Against this background McGeorge Bundy argued that events forced the United States to act. He said that "a rolling consensus as to the proper course of action" had emerged following his return to Washington.[56] When House Minority Leader Gerald Ford asked if the administration intended merely to react to enemy provocations, the president replied that, while all Vietcong actions called for a response, the administration did not intend to limit its actions to retaliation. In this way, the president provided a nice back-door definition of "sustained reprisals." It was clear what the United States would be doing; none of the congressional leaders dissented.

The formalization of the nascent air war continued on 10 February. Several salient points defining the "rolling consensus" were obvious in the NSC meeting that day and the meeting of the principals preceding it.[57] First, the Far East was vulnerable to Communist penetration, even domination, in the event of a U.S. defeat in South Vietnam. Second, the investment of U.S. prestige and influence was of such a magnitude that an American pull-out would have global consequences. Third, with the possible exception of a ground force intervention, the United States could do nothing in the short term directly and positively affecting governmental stability and military effectiveness in the South. Fourth, the evil guiding genius behind the Vietcong was Hanoi in this partisan war. Fifth, the only actions the United States could take having a positive impact on the situation in the South were those having the potential of eroding the material capacity of North Vietnam to provide assistance to the Vietcong or which might enervate the political will of Hanoi. From these points the NSC decided to proceed into "Phase II" and begin a graduated increase in military pressure.[58]

The extent to which information available to the administration supported linking the war in the South to the actions and assistance of Hanoi is open to question. The intelligence reports circulated to the Departments of State and Defense and the White House provided ample reason to conclude the war was running against the South Vietnamese government. There was repeated and convincing evidence of continued political deterioration within the Saigon government. Report after report demonstrated increasing Vietcong success on the battlefield. The intelligence record concerning the extent and the significance of infiltrated men and supplies to the improving fortunes of the Vietcong was less clear, but tended to support the contention the guerrilla movement was not dependent upon external sponsorship. The intelligence record was also unclear as to the nature and character of Hanoi's interest in the success of the Vietcong: Were they Hanoi's auxiliaries, potential rivals for power in the South, or simply a means of bringing about the neutralization of Saigon?[59]

There were close political harmonies between Hanoi and the National Liberation Front for South Vietnam (NLFSVN). Hanoi would have been gratified by an American withdrawal from the South. However, political commonality, even when coupled with geographical proximity, did not automatically imply that Hanoi was providing significant military assistance let alone adopting the role of external sponsoring power. The NLFSVN contained within its leadership ranks genuine Southerners, and its popular support had steadily increased.[60] These two factors are important considering the intense regional identification in Vietnamese society. An early 1965 CIA study of the NLFSVN saw little influence from Hanoi in the growing competence of the NLF in propaganda which effectively exploited the domestic disaffection within South Vietnam. Hanoi was not seen as the reason for NLF success in seizing the opportunities provided by the turmoil within the South Vietnamese government. Hanoi was given no credit for the NLF's ability to effectively govern areas dominated by the Vietcong. In short, the agency saw the reasons for the political and military effectiveness of the guerrillas as arising more from Southern factors than from Northern sponsorship.[61]

Hard evidence of militarily significant infiltration in 1964 was thin. Assessments generally agreed that the majority of guerrilla manpower and materiel came from Southern sources with the contribution from the North being limited to cadre, specialists, and certain types of ordnance and equipment.[62] Both Cambodia and Laos, with their significant base camp and training areas, contributed more to Vietcong military competence than North Vietnam. The Vietcong and NLFSVN had the capacity to operate independently of Hanoi's supplies and without regard to Hanoi's interests.

By late 1964, evidence was accumulating that PAVN units had infiltrated into the northernmost province of South Vietnam potentially changing the character of the war. The initial indications came from the often self-serving and unreliable South Vietnamese intelligence services and were not given great credence. From December 1964 the introduction of American-controlled "roadwatch" teams in combination with Yankee Team and Barrel Roll provided far more reliable information on the looming first clouds of the infiltration storm yet to break.[63]

Just prior to the February NSC meetings authorizing the "Phase II" program's air attack on North Vietnam and the infiltration routes, a draft SNIE stated that "there has also been a steady improvement in the capabilities of the Vietcong forces in South Vietnam. Some of the improvement results from stepped up North Vietnamese support, though detailed judgements are complicated by the spotty and frequently ambiguous evidence available."[64] In general, the position of the Board of National Estimates was that the situation in South Vietnam was becoming increasingly tenuous because of conditions in the South. This assessment was reinforced by a contemporaneous SNIE which considered the political turmoil in Saigon and the other major cities and its negative impact upon social cohesion throughout South Vietnam.[65] On 11 February 1965, the CIA cautioned that the North Vietnamese would not be motivated "to restrain the Viet Cong" by the initiation of the new policy.[66]

The pattern developed by all intelligence reporting through mid-February 1965 demonstrated an insurgent guerrilla conflict in which support from North Vietnam did not constitute the critical component in the successes enjoyed to date. The Vietcong and NLF had been able to capitalize on the pervasive governmental weaknesses in Saigon since the coup against Diem nearly eighteen months earlier. This chronic turmoil, coupled with the relative inefficiency of the Army of the Republic of Vietnam (ARVN), gave the insurgents all the help they needed, and assistance from Hanoi was a bonus. At most Northern political cadre polluted the insurgency, but pollution was not control.

A strong argument might have been made for the proposition that the NLF/Vietcong, regardless of their original relationship with Hanoi, had emerged as an independent Southern force by late 1964. As such the NLF/Vietcong were immune to dictates from Hanoi and, in the view of the politburo, might have become rivals for power in a unified Vietnam. The initiation of "Phase II" actions against the North and the infiltration routes could have only a marginal effect on the battlefield capabilities of the Vietcong, and carried no potential to facilitate a political solution to the war.

"Phase II" actions held a great potential for counterproductive effects. The air attacks might bring the North more directly and vigorously into the war in pursuit, not of success by the Vietcong, but of a North Vietnamese victory. U.S. policy interests would have been better served by ignoring the North Vietnamese pollution of the Southern insurgency than by inviting Hanoi into the war in pursuit of its own goals. The American air war constituted an invitation best left unissued.

The intellectual myopia within the administration not only obscured the counterproductive nature of the "Phase II" program, it made the number of apparent policy alternatives seem quite limited. Through February all indications pointed to a worsening situation.[67] The one bright spot reported by the MACV commander (COMUSMACV) was the improvement in ARVN command morale in the wake of Flaming Dart I and II.[68] The sinking of a coastal freighter laden with arms and other supplies in South Vietnamese territorial waters on 16 February sharply focused attention on the North Vietnamese–Vietcong linkage.[69]

On 19 February 1965, the United States employed jet aircraft in ground attack missions within South Vietnam for the first time. This action constituted a change in policy and might have been seen as an American escalation by the other parties in the war. The new authorization was used heavily.[70] The initial evaluation of U.S. close air support and similar tactical employments in South Vietnam was generally favorable, a judgment that would remain largely accurate for the next several years.[71] Tactical successes notwithstanding, the new use of American jet fighter-bombers did nothing to alter the unfavorable overall trends in South Vietnam.

Inhibitory considerations, such as the possibility of Chinese intervention, were overridden by the apparent lack of viable options and the long-delayed "sustained reprisal" or "Phase II" program was finally activated on 2 March 1965. One hundred U.S. and South Vietnamese aircraft executed Rolling Thunder V against the North Vietnamese ammunition depot at Xom Bang and the naval base at Quang Khe. This attack was followed by twelve more during the rest of March. Overall, 513 sorties were flown against seventeen targets. Damage ranged from none to heavy.[72] The operational planning, execution, and results were carefully monitored at the White House, a practice which would prevail over the next several months.[73]

Starting in mid-March, the administration attempted to assess the effectiveness of Rolling Thunder. Indications were mixed at best.[74] There was no immediate intelligence intimating that the program had impaired either the will or the ability of the North Vietnamese to encourage or assist the Vietcong. The United States suffered some adverse diplomatic and public relations consequences. More ominously, in a memorandum to the president, McCone raised a possibility that, if borne out by later developments, would severely undercut the entire basis of Rolling Thunder and Barrel Roll. The Vietcong might possess "military strengths and capabilities greater than we have supposed as a review of the data now in process suggests."[75]

At the NSC meeting of 26 March, McCone took an upbeat position on the effects of Rolling Thunder, suggesting that the bombing effort had "greatly improved military morale and stabilized the government situation in Saigon."[76] He acknowledged the consensus within the intelligence community that the bombing had not convinced either Hanoi or the Vietcong they could not win the war.[77]

At the next NSC meeting on 5 April, McCone modified his earlier position. He now agreed with CIA analysts who had concluded the "Communist position was hardening rather than the reverse as a result of the air strikes."[78] McCone's position was reinforced three days later by a report of the U.S. Intelligence Board, the senior analytical component of the intelligence community. The board concluded that the bombing campaign had served to stimulate the Hanoi politburo not only to deliver diplomatic and rhetorical responses to the attacks but also to enhance the North Vietnamese military position along the Demilitarized Zone (DMZ), in the Laotian Corridor and in northern South Vietnam. The North had moved within weeks to match and raise the American escalation: "This buildup in capabilities almost certainly indicates an intention to undertake offensive operations of greater scope and significance than hitherto attempted in this area. The security situation in this area has so deteriorated that an accelerated sustained effort by the VC or an attack on some key point could have grave consequences for the GVN."[79]

No longer inhibited by fear of provoking an American response and with a popular political will stimulated by the lash of bombs, Hanoi could be expected to continue matching any further U.S. escalations.[80] It could have been concluded in the first month of the new air campaign that the addition of Rolling Thunder to the ongoing programs of armed reconnaissance and strikes in Laos had impaired neither the will nor the ability of the Vietcong to prepare for and engage in effective military action. There was no indication that Hanoi was willing, or even able, to leash the dogs of war in the South. There were many reasons to conclude that the Vietcong and Hanoi, perhaps for quite disparate reasons, were each in the process of matching the U.S. escalations in the air war by actions on the ground.

In response to indications that Rolling Thunder was failing in its coercive thrust, the administration adopted several proposals made by Army Chief of Staff Harold Johnson in mid-March. The general's recommendations included a reorientation of Barrel Roll to increase the military effectiveness of the program and an increase in the tempo and scope of attacks under Rolling Thunder.[81] His proposals were supported by McCone and the military command structure.[82] Barrel Roll was expanded, with the presumption that this would increase its effectiveness against infiltration. The tempo of Rolling Thunder was to increase slowly.[83] The JCS disagreed with this decision, preferring an approach they called the "sharp knock," implying a rapid, violent, and relatively short campaign. Management of the bombing campaign would continue to rest with the administration, as would significant restrictions regarding munitions, targets, and routing. Following a pause in the bombing program to allow damage assessment and target reconnaissance, May became the month of Rolling Thunder.[84]

With U.S. troops on the ground in South Vietnam, interdiction of the flow of men and supplies had acquired a fresh urgency.[85] The increasing combat power of the Vietcong was seen by the administration and the commanders in the field as making the American interdiction effort the single highest priority. In April 1965 the CIA informed the Johnson administration that while the introduction of U.S. ground combat forces into the South presented a new problem for the Vietcong and the increased use of American air power in the South had likewise challenged the flexibility of the guerrillas, "there was no evidence that Viet Cong capability to increase military activity had been reduced."[86]

Three weeks later, events reinforced this initial assessment. In a memorandum sent to President Johnson by McGeorge Bundy, the CIA reported in mid-May that Vietcong-initiated incidents had surged to 542 during the first week of May, more than 100 higher than the spring 1965 average.[87] According to MACV, the Vietcong had increased their main force strength from 39,000 to 47,000 and the presence of a battalion of the 325th PAVN Division had been confirmed in Kontum Province. These data were taken by the CIA to mean that U.S. intelligence on the ground had become more efficient in identifying the Vietcong order of battle, that the Vietcong were successful in their local recruiting, and that the counterinfiltration operations had not yet succeeded although the attacks on the North had improved ARVN morale.[88]

With strength and momentum available to them, it seemed likely that the Vietcong would attempt to mount a major, perhaps decisive, offensive in the summer of 1965.[89] U.S. troops would be light on the ground through the early rainy season. The effectiveness of tactical air operations in the central highlands of South Vietnam would be reduced greatly by poor weather conditions.

At the end of April in an attempt to forestall a Communist offensive, the weight of the attacks shifted increasingly to the interdiction of lines of communication associated with the perceived North Vietnamese support capacity. Targets included ammunition dumps, petroleum depots, logistics facilities, and transportation system choke points. The majority of sorties conducted from May onward emphasized armed reconnaissance. These missions were assigned a particular route or geographic area with blanket authorization to engage all targets of opportunity, particularly those associated with transportation.

The White House monitored and controlled the Rolling Thunder program very carefully, with the president receiving regular reports on the results of strikes.[90] Weather and the redirection of strikes from designated targets to armed reconnaissance often reduced the number of sorties, but the effort could never be described as light or its prosecution as irresolute.

The increase in bombing efforts did not have any immediate or obvious effect upon the course of the war in the South. A monthly CIA situation report observed that "the violence of the Viet Cong actions was greater in May than in any month this year," and, despite the bombs, "the Viet Cong sharply intensified their activities and dramatically shifted their activities northward" during the last few days of May.[91] Other than the morale boost given to ARVN by news of the campaigns, the bombing showed no benefits to the troops in the South or to the policy-makers in Washington.

In mid-June the administration considered another option: the use of B-52 strategic bombers against targets in South Vietnam.[92] The B-52 could deliver devastating attacks against Vietcong base complexes, destroying their networks of deep tunnels and fortified bunkers. The psychological effect of the unheralded arrival of hundreds of tons of high explosives dropped by planes flying too high to be seen or heard from the ground would be as intense as the physical destruction. Under the code name Arc Light, these operations began in summer 1965.

The B-52s were expected to destroy major supply dumps and hardened base camps deep in the bush, striking directly at facilities beyond the reach of ground combat forces. It was believed that the massive caches of supplies, arms, and munitions served to mitigate the effectiveness of the interdiction campaign.[93] Because of potential political sensitivity, all Arc Light missions had to be cleared through and approved by the NSC staff.[94]

Arc Light operational effectiveness assessments were not regularly reported to the White House except in the form of routine and often misleading bomb-damage assessment photography. Effectiveness of the program had been difficult to assess because there had been only rare follow-up by ground units.[95] The conclusion reached was that "an overall evaluation of the effectiveness of B-52 strikes must be measured in a broad abstract sense, and—from this viewpoint—there is sufficient evidence to reach the conclusion that they are contributing significantly to the war effort."[96] Fainter praise would be difficult to imagine.

The decision to deploy significant additional troops to South Vietnam did not alter the priority given the air war over the North. Secretary McNamara responded to a presidential request on 30 July 1965 with a lengthy memorandum concerning the efficacy of Rolling Thunder.[97] He described the major purposes of the effort as being to influence Hanoi to negotiate "explicitly or otherwise" and to "reduce the flow of men and supplies from North to South" so as "to put a ceiling on the size of the war which the enemy could wage in the South."[98] While granting that the first purpose had not been accomplished in the slightest, McNamara believed that the second had produced some significant results:

(1) *For regular North Vietnamese and Pathet Lao forces.* The interdiction program has caused North Vietnam increasing difficulty in supplying their units in South Vietnam and Laos. How severe this difficulty is or how stretched North Vietnam's supply capabilities are, cannot be estimated precisely. Our interdiction efforts may have prevented or deterred the North from sending more troops than they already have. The interdiction programs in North Vietnam and Laos also may have influenced a Communist decision to forego a 1965 offensive in Laos.

(2) *For Viet Cong forces.* Because the VC require significantly less infiltrated arms and ammunition and other supplies than do the North Vietnamese and Pathet Lao forces, the interdiction program probably has had less of an adverse effect on their operations. By raising VC fears concerning adequacy of supplies, however, the program may have caused the summer offensive to be less intense, aggressive and unrelenting then it would otherwise have been.[99]

Leaving aside the question of proof by negatives—the absence of the Laotian offensive and the perhaps less intense Vietcong summer offensive and the paucity of intelligence information substantiating the secretary's conclusions—McNamara supported the bombing campaign because of a consensus in favor of Rolling Thunder within the military high command and his own office. The only concrete support offered for the campaign was the positive effect that the bombing campaign had produced on the morale of ARVN and the Saigon government. McNamara concluded by recommending continuation of the effort.

In a related memorandum John McNaughton concluded that Rolling Thunder had not measurably affected the capability of the enemy forces in the South to fight or the ability of North Vietnam to meet its civilian and military needs. He concluded that instead of splitting efforts between coercion and interdiction, the United States should throw the entire weight of the attack behind the interdiction mission.[100]

In mid-July 1965 a study group within the Office of the Chairman, JCS, recommended increased ground combat in the South to overtax the supply lines and supporting infrastructure used by the PAVN and Vietcong.[101] The conclusions of this ad hoc study group must be seen in terms of Army doctrine. That doctrine listed three basic requirements for providing security: find the enemy, fix the enemy in place, and fight and finish the enemy. Army doctrine was thus fundamentally Clausewitzian in focus: "The *military power* [of an enemy] must be destroyed, that is, reduced to such a state as not to be able to prosecute the war. This is the sense in which we wish to be understood hereafter, whenever we use the expression 'destruction of the enemy's military power.'" And "in this manner we see that the destruction of the enemy's military power, the overthrow of the enemy's power is only to be done through the effect of the battle."[102]

All editions of FM 100-5, *Field Service Regulations-Operations,* published prior to the Vietnam war, maintained this focus. All U.S. Army officers were steeped in the cult of battle with its single-minded focus upon closing on the enemy and destroying his forces in the field through decisive combat. Not even the introduction of nuclear war and the concomitant cautionary notes against allowing limited [nonnuclear] war to cross the nuclear threshold served to diminish the Clausewitzian tone or modify the focus upon destroying the enemy's force in the field and thus his capability to conduct war.[103] The Clausewitzian approach was not limited to the higher operational levels but extended to the conduct of tactics even at the company level.[104]

When considering guerrilla war, Army doctrine continued its concentration on destroying the enemy force in the field. Guerrillas might impose some modest changes in tactics or organization, but they were not immune to destruction through the application of superior mobility and firepower. Aggressiveness, mobility, and firepower represented the solution to the problems presented by guerrillas.[105] Aggressive patrolling, the maintenance of contact, the use of high mobility ground and air tactical transport systems, the coordinated movement of air and ground mobile elements, the careful use of well-prepared artillery fire patterns as well as the use of artillery in long range, unobserved harassment and interdiction missions were all stressed as appropriate operational modalities to find, fix, and destroy the guerrilla. Above all else the potential of the new Army airmobile forces was accentuated. Offensivemindedness was a universal in the American Army.

Counterguerrilla, particularly counterinsurgent, warfare is essentially defensive in nature at least at the strategic and operational levels. The limited historical experience with successful counterinsurgency shows the strategic defensive should be expressed in offensive small unit operations in which the goal was not so much killing as demoralizing the enemy by depriving him of sanctuary. The Army did not understand this as it conflicted with the cult of the offensive: "Superior mobility is essential in counterguerrilla operations to achieve surprise and to successfully counter the mobility of the enemy force. The extensive use of airmobile forces, if used with imagination, will ensure the military commander superior mobility."[106]

Thus, doctrine ensured COMUSMACV and his field commanders would use mobility and firepower to take the battle to the guerrilla either in the bush or within what the enemy considered to be safe havens using superior air and ground mobility to fix him in place. The application of superior firepower, both ground and air delivered, would destroy him whether he attempted to stand or to run. It was equally certain that U.S. forces would not attempt to hold the land they swept in offensive operations. Holding territory would be too demanding on scarce manpower and erosive of the offensive spirit held to be so important.[107]

The study group accepted the argument that the Vietcong were primarily indigenous Southerners, led primarily by native Southerners who "procure most of their supplies in South Vietnam and are not solely dependent on an external supply system."[108] They noted that only 20 percent of the weapons recovered from the Vietcong in 1964 were of PRC origin while 34 percent were French and 31 percent were American.[109] The report concluded that the entire Vietcong main force of 125 battalion equivalents required only 10 tons of supplies per day from North Vietnam given the level of combat intensity which had prevailed through mid-1965.[110] This requirement was too small to allow for easy interdiction by either ground or air attack.

The study group was conservative in its assessment of the presence of PAVN units in South Vietnam. They accepted intelligence indicating that one regiment, the 101st of the 325th division had entered South Vietnam starting in January 1965, a date after the start of the U.S. aerial interdiction and coercion effort.[111] Elements of two other regiments of the 325th might also be present in the central highlands. The purpose and role of the PAVN units was uncertain, and their troops had not been engaged in combat to a significant extent, which meant that the forces required no more than 4 tons of supplies per day per division.[112]

These small logistics requirements, not more than 14 tons per day, coupled with the wide array of land and maritime infiltration routes explained why the aerial interdiction campaign had not impaired the ability of North Vietnam to supply its forces and assist the Vietcong in the South.[113] The CIA agreed with the study group's conclusions.[114]

In an excellent application of "if you can't raise the bridge, lower the water," the study group concluded that the way to make the lines of supply and the North Vietnamese infrastructure more vulnerable to air attack was to increase the demands placed upon them by the consumers in the South. If the level of combat could be intensified, Vietcong requirements would leap from 10 to 125 tons per day and PAVN demands would increase from 12 to 100 tons per day for each full-strength division.[115] At a sustained demand level of 225 tons per day, the logistic system would be far more susceptible to aerial interdiction and the North Vietnamese infrastructure far more vulnerable to Rolling Thunder.

Ground combat operations would serve to magnify the effect of the air operations against infrastructure and infiltration target systems by increasing the demands placed upon them by Vietcong and PAVN forces.[116] The study group proposed that ground combat forces operate in support of the air forces as a matter of deliberate strategy. Not only was this a first in military history, it also represented an inversion of the customary relationship and carried profound ramifications.

The study group defined winning in South Vietnam as:

> . . . achieving an outcome somewhere between, as a maximum, an end to the insurgency by DRV/VC decision and as an acceptable minimum, containment of the insurgency, except for minor areas and minor acts of violence, with an end to the need for the presence of substantial US forces. . . . Hopefully, the VC/DRV will become convinced that they cannot win in SVN, that continued efforts will be extremely costly and that time is on the side of the Free World.[117]

It developed a theory of victory which had three main components: ground combat operations against the Vietcong main forces and any PAVN units which entered South Vietnam; interdiction of infiltration routes by air, sea, and ground efforts; and air attacks upon infrastructure and economic target systems in North Vietnam. The theory of victory focused on the use of U.S. air power against infiltration routes and support facilities in North Vietnam. Matters such as pacification, military civic action, regeneration of ARVN, or how the pace and scope of the air war might be modulated to facilitate diplomatic exchange were not considered.

The study group was alone among military planners in accurately seeing the Vietcong as an insurgent force with tenuous connections to the North. Having seen the situation in the South accurately, they did not develop a theory of victory directed at countering an insurgency, but produced a theory based on the standard view of guerrilla war as partisan conflict with North Vietnam in the role of external sponsoring power and, therefore, the main enemy. Instead of asking the correct question—what does history show about the use of military force in countering insurgency?—the study group simply accepted the embedded misconceptions and designed a theory of victory for partisan war.

There are several plausible explanations for this apparent lapse of intellectual courage on the part of the group members. They were participants in the shared intellectual heritage which saw insurgency as an impossible phenomenon. As members of the military services, they were aware of and conditioned by Air Force and Army doctrine which emphasized the physical destruction of the enemy's force in the field or his material capacity and political will to continue the war. As military officers of field rank they were also well aware of the utter impossibility of altering doctrine or organizations and tactics quickly. The United States had no alternative except to fight with the forces and doctrine it had in 1965. As Americans, they undoubtedly had a high opinion of the efficacy of U.S. weapons systems, and as a corollary they repeated the fundamental mistake of earlier generations of planners who relied on air power. In World War II, Germans, British, and Americans had all assumed with a profound but baseless conviction that the government and civilian population against which the planes were sent and on whom the bombs fell would suffer a collapse of structural integrity and political will. Finally, as officers well tied to the bureaucracy, they were aware of what was wanted and needed up the chain of command. They provided an assessment which comported itself well with the perspective of JCS chairman Gen. Earle Wheeler, John McNaughton, and Robert McNamara.

Given this shared intellectual heritage, the senior policy-makers and the military commanders could not help seeing the war as a partisan conflict in which the stakes were greater than a South Vietnam that was non-Communist. The study group reflected all the aspects of the heritage in a convenient package. There can be little doubt that General Wheeler and others read the report with a great degree of satisfaction for it contained a recipe for victory they were quite well prepared to cook.

At the end of August 1965, the JCS sent a memorandum to Secretary McNamara in which the joint chiefs laid out a general concept of operations for Vietnam.[118] Working from the statement of goals contained in NSAM 288, they identified the basic tasks for the military as: forcing the North to cease its direction and support of the Vietcong, defeating the Vietcong so as "to extend GVN control over all of the RVN," and deterring "Communist China from direct intervention."[119] Their theory of victory mirrored that of the Ad Hoc Study Group report. They emphasized air power and destroying the infrastructure, industrial base, and political will of the North. The joint chiefs agreed, at least implicitly, that the role of the American ground forces in the South was to act as a force multiplier in support of the air war over Laos and North Vietnam. Despite a series of war games in which all the senior members of the administration, including Secretary McNamara, participated that demonstrated powerfully the dangerous irrelevance of an air campaign against the North, the secretary of defense accepted the JCS position.[120]

This made an advantage of doctrinal necessity. All the troops had to do was increase the tempo and intensity of combat. They need not seize and hold ground. They did not even have to win battles, kill the enemy, or capture his supplies. The only thing the ground forces had to do when they went out to bash the bush in the big battalions was to increase the enemy's logistics requirements. If this could be done successfully, then air power over the North and the trails of Laos would win the real war. It is probably a good thing that the grunts did not know why they were risking their lives in the bush.

By late summer 1965 U.S. ground combat forces were arriving in South Vietnam in ever-greater numbers to fulfill the Ad Hoc Study Group's prescription for using ground combat to enhance the impact of the air war. At the same time, the interdiction efforts and Arc Light operations became central to the American pursuit of victory.

In a major report on infiltration in June 1965, the CIA reported new Soviet bloc and Chinese weapons, which had first appeared in South Vietnam in December 1964, were entering the country in ever-larger numbers. These arms were apparently part of a plan to standardize weapons to increase Vietcong firepower, but they might also make the Vietcong ammunition supply vulnerable.[121] However, many of the new weapons and their ammunition were being infiltrated by sea, and the bombing campaigns were irrelevant in interdicting a coastline more than 1,000 miles in length and used by some 50,000 junks of various descriptions.[122]

Regarding Laos, the CIA concluded that despite "strenuous efforts" to stem the traffic flow the traffic had continued to move, "if at a somewhat reduced rate."[123] It conceded that measuring the effectiveness of interdiction was difficult because it was impossible to determine the percentage of supplies crossing the border from North Vietnam into Laos destined for South Vietnam rather than for use by the Pathet Lao or PAVN forces in Laos. Furthermore, CIA analysis had been hampered by the inability to maintain Roadwatch teams on two critical highways and the limited the utility of aerial imagery.[124]

In southern North Vietnam, the transportation system had been systematically and continuously bombed since 3 April so that by June "almost all" of the major bridges and many of the secondary ones had been "destroyed or damaged." The overall effect was interpreted as constricting of the North Vietnamese transportation system throughout the southern part of the country. It was thought that the need for constant repairs and improvisations placed "considerable strain" upon North Vietnam, making support of the war in South Vietnam more expensive.[125]

An important effect of Rolling Thunder overlooked by the CIA had been accurately reported by the State Department. The bombing had not significantly undermined popular morale in the North and might have had just the opposite impact, improving the political will to continue the war by focusing hatred on the United States.[126]

In another assessment of the bombing, Ambassador Maxwell Taylor confirmed that the Vietcong had shown themselves "quick to adapt" to American weapons and tactics. Their logistics system continued "to provide adequate—or apparently adequate—support in the form of ammunition and weapons despite air strikes against land routes of supply and the efforts of the Seventh Fleet to blockade the coast of South Vietnam to prevent gunrunning."[127] Taylor concluded that everything the United States was doing was correct. The problem was that not enough of it was being done: "The weight and duration of our air attacks in North Vietnam have been insufficient to produce tangible evidence of any willingness on the part of Hanoi to come to the conference table in a reasonable mood."[128]

The most noticeable result of Rolling Thunder had been the increase in North Vietnamese anti-aircraft capabilities. The Soviet Union had furnished surface-to-air missile (SAM) batteries along with the necessary surveillance and target acquisition radars. Soviet technicians were in North Vietnam instructing PAVN personnel in the operation of these systems as well as in the use of new anti-aircraft artillery. U.S. military commanders correctly determined the SAM-2 batteries constituted an unacceptable threat to Rolling Thunder missions and ordered strikes against SAM sites.[129] The North Vietnamese had made it quite clear how they intended to respond to the messages of Rolling Thunder.

Despite an increase in raids on the North, the trend of increased infiltration indicated in June had accelerated by October 1965.[130] The land routes through Laos from North Vietnam had been continuously improved and diversified. It was still not possible, however, to estimate accurately the volume of traffic moving along them.[131] Maritime infiltration had also expanded using small, inconspicuous junks, although the amount of maritime infiltration was unknown.[132] Cambodia had also become more important as an infiltration route because of the lax attitude of the Cambodian government, the maze of minor waterways forming much of the border area, and the number of Vietcong base camps close to or even across the Cambodian border.[133]

These three complementary infiltration systems were individually difficult and collectively impossible to close. Exacerbating the difficulty of meaningfully interdicting the flow of external supplies was the low demand the Vietcong placed upon the system. Even considering the continued influx of modern Soviet Bloc and Chinese weaponry, the guerrillas' requirement for external arms and ammunition was moderate. The CIA reported that the Vietcong had an organic capability to reload cartridges and manufacture grenades and mines from captured explosives.[134] While there was an ongoing need for medical supplies, the small bulk and weight of most pharmaceutical and medical equipment made their infiltration easy. In addition, medical supplies were among the items easily obtained from South Vietnamese sources by purchase, diversion, or theft.

Overall, this assessment must have made very depressing reading for anyone in the administration who had placed great store in the interdiction efforts. The Ad Hoc Study Group had assumed that increased U.S. ground combat operations would translate into an increased vulnerability of Vietcong/PAVN supply lines. Unfortunately, these hopes had not yet been borne out in fact.

The best which might be said in support of the interdiction effort was that it *might* have slowed the rate of infiltration in mid-1965 as American troops were entering combat. Perhaps, in its absence the Vietcong would have mounted a much more serious and extensive summer offensive. The overwhelming preponderance of evidence should have led policy-makers to the conclusion that interdiction had not, and would not, become a war-winning concept no matter how much U.S. search-and-destroy operations might succeed in increasing the tempo and intensity of combat in the South. That being the case, the only purpose for Rolling Thunder was coercion directed at Hanoi.

By default, McNaughton's "progressive squeeze and talk" theory of victory was becoming central. By December the administration was giving renewed consideration to this theory. The next round of squeeze had already been decided: General Westmoreland had proposed, with the support of the JCS and McNamara, a large augmentation of U.S. forces deployed to Vietnam during 1966 as well as an increase in the weight of the air attacks on North Vietnam. McGeorge Bundy reminded the president in early December that the Vietnam augmentation already approved would average 15,000 men per month through 1966.[135]

Growing international and domestic concern over the 1965 escalation in both the ground and air wars led McGeorge Bundy to favor a pause in Rolling Thunder to allow for "talk" before the next round of "squeeze."[136] Undersecretary of State George Ball, who had opposed the air campaign from the beginning, suggested the pause. In a mid-November memorandum, he argued that a bombing pause would strengthen the American position in the eyes of the world community and would remove the largest impediment blocking the possibility of negotiations.[137] Ball reported that McNamara was essentially in agreement. The secretary of state, Dean Rusk, did not agree. By 3 December, McGeorge Bundy had become a supporter of the pause, which he termed an "open question" since the president did not yet favor one.[138]

Bundy supported the pause because of Ball's well-honed arguments and the support for these from McNamara. He might also have been influenced by a study of the effects of Rolling Thunder by the deputy director of intelligence, Ray Cline, done at the request of Bundy in early November. Cline concluded that the strikes had been professionally executed and the ordnance delivered with great care, assuring maximum target damage with minimal civilian casualties. However, the "effects of the air strikes against North Vietnam do not clearly indicate how the Hanoi regime will react to various possible future trends."[139] Stripped of its cautious ambiguity, Cline's conclusion was: Rolling Thunder had neither coerced nor interdicted and might never do so.

On 4 December, McGeorge Bundy reported to the president that a consensus within the administration had emerged for a pause. Rusk, McNamara, McNaughton, both Bundys, Cyrus Vance, Tommy Thompson, and Ball all agreed that the pause was the "best single way of making it clear that Johnson is for peace and Ho [Chi Minh] is for war."[140] While there would be both international and domestic complications and while there was uncertainty as to the timing and duration of the pause, the senior policy-makers all agreed that the benefits, including the preparation of opinion for the next round of "squeeze," far exceeded the problems.

Ten days later, McGeorge Bundy wrote the president concerning Ball's argument that the United States should stop bombing the North altogether. While Bundy did not support this radical suggestion, he cautiously favored a broader cease-fire coupled with a mission to Hanoi. Westmoreland, Henry Cabot Lodge, and the JCS unanimously opposed this proposal. They thought a cease-fire would dishearten the Saigon government and surrender American initiative on the ground in South Vietnam.[141] Even with these unpleasant possibilities, Bundy thought the potential rewards worth the risk. Great political and diplomatic advantages would accrue if the North (or, it could be presumed, the NLF/Vietcong) rejected the offer.

The administration's foreign policy specialists discussed the cease-fire and bombing-pause concepts on 17 and 18 December. The initial meeting showed elements of profound disagreement within the State Department with Ball arguing that the bombing had hardened the will of Hanoi and Rusk disagreeing completely with this assessment.[142] Ball had the weight of history on his side. As he knew from his work on the U.S. strategic bombing survey in Germany during 1945, bombing usually increased and solidified the target population's political will to oppose the perpetrator of the bombing. McNamara seemed particularly confused and disheartened. At the beginning of the meeting he stated that increased bombing was "inevitable," but later he seemed to pull back.[143] The president finally decided that he preferred a de facto pause. Rather than define it as a pause, he would use weather and Christmas as factors causing a temporary cessation of raids. The proposed pause would last from 22 December through 22 January 1966.[144]

The next day, the president again expressed reservations. "The military say a month's pause will undo all we've done."[145] Bundy and McNamara countered that the United States had the option to resume bombing at any time. There was much discussion of the possibility that the North Vietnamese would exploit the pause to ship supplies and repair damage. Finally, domestic political considerations convinced the president to accept the military risks.

The discussion turned to the chance of a U.S. military victory. McNamara said the chances were one in three. The president asked, "Then, no matter what we do in [the] military field there is no sure victory?" The secretary of defense replied, "That's right." McNamara either had lost or was in the process of losing faith in the theory of victory of which he had been a principal designer. Rusk was more optimistic but admitted, "I can't prove it."[146] If the pause brought either a North Vietnamese acceptance of negotiations or a tacit withdrawl from the war, the gambit would have worked. If Hanoi made neither move, the United States would be forced to escalate the ground and air operations already underway. It would be necessary to do more of the so far unsuccessful same old thing.

The bombing pause started on Christmas Day 1965. The duration was an open question, depending upon the response of Hanoi and the effects of an American peace offensive. The American diplomatic efforts were intense as George Ball reported at the NSC meeting on 5 January 1966. The United States had contacted all 113 countries with which it had relations; of these, 57 had responded favorably to the U.S. peace initiatives. President Johnson had written personally to thirty-three heads of state; special emissaries had contacted another thirty-four. It was a maximum diplomatic effort with little in the way of immediate result.[147] Ambassador Lodge threw another bucket of cold water on the diplomatic effort in a telegram on 4 January 1966. Rusk had asked him to consider the possibility of another Geneva conference or the use of the International Control Commission to reach a negotiated settlement to the war. Lodge responded that neither option would be appropriate as "the Communists think they can win." He argued that negotiations would become a viable option when the United States had accomplished three tasks: "really punish them in the North, decisively defeat the North Vietnamese Army," and "root out the terrorists and rebuild the political structure in the countryside."[148]

John McNaughton, who had been one of the two main architects of the bombing campaign nearly two years earlier, was having serious doubts about the administration's theory of victory by mid-January 1966. Retreating from the expansive goal he had espoused earlier, McNaughton was now seeking merely to avoid humiliation. Diplomatic efforts had come to nothing because both the United States and North Vietnam were defining victory as being equivalent to "unconditional surrender," and neither side "could give in" to the other without an unacceptable loss of international status and prestige.[149]

McNaughton now doubted the potential of Rolling Thunder to induce negotiations or a North Vietnamese withdrawal from the South.[150] He focused upon the potential utility of the air campaign in the slowing of infiltration. Following the lead of one of his staff, he argued that with the proper selection of target systems, the United States could hope to place a ceiling upon the number of troops the North could support within South Vietnam.[151] He concluded that bombing probably would not interdict any better than it coerced, so the United States should look for another means of interdiction and continue to bomb so as to provide a "bargaining chip."[152] The goal of the air campaign was again changing out of frustration rather than reflection.

On 24 January as the pause neared the one month mark, President Johnson met with Rusk, McNamara, McGeorge Bundy, and Taylor.[153] This meeting was the first of several on the pause and its effects. It considered the duration of the pause, which Westmoreland was urging be brought to an end within a few days. The peace offensive had come to nought. U.S. military commanders increasingly worried about the North Vietnamese taking advantage of the pause. The CIA confirmed this fear in mid-January.[154] Diplomatically, Hanoi had shown no willingness to offer concessions for a continuation of the pause.

On the 25th the president and Secretaries Rusk and McNamara met with the congressional leadership. Senators William Fulbright and Mike Mansfield opposed resumption of the bombing, but Republican Senator Everett Dirksen set the tone for the majority of the participants. After rejecting both withdrawal and a war of patient attrition, he concluded: ". . . you can fight. You go into win. If we are not winning now, let's do what is necessary to win. I don't believe you have any other choice. I believe the country will support you."[155] Gerald Ford, Carl Albert, Richard Russell and most of the rest of the congressional leadership concurred. With Fulbright and Mansfield isolated, the president felt sufficiently secure politically to authorize a resumption of the bombing.

In a memorandum on 26 January, McGeorge Bundy recounted John McCloy, Dean Acheson, and Clark Clifford had all told him the bombing pause had served its diplomatic and political purposes and should now be brought to an end.[156]

In a lengthy meeting the next day, the president along with Rusk, McNamara, McGeorge Bundy, and Wheeler continued the process of developing a new "rolling consensus" on resuming Rolling Thunder.[157] Rusk recommended proceeding with the bombing but under tight control because of the perceived danger of Chinese intervention. There was no dissent. The question of targeting brought some disagreement. McNamara wanted to strike "perishable" targets such as trucks on the move while Wheeler wanted the weight of the attack to fall on infrastructure and industrial targets to ensure the North could not supply a larger force than that already in the South. McNamara questioned the supply figures on which Wheeler based his argument. McNamara also echoed Rusk's concern about the air effort inducing a Chinese intervention and insisted upon careful restrictions to militate against this eventuality. He was not certain if the bombing would do any good or even if the United States would be able to measure its effectiveness, but he concluded that it should be resumed. The United States had no apparent alternative to resuming the air raids on the North. This was the nature of the "rolling consensus" on Rolling Thunder.

On 28 January the senior members of the administration and the "wise men," McCloy, Dulles, Dean and Clifford, met for nearly two and a half hours discussing the resumption of the bombing.[158] McNamara presented a rather pessimistic view of the bombing. General Wheeler was more optimistic. He believed that bombing reduced the flow of supplies if the weight of attack was great enough. By the end of the meeting all the "wise men" expressed agreement with the resumption of bombing. The president concluded, "I am not happy about Vietnam but we cannot run out—we have to resume bombing."[159] Once again the decision was not made on the basis of assessing what the United States should do, but rather, what the United States could do. All that was needed for Rolling Thunder to begin again was NSC approval.

The 556th meeting of the NSC commenced at noon on 29 January. The actors knew their parts and the lines were easy to deliver. The new CIA director, Admiral Sam Raborn, presented a capsule briefing of North Vietnamese exploitation of the pause. UN Ambassador Arthur Goldberg commented on the failure of the peace offensive. Army Chief of Staff Harold Johnson talked about the major fighting in Operation Masher and how the United States needed a new "surge" of troops into South Vietnam. Air Force Chief of Staff Gen. John McConnell, described the proposed air campaign: "There is nothing unusual in the air effort recommended. It involves 330 sorties weekly [over the North], B-52 sorties at the rate of 300 a month [Arc Light] and 1200 weekly sorties into Laos."[160] General Wheeler concluded by recommending the resumption of bombing as soon as was practical. General McConnell's parting shot was, "Our bombing is ineffective because of the restrictions placed upon the Air Force. We should lift these restrictions and we would then get results."[161] Restrictions still in place, Rolling Thunder resumed two days later.

Target selection for the renewed Rolling Thunder depended upon the goal of the effort: interdiction or coercion. No consensus had been reached on that key issue during the January meetings. As a result the campaign resumed without a clear targeting focus. There were several alternative target systems that could be engaged, including the lines of communication south of the Hanoi-Haiphong line, the lines of communication north of Hanoi, petroleum storage and delivery facilities, military infrastructure, industry, and key agricultural support facilities such as dikes and levees. The 1965 campaign had been characterized by a diffusion of effort with a percentage of the raids assigned to all target categories except agriculture. In an effort to resolve the targeting issue, the CIA was asked to assess four different programs: one following the pattern of the pre-pause attacks, a second focusing on lines of communication in southern North Vietnam, a third including bulk petroleum storage with a lines-of-communication focus, and a fourth including all target systems except urban population centers and agricultural facilities. It was told that the bombing program should be measured in terms of securing two objectives within the near term (ten weeks): coercion and interdiction.

The response came on 11 February 1966. It concluded that interdiction was an impossibility:

> We do not believe that even the most extensive of the programs of air attack would prevent the movement of men and supplies in quantities sufficient to sustain or even increase the scale of VC/PAVN activity. Our best judgement is that an average of about 12 tons daily has been required by the VC/PAVN from external sources over the past year . . . . The principle effect of different bombing levels probably should be measured in terms of slowing the supply effort . . . and setting a ceiling on future expansion of the supply rate. Critical to the significance of any ceiling . . . would be the rate of consumption of men and materiel which GVN/allied forces impose on the VC/PAVN forces.[162]

The CIA had come to the same conclusions as the Ad Hoc Study Group. By dictating the tempo and intensity of combat, U.S. ground combat forces could play

a crucial role in determining Vietcong and PAVN supply and manpower requirements. The CIA, however, placed the air effort in its traditional role, supporting
the ground forces by limiting the resources immediately available to the enemy on
the battlefield. After an exhaustive examination of the alternative programs, Dr.
Sherman Kent and the Office of National Estimates (ONE) concluded the best
option was the second, focusing on the lines of communication south of the Hanoi-
Haiphong line.[163] The CIA assessment was sent to the president by McGeorge Bundy
on the 25 January.[164]

The course of Rolling Thunder did not show the focus recommended in the
ONE assessment. In May General Wheeler assured the NSC that "the air operations in the north have hurt the North Vietnamese. They are having transportation
difficulties and are using at least 80,000 men to repair their LOCs [lines of com-
munication]. They are calling for more trucks and have stepped up their imports of
POL [petroleum, oil, and lubricants]."[165] He also informed the NSC that the North
Vietnamese had used the pause of 25 December through 31 January to repair the
damage inflicted upon their lines of communication, expand their infiltration routes,
and improve their road networks. He did not remind the NSC that the CIA had
demonstrated the North Vietnamese had accomplished precisely the same under-
takings while the bombs had been falling.[166] Sherman Kent had predicted in February
that the United States had little chance of accomplishing the interdiction task successfully. In April the agency reported their pessimistic prediction had been proven
correct. Infiltration of PAVN units was still on the increase, and the North still had
considerable unused capacity to introduce even more troops into the South.[167]

The United States had started and the North had matched another escalatory
round. In monthly assessments on the effectiveness of the air campaigns for May
and June, the CIA determined that infiltration continued, perhaps at an increased
rate, and the North Vietnamese had been repairing damage and extending their
lines of communication as the attacks continued.[168] The obvious dichotomy between General Wheeler's optimism and the CIA assessment underscored the growing
divergence between the military's view of the war and that of the agency which
would dog the administration through the 1968 Tet Offensive. Events bore out the
CIA position.

The next month, the administration considered shifting the focus of Rolling
Thunder from North Vietnamese lines of communication to their petroleum storage facilities.[169] The president informed the NSC on 17 June that the decision to
strike POL targets was imminent.[170] The United States had identified between sev-
enty and eighty POL dispersal sites and was prepared to strike the main POL
off-loading point in the port of Haiphong. By bombing Haiphong the United States
would be crossing a psychological Rubicon. The new national security adviser,
Walt Rostow, strongly supported the POL strike concept, while Vice President Hubert
Humphrey was far more cautious and worried aloud about the possibility of killing
Soviet personnel on board a Russian ship in Haiphong harbor. Rostow had the final
word: "The decision is a rational one. Taking out the petroleum supplies sets a

ceiling on the capacity of the North Vietnamese to infiltrate men into South Vietnam. A sustained POL offensive will seriously affect the infiltration rate." [171] Reports from Ambassador Lodge emphasized the continuing combat capabilities of the Vietcong, however the linkage between Vietcong proficiency on the battlefield and POL supplies in the North was based more on assumptions and desperation than on intelligence. [172] A decision on the POL campaign was deferred.

A week later the NSC again discussed the matter. General Wheeler rehearsed the ceiling imposition argument in favor of the POL strikes, noting that the PAVN had another three divisions ready to go south. He also wanted to mine Haiphong harbor to inhibit shipments of weapons and petroleum. All present, except UN Ambassador Goldberg, agreed to the POL campaign. Only Admiral Raborn supported Wheeler on the question of mining Haiphong. [173] The POL strikes would be made, but the time had not yet arrived to mine Haiphong harbor.

In mid-October 1966, McNamara returned from a trip to Vietnam. He presented the usual lengthy report to the president in which he made several recommendations regarding the air war. [174] He wanted to stabilize Rolling Thunder, which had grown like a malignant weed from 4,000 sorties per month at the end of 1965 to 12,000 per month in October 1966. Some 84,000 attack sorties had been flown against North Vietnam. Forty-five percent of the total occurred in the seven months between March and October 1966. Despite this immense effort:

> It now appears that the North Vietnamese–Laotian road will remain adequate to meet the requirements of the Communist forces in South Vietnam—this even if its capacity could be reduced by one-third and if combat activities could be doubled. . . . Furthermore, it is clear that, to bomb the North sufficiently to make a radical impact upon Hanoi's political, economic and social structure, would require an effort which we could make but which would not be stomached either by our own people or by world opinion, and would involve a serious risk of drawing us into open war with China. [175]

The intellectual predicates of the Ad Hoc Study Group and of the administration fifteen months earlier had been proven incorrect. The CIA's relatively pessimistic assessment of February 1966 had been validated. McNamara wanted Rolling Thunder stabilized at some level well below 12,000 sorties per month. He hoped negotiations would allow discontinuing all bombing in the North or, at the least, bombing above the Hanoi-Haiphong line. [176]

The JCS disagreed with the secretary of defense. For them Rolling Thunder was "an integral and indispensable" portion of the overall war effort. The JCS believed: "To be effective, the air campaign should be conducted with only those minimum constraints necessary to avoid indiscriminate killing of population." [177]

General Westmoreland was in complete agreement with the joint chiefs. He offered a tightly argued justification of Rolling Thunder to Rostow in late October 1966. Westmoreland maintained its cessation would "adversely affect the war in the South to a serious degree" allowing the movement of men and materiel with impunity. [178] Ending the effort would adversely affect ARVN's morale. The general believed that the gradual escalation of Rolling Thunder had been inefficient and expensive. He strongly urged empolying greater shock effect and flexibility of targeting.

At McNamara's request the CIA produced a study of the effectiveness of Rolling Thunder.[179] In the eighteen months since the inauguration of Rolling Thunder, U.S. aircraft had flown a total of just under 84,000 sorties against North Vietnamese targets delivering approximately 125,000 tons of ordnance. The loss rate had been low with only 396 aircraft destroyed. An analysis of the damage inflicted compared to U.S. costs of inflicting the damage concluded that it cost $8.70 to cause $1.00 worth of damage upon North Vietnam in 1966 alone.[180] The results had been disappointing:

> Despite the increased weight of air attack, North Vietnam continues to increase its support of the insurgency in South Vietnam. The Rolling Thunder program has not been able to prevent about a three fold increase in the level of personnel infiltration in 1966. The external logistic support needed to maintain the expanded VC/PAVN force in South Vietnam has been adequate. In particular, despite the neutralization of the major petroleum storage facilities in the North, petroleum supplies have continued to be imported in needed amounts. . . . Nor has Rolling Thunder served visibly to reduce the determination of Hanoi to continue the war. We see no signs that the air attack has shaken the confidence of the regime, and with increased Soviet and Chinese aid to bolster its capabilities, North Vietnam in the short term, at least will apparently take no positive step toward a negotiated settlement.[181]

The CIA came to an even more disturbing conclusion concerning the limits of air power: "Since the bombings of North Vietnam began . . . there appears to be more enthusiasm for supporting the war in the south."[182] Rolling Thunder had failed to interdict or coerce. McNamara was right in his loss of faith.

The CIA issued a second, longer, and more detailed examination of Rolling Thunder in December 1966.[183] It recounted that over 98 percent of 104,000 sorties flown over North Vietnam and 57,000 of those sent to Laos had been allocated to the interdiction effort in the first nine months of 1966.[184] The cost of the interdiction effort to the North Vietnamese had not been excessive. Despite the interdiction campaign, the North Vietnamese had been able to expand the road net in the Laotian Corridor and to make improvements in their ability to move supplies during bad weather.[185]

In September 1966, MACV's own assessment confirmed the CIA's pessimistic assessment. MACV Chief of Staff, Maj. Gen. W. B. Rosson, stated that the enemy had the capability to infiltrate a daily average of 458 tons of supplies but required only 30 tons per day of infiltrated materiel.[186] MACV hoped this consumption could be forced to a higher level in 1967 by greatly expanded ground combat.[187] Recall the CIA had concluded earlier that MACV was overestimating the external supply requirements of the Vietcong/PAVN, which the agency believed was only 12 tons per day.[188]

In December a Rand study done for John McNaughton considered the domestic political consequences of Rolling Thunder within North Vietnam. The civilian casualties were seen as being sufficiently large and well distributed to ensure "acute hostility to the attacker."[189] The morale factor assured the bombing campaign had not achieved any useful result. The Rand report concluded: "It becomes increasingly doubtful that the advantages of continuation or intensification of the attacks outweigh the potential net gains from cessation or, at least, drastic and demonstrative de-escalation."[190] These words were almost heretical coming from a long-time bastion of pro–Air Force thinking, but words which deserved a hearing.

The bombing continued, regardless of the assessments calling its effectiveness into question and despite the doubts expressed by McNamara and probably felt by others. It continued because it had been started, and to stop it without some concession from the North would appear perilously close to a partial American surrender. The bombing had trapped the United States and significantly limited its options. It is ironic that the air war had been conceived because it appeared to be so manageable, so capable of assuring Washington policy-makers maintained control. Now, after eighteen months, they had lost control and were running out of options.

The administration had grown dissatisfied with the course of the war. As the bombs fell and the search-and-destroy operations increased in 1967 according to the old, and so far quite unsuccessful theory of victory, so also did the search for a new theory which might produce an end to the war. A theory of victory must be found which would allow the war to be won without further damage to the global policy matrix on whose behalf it was being waged.

The air campaign against the North took center stage at an NSC meeting on 8 February 1967. General Wheeler recounted that during 1966 U.S. aircraft flew 81,000 attack and 48,000 combat support sorties against the North, 48,000 attack and 10,000 combat support sorties against targets in the Laotian panhandle, 130,000 attack and 31,000 combat sorties in South Vietnam, and 5,000 B-52 sorties, most in South Vietnam.[191] He contended that the air campaigns had positively altered the course of the war in the South by effectively interdicting the flow of men and supplies. The bombing imposed a heavy drain on North Vietnamese manpower in manning air defense systems and repairing extensive bomb damage. General Wheeler concluded that the air campaign against North Vietnam in conjunction with the "vigorous and aggressive" ground combat actions in the South assured that the Communists could no longer win the war. Obviously, the chairman and the joint chiefs as a body had not accepted the pessimistic appreciations of the CIA and Rand.

At a lunch on 22 February, Rostow, Rusk, McNamara, and the president made no progress in resolving the difference between the assessment of the air war offered by the JCS and the CIA. They discussed four potential courses of action: air and naval attacks on North Vietnamese targets, interdiction efforts within Laos including increased use of small ground units and cloud seeding over the Ho Chi Minh Trail, expansion of the search-and-destroy operations, and improvements in pacification.[192]

The JCS also examined alternatives in May 1967. The joint chiefs wished to continue and increase the air campaign against North Vietnam. They recommended that Rolling Thunder be oriented toward isolating the "Hanoi-Haiphong logistics base" by an integrated air interdiction effort against all means of transportation and imported "war-supporting materials."[193] In addition, the joint chiefs urged the expansion of Laotian interdiction and the initiation of similar programs directed at Cambodia.[194] Finally, the joint chiefs advised doubling the B-52 strikes in North Vietnam and Laos from 800 sorties per month to 1,600.[195] The joint chiefs were not impressed by the lack of positive results so far demonstrated by any of the air interdiction campaigns.[196] They were opposed to any restriction or cessation of Rolling Thunder.[197]

In their June examination of the air war, the joint chiefs continued to recommend an unrestricted campaign. They still saw the air war as the key to American success.[198] The correctness of the premises upon which their assessment was based were left unexamined.

The CIA at McNamara's request examined a number of alternative bombing options. It concluded that none would be effective. Rolling Thunder would have to be either canceled or greatly expanded as the joint chiefs recommended.[199] Rarely were choices presented as such stark extremes.

Secretary of the Air Force Harold Brown entered the assessment arena in June. He equivocated, recommending "from a purely military point of view" an all-out attack on the northeast and northwest land lines of communication and closure of the ports, but concluding diplomatic and other risks militated against this course.[200] He advised continuing harassing attacks on railroads and an effort to sever Haiphong from the internal communication system. In a memorandum to McNamara, he engaged in an exercise in cost accounting. Brown concluded if the requirement for U.S. ground troops was reduced by 300 men for every 1,000 attack sorties in Laos and North Vietnam assuming that each 1,000 sorties killed 37 infiltrators, the air war had paid its way.[201] In defense of the air war, Brown offered an involuted exercise in assumptions disguised as facts by the questionable use of statistics, having little relevance to the requirements of policy definition or the realities of war.

General Westmoreland supported the joint chiefs' recommendation for the expansion of Rolling Thunder. He argued that the bombing had two purposes: the curbing of infiltration and logistical support for the Vietcong, and acting "as an instrument for concession in return for negotiations."[202] The general asserted that the latter purpose was the more important, now agreeing with the earlier thinking of John McNaughton. In Westmoreland's evaluation bombing could not halt infiltration, destroy North Vietnamese morale, endanger the Hanoi regime, or debilitate the Vietcong, but it could, he believed, erode the North Vietnamese economy and raise the costs of supporting a large expeditionary force in the South. Westmoreland concluded that this had already happened, noting that a "plateau of about 110,000 main force Viet Cong and North Vietnamese Army units in SVN has been maintained since September 1966."[203] The air war might bring Hanoi to the negotiating table. Interestingly, Westmoreland had used the threat of open-ended escalation by the North as an argument for large troop increases, and now he used the apparent Communist troop plateau as an argument in favor of Rolling Thunder.

General Westmoreland's monthly assessment for August 1967 was sanguine.[204] He noted that the expected Communist offensive in the north of South Vietnam had not occurred. He believed that aerial interdiction just north of the DMZ had been particularly effective. As he reviewed events in each of the Corps Tactical Zones (CTZ), Westmoreland presented a picture of growing military success. Progress in pacification and revolutionary development was slow, but he saw this as a manageable problem. The prospect conveyed by COMUSMACV was of slow, but steady and measurable progress toward victory.

In a telegram not transcribed and forwarded to the White House, General Westmoreland expressed a tone of anxiety which had been absent in his monthly reports.[205] He was "concerned over" the situation in I CTZ for two reasons: high friendly casualties and "the grave possibility" the unpleasantness along the DMZ would be viewed "out of perspective" by the American public.[206] To help reduce casualties, he desired approval by PACOM and the JCS of an increase in B-52 sorties with a goal of 1,200 sorties per month in the DMZ and bordering areas and the employment of 2,000-pound and larger bombs.[207]

The air war continued to be a locus of debate in the fall of 1967. The central question concerning the air campaign against North Vietnam remained its effectiveness. There had been no doubt expressed concerning the way in which Rolling Thunder had been executed. Observers generally agreed that the implementation of the air campaign reflected high levels of skill, professionalism and courage by the pilots and air crew involved. The qualms expressed within the administration had been caused by the lack of effectiveness and seeming irrelevance of the effort. These reservations increased with the growing domestic and foreign reaction against American bombing.

In early fall 1967, the underlying assumption was the air campaign would continue. In an outline of programs and proposals for the future, a fundamental postulate was the continuation of Rolling Thunder. Air operations were credited with having produced a great reduction in the transportation capabilities of the North, a reduction in the PAVN order of battle, and destruction of a major portion of the North Vietnamese infrastructure. However, a blueprint evaluating the American position in Vietnam noted: "In spite of such airstrikes a substantial amount of equipment and large numbers of men are still moved into South Vietnam from the North."[208] Instead of examining this dichotomy and assessing options for policy change, the authors recommended "intensification of our bombing efforts and destruction of all targets that can be hit without unacceptable risk or extending the war to Soviet Russia or Communist China."[209] Unaddressed by the "Blueprint for Vietnam" was the central puzzle: in spite of the heavy weight and high tempo of the bombing campaign, the North had been able to enter the war in South Vietnam in an increasingly effective manner. The military situation in I and II Corps made abundantly clear the unpleasant reality that the war had become increasingly a contest between North Vietnam and the United States, even as the bombs had fallen in an ever greater rate and weight.

The Bureau of Intelligence and Research came very close to solving the puzzle. The Bureau concluded that Hanoi viewed its losses as not being disproportionate to the goals it sought.[210] Inverting this, the losses suffered by North Vietnam, primarily to Rolling Thunder, demanded a commensurate reward. Against this, an assumption, the falsity of which could not be proven, was offered: without the bombing, the military situation in South Vietnam would be much worse.

Diplomatic activities in late summer 1967 provided mixed signals regarding the air war against the North. Henry Kissinger had been engaged in highly secret preliminary conversations through intermediaries with North Vietnamese representatives.[211] In late September, Kissinger's interlocutor reported that the North Vietnamese prime minister had "made it clear that there could be no *formal* discussions between North Vietnam and the United States as long as *any level* of bombing continued in the North."[212] There was some debate over whether this implied that the bombing campaign was working in its coercive intent or not. It appeared that the North was not yet serious concerning negotiations other than time-consuming preliminary, informal, and secret conversations. Rolling Thunder was not yet coercing, although it might have served Hanoi to convey that impression in order to halt the bombing. Rolling Thunder was not hurting the North so much they were willing to accept a reduction of their efforts in the South as the price for halting the bombs.[213]

Not surprisingly, the JCS dissented vigorously from the position of the CIA and the State Department that bombing continued to fail in its objectives of coercion and interdiction. In early October 1967, the JCS staff stated: "The fact is that *there is not sufficient evidence in CIA, DIA* [Defense Intelligence Agency] *or any other US agency upon which to base any reasonable conclusions on the military effectiveness of the bombing campaign upon NVN.*"[214]

Without going into the details of the convoluted reasoning and the blind rejection not only of the CIA's assessment methods, but also of previous JCS staff statements concerning the thrust of the Rolling Thunder interdiction attacks, suffice it to say that the protest was wrongheaded, unjustifiable, and tendentious. The agency responded two weeks later restating the already painfully obvious. The interdiction effort had not placed a meaningful ceiling on North Vietnamese supply capabilities, and the North pursued its strategy in the South "with little reference to the air war in the North."[215]

Against this background, on 1 November 1967, McNamara wrote a lengthy memorandum regarding military operations over the next fifteen months.[216] He observed that any intensification of the air campaign, including the removal of all restrictions, would not be likely to prove effective: "expansion could not produce results which would offset the loss of support for our effort."[217] He recommended

Rolling Thunder be halted, arguing that this would serve to "clear the atmosphere," improve American standing in the world and administration standing at home, and place great pressure on Hanoi to end overt efforts in the South, thus facilitating negotiations.[218] While his optimistic expectation of a favorable reaction from Hanoi to an end of the bombing might not have been realistic, his conclusion that the bombing program, even if extended, would not be likely to have positive effects was well founded. There had been no objective indications of success.

McNamara was virtually alone in his appreciation and recommendation. McGeorge Bundy opposed both an intensification and any unconditional pause or cessation of the air campaign. He believed that the bombing had real military advantages and recommended that the United States look for a way of maintaining these advantages while giving the appearance of reducing the attacks.[219] Walt Rostow opposed McNamara's proposition primarily on the basis of its presumed domestic political effects. He also believed that the bombing had exercised some degree of coercion and helped the ground war in the South.[220]

Clark Clifford violently attacked McNamara's position, arguing that the end of the bombing, or for that matter any reduction or stabilizing of the military effort, would be tantamount to signaling to Hanoi that the United States was losing its political will, thus playing into Hanoi's hands.[221] Clifford adopted the position that the effectiveness of the bombing was irrelevant. It had to be continued or Hanoi's strategy of winning through the weakening of American political will would succeed. At least he understood that Hanoi intended to win through enervation, even if he did not understand the implication of the bombing for North Vietnamese political will.

At the 2 November 1967 meeting between the president and his foreign policy advisers, opinion on the efficacy and necessity of Rolling Thunder ran against the position taken by the secretary of defense.[222] Dean Acheson commented that the importance of the bombing was not its military effect, but its value as a signal to Hanoi.[223]

This view failed to address the simple reality that the capacity to bomb did not reflect political will as much as the ability to tolerate being bombed. Reviewing the record of Rolling Thunder suggested bombing assisted the consolidation of political will in North Vietnam. Even at this late date of December 1967, a bombing halt could have exercised a corrosive effect on Northern cohesiveness.

In a memorandum to the president the next day, Taylor strongly opposed an end to the bombing, stating that its effect would be to demoralize the South Vietnamese. He contended that "our own forces would regard this action as a deliberate decrease in the protection which, they feel, is afforded them by the bombing."[224] The perception, rather than the reality, of effectiveness governed Taylor's position. Taylor amplified his position in a memorandum sent to the president on 6 November 1967. He understood that the war was a contest of political will more than of military force.[225] He did not realize that Hanoi already had a very good feel for the American political dynamic, and their use of military force showed this quite well.

Walt Rostow agreed with Taylor, Abe Fortas, and the other supporters of continuing the present course in mid-month. In a memorandum addressing "seven key difficult questions," Rostow attempted to demonstrate that U.S. efforts were resulting in genuine progress.[226] Rostow employed statistics to address questions on the number of South Vietnamese under government control, enemy losses of strength, Vietcong loss of morale, and improvements in the South Vietnamese government and armed forces. Rostow stated one very important sign of progress toward victory made by the United States: "The enemy has been unable to mount a major offensive although intelligence indicated he planned to do so last May and June."[227] This was true up to a point, but misleading to the point of danger.

By the end of the month Bunker and Westmoreland weighed in against any cessation of the bombing campaign.[228] They were joined by Rusk who strongly supported "intensive bombardment of infiltration routes" but rejected "the political judgement that a continuous escalation of the bombing will break the political will of Hanoi."[229] Only Undersecretary of State Nicholas Katzenbach swam against the stream. He joined his predecessor, George Ball, in recommending that Rolling Thunder be reconsidered: "Nobody really believes that the war can be won with bombs in the North. We may lose it with bombs—here in the United States."[230]

In mid-December the president decided to continue Rolling Thunder with some slight modifications, hoping to make the program more effective and less visible and controversial in the public mind.[231] He was wrong. President Johnson had been trapped by a classic Goldilocks gambit offered by his foreign policy advisers. He had been presented with one option that was too hot, the virtually unrestricted air campaign favored by the JCS, General Westmoreland, Clifford, and Rostow. He had been handed another option which was too cold, the unconditional pause or cessation favored by McNamara, Ball, and Katzenbach. He had chosen the option that was "just right," the continuation of Rolling Thunder with changes at the margin which might make it less high profile and less unsuccessful. In the one area of American strategy where happy numbers could not conceal unhappy reality, in the one area where there should have been no ambiguity on the question of progress toward an American victory, the president chose to ignore fact and opt for hope, no matter how forlorn or desperate.

The intelligence assessments continued to show that the air war was not succeeding. The monthly appraisal for the period ending 16 November concluded that even with good weather over central and northern North Vietnam, even with a heavy weight and tempo of attacks, there had been no productive result beyond the routine destruction of vehicles, facilities, factories and infrastructure.[232]

On 13 December 1967, Rostow forwarded to the president two "major CIA studies" published five days earlier that had been recommended by Secretary McNamara.[233] The first of these constituted a complete evaluation of the progress of American policy in Vietnam to date. Concerning the air war, the conclusion was quite straightforward and unambiguous: "Despite the achievements of the bombing program, however, no significant deterioration in North Vietnam's military capabilities or its determination to persist in the war can be detected. The flow of men and supplies to the South has been maintained; and the cost of damage has been more than compensated by deliveries of foreign aid." [234]

In the second study, the CIA reinforced the conclusions offered in the first. The analysts concluded that the bombing had killed not more than 2 percent of the personnel infiltrating into the South during 1966 and that it had not impaired the ability of the North to meet the supply requirements of PAVN and Vietcong forces which were estimated to be approximately 55 tons per day by late 1967. [235] The figure of 55 tons represented about 25 percent of the daily requirements, so roughly 165 tons per day were acquired within South Vietnam. [236] There was no evidence that the bombing had weakened the will of the North Vietnamese leadership or was causing significant dissent within the North Vietnamese population. [237] The North Vietnamese economy, manpower reserves, and foreign assistance levels were sufficient to continue the war effort even in the face of increased air attack. [238] In short, the CIA concluded that the air war against the North had been a failure.

One-time architect of the air war John McNaughton had authorized the Institute of Defense Analysis (IDA) to conduct a far-ranging review of Rolling Thunder and the several aerial interdiction campaigns. A four-volume report, the JASON study, was issued 16 December 1967. [239] While there were differences of detail between this study and the assessments performed by the CIA, the general conclusions were identical. "As of October 1967, *the US bombing of North Vietnam has had no measurable effect on Hanoi's ability to mount and support military operations in the South.*" [240] The bombing had "not discernibly weakened" Hanoi's determination to persevere. [241] The IDA analysts agreed with the CIA: "no bombing campaign can be designed that can either reduce the flow from North to South significantly or raise the cost of maintaining the flow to some unbearable level." [242] Finally, the JASON study analysts came closer than those of the CIA to understanding Hanoi's strategy was not one of simple attrition but rather one of enervating American and South Vietnamese political will. [243]

Robert Ginsburgh, an assistant of Walt Rostow, wrote a five-page critique of the JASON study in mid-January 1968. He characterized the effort as "intellectually dishonest" and then twisted the conclusions and much of the analysis out of all recognizable form. [244] While there were some questionable uses of statistical analysis within the JASON study, these in no way obviated the essential thrust of the argumentation and conclusions. Further, Ginsburgh was wrong in asserting that the JASON study misrepresented the American air effort as an attempt to seek victory through air power. While the IDA team never made such an assumption, both the administration and the Ad Hoc Study Group had more than two years earlier when Rolling Thunder was initiated. The air war had been the focus of effort, and the air war over the North had largely driven policy. Now the air war had failed. JASON and the CIA had both brought that message unmistakably to the administration. It was too late to cry foul. It was too late to expect the air war to succeed.

In another of the high points of irony within an irony-ridden war, the air war was the only major component of the American effort about which there was no ambiguity. There was no way in which smiling numbers could bemuse and distract from the unpleasant reality of failure. The answer to the question, "Are we winning?" was a clear, obvious, and unavoidable "no." Yet it was the only portion of the war for which the president gave a clear authorization to continue.

The administration, especially the president, is open to a more damning indictment with regard to the air war. It was clear from all the intelligence assessments that the air war over the North was a counterproductive failure which should be terminated. There were good pragmatic reasons for its ending and a real possibility that benefits would accrue from stopping the bombing. The president chose to reject or ignore excellent counsel and intelligence and authorize a continuation of an aerial campaign which had all too obviously failed. He may have had political reasons for doing this, but that constitutes no justification. At root, the president demonstrated a lack of intellectual, moral, and political courage when he chose to continue the air war.

Robert McNamara's successor as secretary of defense, Clark Clifford, had been a consistent and robust supporter of American policy and its means of implementation during the preceding months. It had been Clifford's resolute rejection of the McNamara memorandum of 1 November 1967 which led to his designation as secretary of defense.[245] President Johnson saw Clifford as a loyal supporter of administration policy in South Vietnam, an appropriate replacement for the architect who had lost faith in his own vision and creation.

Clifford was sworn in as secretary of defense on 1 March 1968. That afternoon he started work with a task force which included experienced men such as Nicholas Katzenbach, William Bundy, and Maxwell Taylor.[246] This task force's analysis of required additional force deployments to Vietnam led inexorably to the larger question: "Why and to what purpose?"

Taylor set forth the policy parameters and alternative force structures.[247] He recognized several different definitions of victory might be employed ranging from the unconditional surrender of North Vietnam to a unilateral American declaration of victory as a prelude to a total pull out. Depending upon the definition of victory employed, the theory of victory and force structure needed to implement it could be selected. Taylor believed that the United States should stick to the San Antonio formula announced by President Johnson in a speech in San Antonio, Texas, on 29 September 1967. It promised that the United States would stop bombing North Vietnam in exchange for an undertaking by the North to enter into negotiations and to refrain from infiltrating men or supplies into South Vietnam. There must be no reduction in the air effort directed at the North without Hanoi's acceptance of the San Antonio formula.

William Bundy saw matters in a larger context. He asserted that the United States had two goals in South Vietnam. The first was to avert a "forcible takeover" by Hanoi and the second was the maintenance of a non-Communist Southeast Asia.[248]

Undersecretary Katzenbach assessed the state of American public opinion. He predicted that without indication of genuine progress within a few months, public opinion would coalesce into a "win or get out" mentality.[249] American public opinion placed severe constraints upon the options available to the administration.

As the debate over alternatives within the Clifford task force raged, the secretary conveyed his doubts to the president. He was becoming convinced that the United States was on "the wrong road" and the time had come to try another.[250] On 18 March 1968 the second version of the Draft Presidential Memorandum on Vietnam was floated, analysizing different force structures and bombing campaign designs to determine which of two alternative American goals was more achievable and which of several operational concepts was most relevant to securing that goal.[251] The final recommendation was: hold U.S. force levels to the 525,000 already authorized, emphasize population security, work on improving ARVN, concentrate bombing on the southern portions of North Vietnam, and seek early negotiations after consultations with the government of South Vietnam. The recommendations constituted a major shift in the American theory of victory, rejecting a continuation of the search for victory through attrition and erosion and substituting an American version of protracted conflict in which enervation of political will was the way to success.

The nature of Hanoi's theory of victory had become apparent, but not the relationship between North Vietnam and the expendable Vietcong.[252] Population security coupled with improving ARVN would present the North with a clear demonstration of American political will. It would also lower U.S. casualties, reduce domestic expectations for a quick victory, and place pressures upon the Northern political will by removing the bomber as a reinforcement of cohesion. Not only was the American theory of victory altered, so was its goal, now stated as "a settlement we would consider honorable."[253] It was still too early to say the North was winning, but it was not too soon to say Hanoi could not now lose.

The advice was for disengagement. Ball recalled the theme of the majority was: "you've got to lower your sights. We can't achieve these objectives."[254] Dean Acheson "summed up the majority feeling when he said that we can no longer do the job we went out to do in the time we have left and we must begin to take steps to disengage."[255] This position was shared by George Ball, Arthur Dean, Cyrus Vance, Douglas Dillon, Henry Cabot Lodge, Omar Bradley, and McGeorge Bundy. Ball thought the president "was greatly shaken" by the consensus and particularly by Acheson's participation.[256]

George Ball, the long-time opponent of bombing, now saw his position become the majority view. A more cold comfort is difficult to imagine. Ball urged the air war against North Vietnam be stopped at once. Omar Bradley agreed. "We do need to stop the bombing, if we can get the suggestion to come from the Pope or [UN General Secretary] U Thant, but let's not show them that we are weakening."[257] Cyrus Vance echoed the call to end Rolling Thunder. Henry Cabot Lodge urged shifting from search and destroy to using the American military as a shield for South Vietnamese nation-building. Douglas Dillon concurred. Taken as a whole, the position of the majority of senior foreign policy advisers was virtually identical to the Clifford proposal embodied in the 18 March Draft Presidential Memorandum. Maxwell Taylor dissented: "I am dismayed. Let's not concede the home front; let's do something about it."[258] He was joined by Robert Murphy: "This is a giveaway policy."[259]

Murphy was wrong. The changes in the American theory of victory recommended by the Clifford Committee and subscribed to by the majority of the "wise men" were a realistic response to the realities which had developed on the ground. The lonely prophet, George Ball, had been right all along; now the administration had caught up with him. It was a painful process. There was no one for whom it was more painful than the president. For him and him alone among the administration some sympathy was and is due.

After 31 March 1968, bombing North Vietnam was restricted to the southern portion of the country. The residual Rolling Thunder continued to be a matter of concern within the administration as the continuation of the bombing was linked to negotiations by the North Vietnamese. On 9 April 1968, the president met with his senior advisers at Camp David. General Wheeler stated the restriction of the interdiction effort to the Laotian Panhandle and North Vietnam south of the 19th parallel had not resulted in a lessening of the sortie rate, nor had it given the North Vietnamese any significant advantage.[260] Hanoi was exploiting the American desire for negotiations to bring the bombing south of the 19th parallel to an end. Rump Rolling Thunder would have to continue not only for reasons of domestic public opinion and military necessity, but as a demonstration of political will to the adversary during the initial period of tough negotiations. The problem lay in the reality that continued bombing enhanced the position of the North Vietnamese in the mind of the American population.

The difficult interlocking of bombing and negotiating was the focus of meetings between President Johnson and his foreign policy advisers and the JCS on 14 October 1968. In short, Hanoi was demanding a total halt to Rolling Thunder in exchange for concessions on key points such as the inclusion of the South Vietnamese government in the Paris talks. If Hanoi did not take advantage of the bombing termination by moving large forces into or across the DMZ, and neither Hanoi nor the NLF/Vietcong attacked the South Vietnamese cities, then ending the bombing would be an appropriate tool to assure that the South Vietnamese government was included in the Paris talks. The joint chiefs concurred in the total halt after a lengthy discussion in which General Westmoreland's observation that the flying weather at that time of year was poor, thus impairing bombing effectiveness.[261] The general shared with his colleagues and the administration the notion that negotiations would proceed swiftly along the lines of the 1954 Geneva talks. This notion assumed that the air campaign and the losses suffered during the Tet Offensive prevented the North from mounting a third and final offensive. Thus, Hanoi was eager to bring the stalemate to an end. There was no intelligence support for this assumption. A review of the weekly intelligence summaries for the months of August and September shows clearly that the North Vietnamese and their greatly diminished clients, the NLF/Vietcong, were prepared either to pursue a protracted military effort or to use a period of armistice for political consolidation.[262]

In short, there was no evidence to support the proposition that the North Vietnamese were seeking a quick resolution to the conflict. There was no reason to believe that bombing had accomplished its ultimate goal of coercing the North Vietnamese to the bargaining table. Rather, evidence was clear that the United States had no choice but to end Rolling Thunder in the hope negotiations would start at last. The North Vietnamese strategy of enervation had been successful and Rolling Thunder would shortly be placed in a body bag and buried without honors.

In the beginning discussions within the administration had not focused so much on what the United States should do as on what the United States could do in support of the threatened containment policy. To his credit President Johnson did not immediately accept the advice of McNaughton, McNamara, and McGeorge Bundy. Eventually persuaded by the continued Vietcong battlefield successes and the belief that South Vietnam represented a major challenge to containment, the president authorized the use of air power against the North. From February 1965 American air operations against North Vietnam became the prime determinant of policy in prosecuting the war. Air power seemed to promise so much. It was easily and precisely managed. American casualties would be low. It was expected to inflict insupportable damage on North Vietnam.

The tit-for-tat and graduated escalation of military pressure were not only massively irrelevant to the real war in South Vietnam, they were completely counterproductive in effect. Far from coercing Hanoi, the bombers issued an invitation to the North to enter the war in pursuit of its own goals. Within weeks the irrelevance of the air campaign to the course of the war in the South had been demonstrated by the Vietcong attacks against U.S. installations in the South which necessitated the introduction of ground combat forces. The counterproductive effects of the bombing campaign took longer to become obvious, but by late 1965 it had become evident that North Vietnamese armed forces were entering South Vietnam. Rolling Thunder had changed the character of the conflict from an insurgency to a partisan war.

From the Christmas bombing pause of 1965 on, one intelligence report after another demonstrated that the air war had failed in its objectives of interdiction and coercion. Several major assessments concluded that the American bombers served Hanoi well by reinforcing North Vietnamese political will and allowing Hanoi to seek its own goals in the South. Despite the intelligence picture, the administration was powerless to end the bombing. There were two reasons for this unpleasant state of affairs. The first was a lack of moral courage. The administration and president simply could not act upon their knowledge for fear that by ending the bombing without a concession from the North, the United States would give the appearance of political irresolution. The second was fear of the political power of the JCS. Civilian control of the military had run against a real limit. The joint chiefs had independent access to Congress and the press. As a result, the administration could be attacked for placing the lives of American servicemen in South Vietnam at risk by halting the bombing of the North.

The senior military command structure had a limitless faith in the efficacy of the air war. A monolithic resistance to reevaluating Rolling Thunder existed throughout the senior commanders. If the bombing had not accomplished its objectives of coercion and interdiction, the United States had not bombed with sufficient intensity and duration. The JCS called continually for a removal of the administration's restrictions on bombing. The joint chiefs discounted completely the effects of the air war upon North Vietnamese political will. They discounted completely the impact of the American air war on public opinion in the United States and around the world. Indeed, the joint chiefs demonstrated repeatedly that they could not understand that the war in Vietnam was a war in support of policy and that as such it made no sense to destroy the policy matrix in order to win the war.

The pilots and air crew who executed the air wars over North Vietnam, Laos, and South Vietnam did so with the highest standards of professionalism. Throughout, they exhibited courage and dedication of the highest order. The rules of engagement were calculated to reduce civilian casualties and destruction of purely civilian facilities. The administration monitored and managed air operations closely. Nonetheless, the air war against the North, the interdiction efforts in Laos, and much of the effort in the South were not only unsuccessful but actually counterproductive. The reasons for this was the American theory of victory, which emphasized the efficient delivery of firepower. While the hoary aphorism, "firepower kills," was fully applicable, the tragedy came in the simple fact that the question, "but can it win?" was never asked. The failure of intellectual, moral, and political courage implied by the absence of that single question became manifest in the ultimate failure of President Johnson's air war.

Notes

1. "Report on General Taylor's Mission to South Vietnam," 3 November 1961, app. F:1, Box 210/Folder: Taylor Report/Document 1 (hereafter cited in the format 210/Taylor Report/1), Country File: Vietnam, National Security Files, Lyndon B. Johnson Papers, Lyndon Baines Johnson Library, Austin, Texas (hereafter cited as CF:VN/NSF/LBJ).

2. Ibid., app. F:3–5, and summary report, 13.

3. Joseph Zasloff, "The Role of North Vietnam in the Southern Insurgency," Rand Memorandum RM-4140 PR (July 1964), 43, 8/M17/90b, ibid. This report was prepared for the Air Force and was sent by Air Force Chief of Staff Curtis LeMay to the Joint Chiefs of Staff on 17 August 1964. A copy was forwarded to the National Security Council.

4. Ibid., 74–81.

5. Ibid., 2–3.

6. "The Outlook for North Vietnam," 4 March 1964, 5, Special National Intelligence Estimate 14.3-64, Folder NIE/1/14.3, Document NVN/3b, NSF/LBJ.

7. Ibid., 6–7.

8. Ibid., 9.

9. Ibid., 8.

10. Ibid., 11.

11. Ibid., 13–15.

12. State Department Bureau of Intelligence and Research, Memorandum to secretary, 17 July 1964, 6/M14/230, CF:VN/NSF/LBJ.

13. "Situation in South Vietnam," 20 and 28 February, 6 and 13 March, 1964, 2/M4/86, 2/M4/87, 2/M4/88, 2/C5/67, ibid.

14. Colby to McGeorge Bundy, Rusk, McNamara et al., 11 February 1964, 1/M3/111a, 111b, 111c, ibid.

15. McNamara to president, 13 March 1964, esp. 2, note a, 2/C5/55/a, ibid.

16. "Summary Record of the NSC Meeting No. 524," 1/T5/2 plus attachments, NSC Meetings/NSF/LBJ.

17. Ibid., esp. doc. 9:6–8, 15.

18. Summarized in Office of the Secretary of Defense, *United States–Vietnam Relations, 1945–1967* (Washington D.C.: Government Printing Office, 1971), vol. 4, chap. 3:2–3 (hereafter cited as *USVR*). See also McNamara to president, 14 May 1964, 4/M9/2a, CF:VN/NSF/LBJ, in which he summarizes conversations with General Taylor and states the position of Ambassador Henry Cabot Lodge who "wishes to carry out air strikes against the North . . . not only to cut off the supply of men and equipment from the North but also to destroy the morale of the North Vietnamese."

19. "Probable Consequences of Certain US Actions with Respect to Vietnam and Laos," 23 May 1964, esp. 12–15, CIA SNIE 50-2-64, 18/Meetings on SE Asia/42, Papers of McGeorge Bundy/LBJ (hereafter cited as Bundy Papers).

20. Ibid., 16.

21. "Summary Record of NSC Meeting no 533," 6 June 1964, II/T6/2, NSC Meetings/1/V, NSF/LBJ.

22. Ibid., 1.

23. "Viet Cong Activity January through June 1964," II/T9/9a, NSC Meetings/1/V, NSF/LBJ.

24. See CIA weekly and monthly reports, 4/M8/35, 36, and 37; 4/M9/36; 5/M11/8; 5/M12/9, 10; 6/M13/47, 48a, 49; 6/M13/47; 6/M14/233a, 234. CF:VN/NSF/LBJ.

25. "Summary Notes of the 538th NSC Meeting," 4 August 1964, 1, 20/2, III/T19, NSC Meetings/1/V NSF/LBJ.

26. Ibid.

27. Ibid.

28. Ibid., doc. 3.

29. JCS to secretary of defense, 27 July 1964, JCSM 639–64; CINCPAC to JCS, 19 August 1964, 7/C16/130; CINCPAC to JCS, 21 August 1964, 8/C18/114; COMUSMACV to JCS, 22 September 1964, 8/C18/116; CINCPAC to operational elements, 20 September 1964, 8/C18/117, CF:VN/NSF/LBJ.

30. JCS to CINCPAC, 28 September 1964, 268/C10/57, CF:Laos/NSF/LBJ.

31. COMUSMACV AIG 967, and CINCPAC, to JCS, 31 August 1964, 268/C10/80, 80a, 80b, 80c; COMUSMACV to JCS, 11 September 1964, White House clearance slips, and JCS to CINCPAC, 268/C10/74-79 inclusive; all in ibid.

32. State Department to Vientiane, 25 September 1964, 268/C10/22, ibid.

33. Ibid. The RLAF finally did undertake attacks in the northern panhandle or the Laotian Corridor, see USAIRA/VIENTIANE to CSAF, 12 October 1964, 9/M20/151, CF:VN/NSF/LBJ, outlining forthcoming RLAF attack on the corridor scheduled for 14 October; COMUSMACV to CINCPAC, on same date and same subject, 9/M20/150, ibid.

34. Memo for the record, 14 September 1964, Meeting Notes File/1, WHCF/LBJ.

35. COMUSMACV to CINCPAC and JCS, 1 November 1964, 10/C21/90, CF:VN/NSF/LBJ.

36. Telex transcript of Westmoreland press briefing, 1 November 1964, section 1:2, 10/C21/86a, ibid.

37. Intelligence memorandum, 9 September 1964, 8/M17/103, ibid.

38. *USVR*, vol. 4, chap. 3:4.

39. William Bundy and McNaughton to NSC, 26 November 1964, 2, 45,46/Courses of Action SEA/9, CF:VN/NSF/LBJ. See also *USVR*, vol. 4, chap. 3:4.

40. President to state secretary, defense secretary, and CIA director, 7 December 1964, Memos to president, 7/53, Aides Files/2/LBJ. Intelligence memorandum, 3 December 1964, 11/M23/116, CF:VN/NSF/LBJ. This memo took the "quality personnel" approach, arguing that leadership and specialists as well as key supplies made up the bulk of the infiltration. The use of leadership cadre allowed Hanoi to continue control of the movement in the South while the provision of key supplies such as munitions, heavy ordnance and communication equipment greatly enhanced the military potential of the Vietcong. It was believed that the rate of infiltration had increased.

41. "Position Paper on Southeast Asia," 2 December 1964, 1, Memos to President, 7/53b, Aides Files/ 1/LBJ.

42. Ibid., 2.

43. Ibid.

44. Intelligence memorandum, 29 December 1964, 11/M23/28b, CF:VN/NSF/LBJ.

45. Ibid., 102.

46. Ibid., 2.

47. See Intelligence memorandum TS 185793, "Probable Communist Reaction to Option C or C-Prime Measures," 27 November 1964. Copies went to both William Bundy and John McNaughton.

48. Bowman to McGeorge Bundy, 5 January 1965, 12/M25/155, CF:VN/NSF/LBJ.

49. Bundy and Cooper to president, 4 January 1965, 12/M25/122; Bundy to president with attachment, 5 January 1965, 12/M25/132 and 132a; Cooper and Bundy to president, 6, 8, and 18 January 1965, 12/M25/117, 12/M25/113, and 12/M26/188a; Cooper to Bundy and president, 26 January 1965, 12/M26/220, 220a, ibid.

50. Thompson to McGeorge Bundy, 28 November 1964, 202/Meetings of the Principals/9, ibid.

51. COMUSMACV to JCS, 13/C27/7, ibid.

52. Bundy to president, 7 February 1965, AF/II/2, NSF/LBJ. See also, *USVR,* vol. 4, chap. 3:23.

53. "Summary of Air Attacks against North Vietnam," 12 April 1965, 216/Reprisal Program 2/43a, CF:VN/NSF/LBJ.

54. "Summary Notes of the 547th NSC Meeting," 8 February 1965, 1, III/T29/2, NSC Meetings/1/V, NSF//LBJ.

55. See, e.g., E&P DIV INTEL to AIR INTEL OFFUSMACV, 10/C21/154, CF:VN/NSF/LBJ, which warned of possible mortar attack at Danang by imitators of Bien Hoa.

56. "Summary Notes of the 547th NSC Meeting," 8 February 1965, 3, III/T29/2, NSC Meetings/1/V, NSF/LBJ.

57. "Summary Record of NSC Meeting No 548," including attachment, "Meeting of the Principals," 10 February 1965, III/T30/2, 3, and 4, NSF Meetings/1/LBJ.

58. See in addition to ibid., Cooper and Ungar to McGeorge Bundy, 9 February 1965, 13/M28/224, 224a, CF:VN/NSF/LBJ.

59. Consult the weekly and monthly CIA intelligence summaries, "The Situation in Vietnam" for the period September 1964 through January 1965 in ibid.: 8/M17/131, 133; 9/M18/283, 285; 9/M19/107, 108; 9/M20/170, 171; 10/C21/213, 214; 10/C22/110; 11/M23/184, 185, 187; 11/M24/238; 12/M25/178, 179; 12/M26/146, 148, 149; 13/M27/199.   60. CIA Special Report, 10 July 1964, Special Intelligence Material/4, 48/SEA V I, ibid.

61. CIA Special Report, 15 January 1965, 12/M26/169, ibid.

62. CIA Special Reports: 17 January 1964, Special Intelligence Material/21, 48/SEA V I, 23 October 1964, 9/M20/157, 3 December 1964, 11/M23/116, ibid.; CIA Intelligence Memorandum, 13 January 1965, Special Intelligence Materials/26, 48/SEA V III, ibid. On the question of using South Vietnamese intelligence sources to demonstrate infiltration, see Summary Statement of 23 January 1965, 199/Briefing Materials/30, ibid.

63. CIA Special Report, 13 January 1965, Special Intelligence Material/26, 48/SEA V III, ibid.

64. Seltzer to U.S. Intelligence Board, "SNIE 10-65: Communist Military Capabilities and Near-Term

Intentions in Laos and South Vietnam," 1 February 1965, 13/M27/104, CF:VN/NSF/LBJ.

65. SNIE 53-65: "Short-Term Prospects in South Vietnam," 2 February 1965, SNIE 53-65, 13/M27/107, ibid.

66. SNIE 10-3-65: "Communist Reactions to Possible US Actions," 11 February 1965, 13/M28/218, ibid. It should be noted that earlier drafts of the SNIE were circulated to McGeorge Bundy and the NSC staff.

67. See the FISHNET reports for February such as Reprisal Program I/2/171, 169, 168, 167, 166, and 165, NSF/LBJ.

68. COMUSMACV to CINCPAC, 10 February 1965, 13/C28/6, CF:VN/NSF/LBJ.

69. COMUSMACV to JCS, 19 February 1965, 13/C28/51; COMUSMACV to NMCC, CINCPAC, 19 February 1965, 13/C28/67; COMUSMACV to NMCC, CINCPAC, 20 February 1965, 14/C29/4; COMUSMACV to CINCPAC, 21 February 1965, 14/C29/7; COMUSMACV to NMCC, CINCPAC, 21 February 1965, 14/C29/10; all in ibid.

70. COMUSMACV to CINCPAC, reprinted for President Johnson, 2 March 1965, 14/M30/144, ibid. See also COMUSMACV to CINCPAC, 24 February 1965, 14/C29/38, and COMUSMACV to NMCC, 2 March 1965, Reprisal Program I/2/42, ibid.

71. Cline to McGeorge Bundy, 22 April 1965, plus attached CIA/OCI Intelligence Memorandum, "Results of US Air Strikes in South Vietnam," 21 April 1965, Special Intelligence Materials/4 and 4a, 49/SEA V V, ibid. See also the many Combat After Action Reports of U.S. Army and Marine Corps operations through 1967.

72. "Summary of Aircraft Strikes Against North Vietnam (as of 31 March 1965)," 216/Reprisal Program II/54c, ibid.

73. Memo to McGeorge Bundy, 31 March 1965, 216/Reprisal Program II/54b, ibid. The White House received as well copies of the frag orders pertaining to every Rolling Thunder mission.

74. An evaluation of the effects of Flaming Dart I and II was available on 5 March. The CIA noted that as a result of the three attacks on the 304th PAVN Division headquarters at Dong Hoi, the troops of that unit had been dispersed along the DMZ, construction in the region had been halted, civilians dispersed to rural areas, and an internal security program initiated. At Dong Hoi, damage was moderate to heavy while at the other targets it was lighter. Casualties included 185 soldiers and 150 civilians killed. Intelligence Information Cable, 5 March 1965, 14/C30/64, CF:VN/NSF/LBJ.

75. McCone to president, 13 March 1965, 15/M31/195, ibid.

76. "Summary Notes of 550th NSC Meeting," 26 March 1965, III/T33/2, NSC Meetings/1/V, NSF/LBJ.

77. See Cline to McGeorge Bundy, 8 March 1965, 14/M30/134, 143a, and Cooper to McGeorge Bundy, 9 March 1965, 15/M31/220, CF:VN/NSF/LBJ.

78. "Summary Notes of the 551st NSC Meeting," 5 April 1965, III/T33/2, NSC Meetings/1/V, NSF/LBJ.

79. Memorandum, 8 April 1965, 5, 16/M32/222, CF:VN/NSF/LBJ. A draft version had been circulated on 6 April.

80. Intelligence cable, 15 April 1965, C32/141, ibid.

81. Johnson 21-point program, 14 March 1965, 15/M31/199, ibid.

82. McCone to president, 2 April 1965, and McCone to Rusk, McNamara, Bundy, and Taylor, 2 April 1965, 16/M32/231b and 231c, ibid.

83. McNamara to president, 21 April 1965, Meetings of the Principals/1/10/198d, Aides Files/LBJ; see also Harold Johnson to McNamara, 12 April 1965, 16/M32/213, CF:VN/NSF/LBJ.

84. *USVR*, vol. 4, chap. 3:74–80.

85. Ibid., 99–105.

86. Intelligence memorandum, 21 April 1965, 1, 17/M33/120, CF:VN/NSF/LBJ.

87. Intelligence memorandum, 12 May 1965, Special Intelligence Materials/20, 20a, 20b, 50,51/SEA V VIb, ibid.; 20b, p. 1.

88. Ibid., 3.

89. Special memorandum, 30 April 1965, 16/M33/92a, ibid.

90. 217/Reprisal Program/V. II/54b, 54c, 69, 77, 83, 94, 99, 113, 114, 117, 118, 121, 128, 129, 146. Reprisal Program/V. III/21, 23; 41–49; 56, 57, 60, 65, 70, 71, 74, 80, 86, 91, 99, 100–103; 148–158; 161–66; 169, 180–89; 191–97; 202a. All in ibid.

91. Memo to McGeorge Bundy with attached CIA Monthly Report, 4 June 1965, 18/M35/326, 326a, ibid.; cf. Special Intelligence Materials/20, 20a, and 20b, 50, 51/SEA V VIb, ibid. See also Taylor to president, 1 June 1965, 18/M35/320a, ibid.

92. Taylor to McNamara and McGeorge Bundy, 24 June 1965, 19/C36/28, ibid.; "Agenda for 5:30 Meeting with the President," 23 June 1965, Aides Files/MP/3/11/38c, LBJ.

93. Intelligence memorandum, 30 June 1965, VI/Special Intelligence Materials/2, 2a, 49/SEA V, CF:VN/NSF/LBJ.

94. Consult 207, 208/Arc Light I, and 209, 210/Arc Light II, ibid.

95. Smith to Bundy, with report, 10 January 1967, 18/M35b/326, 326a, ibid.

96. Ibid., 3.

97. Reprisal Program/44a, ibid.

98. Ibid., 1.

99. Ibid., 2.

100. 74/RP/43, Ibid.

101. 20/M37/413a, ibid.

102. Karl von Clausewitz, *On War,* trans. J. J. Graham, 3 vols. (London: Routledge & Kegan Paul, 1968), vol. 1, bk. 1, chap. 2:26 (emphasis in original); ibid, vol. 1, bk. 3, chap. 1:26.

103. FM 100-5, *Field Service Regulations—Operations* (Washington, D.C.: Department of the Army, 1962), 4–5.

104. FM 7-10, *Rifle Company, Infantry and Airborne Battlegroups* (Washington, D.C.: Department of the Army, 1962), 3–4.

105. As examples, see Special Warfare Board [Lt. Gen. Hamilton Howze, Chair]. *Final Report* (HQ USCONARC: Ft. Monroe, Va., 28 January 1962), 140, and FM 31-16, *Counterguerrilla Operations* (Washington, D.C.: Department of the Army, 1965), 20.

106. FM 31-16 [1963], 21–22.

107. This was explicitly recognized and accepted by the Ad Hoc Study Group, Summary Report, v.

108. 20/M37/413a, F-4, CF:VN/NSF/LBJ. Secretary McNamara had accepted this contention as early as May 1964. See 1/T4/2, 5, NSC/NSF/LBJ.

109. Ibid., F-5.

110. Ibid., F-6, G-28.

111. Ibid., F-17.

112. Ibid., F-6, F-18.

113. Ibid., G-25-28.

114. 78,79/3 C NVN Infiltration into SVN/7 24 June 1965, CF:VN/NSF/LBJ.

115. 20/M37/413a, G-28, G-29, ibid.

116. Summary Report, v, ibid.

117. Summary Report, iii, ibid.

118. 42/VII/T436/36a, NSCH/NSF/LBJ.

119. Ibid., 2.

120. JCS Wargames/Vol. I (1), Final Report, Sigma I-64, 15 April 1964, and JCS Wargames/Vol. II (1), (2), Final Report, Sigma II-64, 5 October 1964, AGENCY/30/NSF/LBJ.

121. Intelligence memorandum, 24 June 1965, 5–6, VI/Special Intelligence Materials/8, 49/SEA V, CF:VN/NSF/LBJ.

122. Ibid., 7.

123. Ibid., 10.

124. Ibid., 9.

125. Ibid., 11.

126. State Department, Bureau of Intelligence and Research, Intelligence Note, 29 June 1965, 18/ M35/362, NSF/LBJ.

127. Transcribed telex from Taylor with McGeorge Bundy cover memo, 11 July 1965, 6, 190 and 191/ NODIS-MAYFLOWER/2 and 2a, CF:VN/NSF/LBJ.

128. Ibid., 21.

129. I/20, 22, 24, and 25, 201/Special Meetings on SE Asia/V, ibid.

130. For an indication as to the trends in the Rolling Thunder program, consult the following frag and execute orders: I/40, 42a, 50a, 60b, 62, 64, 70, and 71b, 201/Special Meetings on SE Asia/V, ibid.

131. USIB memorandum: 28 October 1965, 19, VIII/10, 50 and 51/SEA V, ibid. See also CIA Intelligence Memorandum, 25 October 1965, 78, 79/3C NVN Infiltration into SVN/48h, ibid. This report details the impressive program of road and trail construction which the North Vietnamese had undertaken in the Laotian Corridor under the weight of the Barrel Roll and Steel Tiger attacks.

132. Ibid., 24.

133. Ibid., 30–31.

134. Ibid., 11.

135. Bundy to president, 3 December 1965, 17/72, 2/V, Bundy Papers.

136. Bundy to president, 27 November 1965, 17/86, ibid.

137. Ball to Bundy, n.d., 17/86a, ibid. This memo was sent to the president by Bundy on 17 November 1965.

138. Bundy to president, 3 December 1965, 2, 17/72, ibid..

139. Cline to McGeorge Bundy with appended report, 8 November 65, 2, (1)/4 and 4a, 83/3H, CF:VN/ NSF/LBJ.

140. Bundy to president, 4 December 1965, 17/68, 2/V, Bundy Papers.

141. Bundy to president, 14 December 1965, 2, 17/55, ibid. See also Ball talking notes, 17/55a, ibid.

142. Jack Valenti notes, 2–3, 12/17/65, 1/Meeting of Foreign Policy Advisors, CF/Meeting Note File, WHCF, LBJ.

143. Ibid., 1.

144. Ibid., 4.

145. Jack Valenti notes, 1/Meetings of Foreign Policy Advisors 12/18/65, ibid.

146. Ibid., 6–7.

147. Memo to Rusk and Ball, 5 January 1966, II/T2/2, NSC Meetings/1/V, NSF/LBJ.

148. Transcript of Saigon 2376, Lodge to the Secretary, 4 January 1966, 1, 18/84a, 6/McGeorge Bundy V, Memos to the President, ibid.

149. "Some Paragraphs on Vietnam—3rd Draft," 19 January 1966, 2, 1/McNaughton Drafts (III)/ 75a, Papers of Paul Warnke–John McNaughton Files, LBJ Library.

150. McNaughton draft memo, 18 January 1966, 2, 1/McNaughton Drafts II (3)/79, ibid.

151. Ibid., 3–4. See Freedman draft, 15 January 1966, 1/McNaughton Drafts (III)/83, ibid.

152. Ibid., 7, 11–13.

153. Meeting in Cabinet Room, 1/24/66, Meeting Notes File/1, WHCF/LBJ.

154. Intelligence memorandum, 18 January 1966, 1, 312/2a, 71/ND CO/CF, ibid.

155. Meeting in the Cabinet Room, 25 January 1966, 2, Meeting Notes File/1, ibid.

156. 312/Situation in Vietnam, Jan-Mar 66, Bundy to president, 26 January 1966, 71/ND CO/CF, ibid.

157. Meeting in Cabinet Room, 27 January 1966, Meeting Notes File/1, ibid.

158. Meeting in Cabinet Room, 28 January 66, Meeting Notes File/1, ibid.

159. Ibid., 10.

160. "Summary notes of 556th NSC Meeting," 29 January 1966, 2, II/T2/2, NSC Meetings/2/V, NSF/ LBJ.

161. Ibid., 3.

162. Office of National Estimates memorandum, 11 February 1966, 2, 27/C47/3, CF:VN/26, NSF/ LBJ.

163. Ibid., 13.

164. Bundy to president, 25 February 1966, 20/15, Memos to the President/6/V, ibid.

165. "Summary Notes of 557th NSC Meeting," 10 May 1966, 1, II/T4/2, NSC Meetings/2/V, ibid.

166. Intelligence memorandum, 21 February 1966, 10, 79/3C NVN Infiltration into SVN/3, CF/VN/78, ibid.

167. Intelligence memorandum, 9 April 1966, 79/3C NVN Infiltration into SVN/2b, CF/VN/78, ibid.

168. Intelligence memoranda, 21 May 1966 and 20 June 1966, CF/71/ND CO 312, WHCF/LBJ.

169. See Rostow to president, 16 June 1966, 3/32, Memos to the President/7/W. W. Rostow V, NSF/LBJ, in which he reported his conversation with UN Ambassador Goldberg regarding the low civilian casualties to be expected from the POL campaign and the means by which a diplomatic confrontation with the Soviets might be mitigated.

170. "Summary Notes of 559th NSC Meeting," 17 June 1966, II/T4/2, NSC Meetings/2/V, ibid.

171. Ibid., 8.

172. Transcript of Lodge Weekly Report, 15 June 1966, V/41a, Memos to the President/8/WWR, ibid.

173. Notes of president's meeting with NSC, 22 June 1966, NSC Meetings/2/II/T7/2, ibid.

174. McNamara to president, 14 October 1966, NSC Meetings/2/II/T9/3, ibid.

175. Ibid., 3.

176. Ibid., 4, 6–7.

177. JCS to president, 14 October 1966, 3, NSC Meetings/2/II/T9/4, ibid.

178. Westmoreland to Rostow, 24 October 1966, 1, 10/11, Papers of William C. Westmoreland/9/V (hereafter Westmoreland Papers), LBJ Library.

179. Smith to Rostow, 5 November 1966, with attached intelligence memorandum, November 1966, CIA Report on Effectiveness of Rolling Thunder/1 and 1a, CF:VN/221, NSF/LBJ.

180. Ibid., 5–9.

181. Ibid., 2, 3.

182. Ibid., 35.

183. Intelligence memorandum, December 1966, Effectiveness of Air Campaign/1, CF/VN/22, NSF/LBJ.

184. Ibid., 19.

185. Ibid., 20.

186. Rosson to Leonhart, 9 September 1966, 8–9, Special Studies/3a, Komer-Leonhart Files/24, LBJ.

187. Ibid., 9.

188. Office of National Estimates memorandum, 11 February 1966, 2, 27/C47/3, CF:VN/26, NSF/LBJ.

189. Oleg Hoeffding, "Bombing North Vietnam: An Appraisal of Economic and Political Effects," December 1966, 17, Rand Memorandum RM-5213-ISA, 3F Memos on Bombing/35, CF/VN/81-84, NSF, ibid.

190. Ibid., 32.

191. Report by Wheeler, "Air Campaign Against the North," 1, NSC Meeting of 8 February 67, NSC Meetings/2/T35/2b, NSF, ibid.

192. "Outline," n.d., Meetings with the President Apr 66-Jun 67/52b, Meetings/1, NSF, ibid.

193. Ibid., 45.

194. Ibid., 48.

195. Ibid., 49.

196. See the arguments of ibid., 77–85.

197. Ibid., 62–63.

198. Ginsburgh to Rostow, 3 June 1967, with JCS to secretary of defense, JCSM-312-67, and "Appendix to Basic Report," Future Military Operations/14, 14a, and 14b, 3E(1)A, CF/VN/81-84, NSF, ibid.

199. Helms to McNamara, 1 June 1967, with CIA memorandum TS 196752/67, 1 June 1967, (2)/33 and 33a, McNaughton Memos XIII, Papers of Paul Warnke–John McNaughton Files/5, LBJ.

200. Brown to McNaughton, 5 June 1967, McNaughton Memos XIII/41, ibid.

201. Brown to McNamara, 9 June 1967, 10, McNaugton Memos XIII/39, ibid.

202. Talking Paper, "Justification of Continued Bombing of NVN," May 1967, 15 (1)/65, 11/V, Westmoreland Papers.

203. Ibid., 2.

204. Telex to Sharp and Wheeler, 6 September 1967, 21 (I)/65, 13/V, Westmoreland Papers. A transcribed copy was forwarded to the White House. Memos to president IV/51d, CF:VN/NSF/LBJ.

205. Telex to Johnson and Sharp, 27 September 1967, 21 (II)/71, 13/V, Westmoreland Papers.

206. Ibid., 1.

207. Ibid., 7.

208. "Blueprint for Vietnam," n.d., 7, with Leonhart to Rostow, "Blueprint for Vietnam," 11 September 1967, Blueprint for Vietnam/2, Komer-Leonhart Files/1, LBJ.

209. Ibid., 7.

210. Hughes to the secretary, 24 October 1967, ii, (1)/29, CF/VN/66/2F, NSF/LBJ.

211. For a brief review of the process see Rostow to president, 9 September 1967, Files of Walt W. Rostow/Pennsylvania/5, NSF/LBJ.

212. Acting state secretary to president, 26 September 1967, 2, Files of Walt W. Rostow/Pennsylvania/3a, NSF/LBJ.

213. Rusk to Kissinger, 12 September 1967, Files of Walt W. Rostow/9/Pennsylvania/8c, NSF/LBJ.

214. Edmunds to Brown, 10 October 1967, 1 (emphasis in original), (1) Appraisal of the Bombing of NVN/2a, CF/VN/81-84/3H, NSF/LBJ. Sent to White House by 2, memo to Rostow.

215. Helms to Rostow, 24 October 1967, 1, (1) Appraisal of the Bombing of NVN/1, CF/VN/81-84/3H, NSF/LBJ.

216. McNamara to president, 1 November 1967, with Draft Memo, (1)/5 and 5a, CF/VN/127/Decision to Halt Bombing, NSF/LBJ.

217. Ibid., 9.

218. Ibid., 7.

219. Bundy to president, 17 October 1967, 5, (1)/Tab J/22, CF/VN/127/Decision to Halt Bombing, NSF/LBJ.

220. Rostow to president, 2 November 1967, (1)/Tab K/-, CF/VN/127/Decision to Halt Bombing, NSF/LBJ.

221. Rostow to president, 7 November 1967, with attached Clifford memorandum, Decision to Halt Bombing/Tab K-1/26, CF/VN/127, NSF/LBJ.

222. LBJ/WHCF/ Meeting with the Foreign Policy Advisors, Thursday 2 November 1967, Meeting Notes File/2, WHCF, LBJ. Attendance at the meeting included Clark Clifford, George Ball, McGeorge Bundy, Bill Bundy, Maxwell Taylor, Omar Bradley, Robert Murphy, Henry Cabot Lodge, Dean Rusk, Nicholas Katzenbach, Averill Harriman, Dean Acheson, Abe Fortas, Arthur Dean, Douglas Dillon, Walt Rostow, Richard Helms, and Robert McNamara.

223. Ibid., 3.

224. Taylor to president, 3 November 1967, 2, (1)/Tab I/20a, Decision to Halt Bombing, CF:VN/127, NSF/LBJ.

225. Rostow to president, with Taylor to president, 6 November 1967, and "An Estimate of the Vietnam Situation November 1967," n.d., 49/6, 6a, and 6b, Memos to the President/25/WWR, NSF/LBJ.

226. Rostow to president, 11 November 1967, with attachment, 50/59 and 59a, Memos to the President/25/WWR, NSF/LBJ.

227. Ibid. 59a, 3.

228. Rostow to president, 21 November 1967, and Rostow to president, 20 November 1967, (1)/Tab E/12 and Tab F/14, Decision to Halt Bombing, CF:VN/127, NSF/LBJ.

229. Rusk to president, 20 November 1967, 2, (1)/Tab D/10, Decision to Halt Bombing, CF:VN/127, NSF/LBJ.

230. Katzenbach to president, November 1967, 12, Tab G/10a, Decision to Halt Bombing, CF:VN/127, NSF/LBJ.

231. Memorandum of the President for the File, 18 December 1967, 1–2, (1)/Tab L/28, Decision to Halt Bombing, CF:VN/127, NSF/LBJ.

232. "An Appraisal of the Bombing of North Vietnam (through 16 November 67)," November 1967, (2) 1967/7a, CIA/DIA Report S-2607/AP4A, CF:VN/84/3H, NSF/LBJ.

233. Rostow to president, 13 December 1967, (2)/General Military Activities/1, CF:VN/68, 69/2C, NSF/LBJ.

234. Intelligence memorandum, 8 December 1967, VIII-1, (2)/General Military Activities/1b, CF:VN/68, 69/2C, NSF/LBJ.

235. Intelligence report, 8 December 1967, 5, 6, 11, (1) General Military Activities/2, CF:VN/68, 69/2C, NSF/LBJ.

236. Ibid., 11.

237. Ibid., 7.

238. Ibid., 48, 49, 58.

239. Institute for Defense Analysis, JASON Study, "The Bombing of North Vietnam," vol. 1: Summary, vol. 2: Accomplishments, vol. 3: Analysis, vol. 4, Evaluation of Various Interdiction Campaigns, 16 December 1967, CF/VN/JASON Study/1, 2, 3, 4, NSF/LBJ.

240. Ibid., 1:1 (emphasis in original).

241. Ibid., 1:7.

242. Ibid., 1:16.

243. Ibid., 2:82.

244. Ginsburgh to Rostow, 13 January 1968, with 4a, memorandum, "JASON Study—The Bombing of North Vietnam," 13 January 1968, (3)/4 and 4a, CF/VN/84/3H, NSF/LBJ.

245. Clifford to president via Rostow, 7 November 1967, (1)/T. K-1/26, Decision to Halt Bombing, CF/VN/127, NSF/LBJ.

246. Tape 3, 14ff, AC74-97, Clark Clifford Oral History, LBJ.

247. Taylor memorandum, n.d., 1/Alternative Strategies vis a vis SEA/25, Papers of Clark Clifford, LBJ Library.

248. William Bundy draft memorandum, 29 February 1968, 2/Memos on Vietnam/3b, ibid.

249. Nicholas Katzenbach, "US Public Opinion," n.d. (probably 1 March 1968), 2/Memos on Vietnam/3d, ibid.

250. CIA ONE memo to director, 13 March 1968, 22, 7/83, NSCH/49/March 31st Speech/V, NSF/LBJ.

251. Warnke to Clifford, draft presidential memorandum, 2nd draft, 18 March 1968, 1/Alternative Strategies and Strategic Guidance/3, Papers of Clark Clifford.

252. Ibid., 6.

253. Ibid., 7.

254. Ball oral history, interview II, tape 1:14. Oral History Collection, LBJ Library.

255. "Summary of Notes," 26 March 1968, 1, Meeting Notes File, WHCF/LBJ.

256. Ball oral history, interview II, tape 1:14.

257. Ibid., 2:2.

258. Ibid.

259. Ibid.

260. Notes of president's meeting at Camp David, 9 April 1968, 5, Meeting Notes File/2, WHCF/LBJ.

261. "Summary Notes of President's Meeting with the Joint Chiefs on Vietnam," 14 October 1968, 17, Meeting Notes File/3, WHCF/LBJ.

262. CIA Directorate of Intelligence, "Intelligence Report," 5 August to 30 September 1968, The Situation in South Vietnam/1, 2, 3, 4, 6, 7, 8, 9, 10, CF/VN/58/1A (8/68-9/68), NSF/LBJ.

Vietnamization: The War to Groom an Ally

Jeffrey J. Clarke

In April 1969 the administration of President Richard M. Nixon began a policy of "Vietnamizing" the war in Southeast Asia. Vietnamization was not a strategy for fighting the war, nor was it a plan for winning it. Instead, Vietnamization was a policy of gradually substituting South Vietnamese troops for American ground combat forces in Vietnam. No change in the tempo of the war was contemplated, and no negotiated settlement was expected. Vietnamization assumed that U.S. casualties would be substantially reduced by an incremental American withdrawal of its ground combat forces; many administration leaders also believed this reduction would mute criticism of the war within the United States, facilitating a protracted commitment to Saigon. With these objectives in mind, American political and military leaders implemented the policy of Vietnamization between 1969 and 1972.

Although Vietnamization appears to be an easily defined policy with limited objectives, its relationship to concurrent policies, programs, and strategies is often confusing and even contradictory. For example, each U.S. troop reduction, normally announced by the White House with much public relations fanfare, eroded the bargaining position of American peace negotiators in Paris, making diplomats such as Henry Kissinger uneasy over the speed of their country's exodus. At the same time, the expansion of the war into Cambodia and Laos seemed to signify a major change in the type of warfare contemplated. For these reasons any analysis of the origins, objectives, and implementation of Vietnamization, as well as any evaluation of its successes and failures, should take place within the larger political-military context. When this is done, Vietnamization suddenly becomes exceedingly complex.

Throughout the Vietnam War, American leaders wavered between two distinct political-military strategies: pacification and attrition. Pacification represented America's original response to third-world insurgencies. It entailed a combination of measures designed to defeat insurgent military and political forces and strengthen the political-military base of the supported regimes. Although exceedingly difficult to implement effectively in South Vietnam during the early 1960s, pacification emphasized measures that could be accomplished by the host country and thus was more closely associated with the policy of Vietnamization. The strategy of attrition, however, was based on an entirely different set of assumptions. Unlike pacification, attrition assumed that the fulcrum of the enemy's war effort was not in South Vietnam but in the North. If enough American combat power could be brought to bear on the southern battlefields, on the infiltration routes from North to South Vietnam, and on North Vietnam itself, then the war could be won. Loss of manpower would force Hanoi to end its support for the southern insurgency, which would then quickly wither without outside assistance. American leaders regarded a negotiated settlement as an event formally ending North Vietnam's participation in the war effort. Thus attrition was tied closely to negotiations.[1]

Both strategies had major weaknesses throughout their long lives. Pacification foundered on the weaknesses of successive Saigon regimes, while attrition was limited by the unwillingness of American political leaders to expand the scope of the conflict. Gen. William Westmoreland's efforts to implement both strategies at the same time—attrition by his American forces and pacification by his South Vietnamese allies—often confused the issue, as did the efforts of Gen. Creighton Abrams, Westmoreland's successor in mid-1968, to meld the two together in his "One War" concept. The two strategies overlapped in many areas, each in many ways contributing to the other. Their ultimate ends, however, were fundamentally different. Attrition was aimed primarily at the willpower of Hanoi's leaders while pacification was directed at the capabilities of the southern insurgents.

The origins of Vietnamization are much debated. As early as 1963, prior to the assassination of President Ngo Dinh Diem, American leaders, optimistic over progress in the war, had begun planning for an early withdrawal of most American advisory and support elements by 1965—an early Vietnamization effort.[2] Such plans, of course, proved unrealistic. Instead, U.S. force commitment rose dramatically in 1965. By the end of that year, attrition had become the accepted American strategy. All efforts to force a military decision on a limited battlefield, however, proved in vain. By 1967 support for the war on the American home front was beginning to decline. In response both General Westmoreland and President Johnson turned their attention to the South Vietnamese. Johnson urged his military commander to increase South Vietnamese participation in (what was to Americans) the main war effort and to devote more publicity to their military achievements. One result was Westmoreland's speech to the National Press Club in November 1967. In his speech he promised the beginning of unilateral American troop withdrawals within two years and their replacement by reinvigorated South Vietnamese armed forces. Another result was a substantial effort to modernize Saigon's military hardware with the M-16 rifle and other lightweight equipment.[3]

The Tet Offensive of February 1968 put a temporary end to these revived Vietnamization proposals. U.S. military leaders pressed President Johnson for more American troops to follow up the enemy's severe battlefield defeats. The president's firm decision not to expand the already large American participation in the war, however, again turned the spotlight on the South Vietnamese forces. Starting in April 1968 and continuing throughout the summer of that year, the American Military Assistance Command, Vietnam (MACV) produced a series of plans to modernize and expand Saigon's military forces. At the time American leaders expected the recently convened peace talks in Paris would produce a negotiated settlement specifying a mutual American–North Vietnamese withdrawal from South Vietnam. With this in mind, U.S. officials scrambled to prepare a pacification-oriented South Vietnamese military force that could handle a "residual" insurgency without direct American assistance. The task put a premium on area security and light infantry forces supported by a decentralized fire support and logistical system.[4] The expectation of an imminent negotiated settlement, in fact, continued throughout the tumultuous Democratic National Convention in Chicago and on into the November elections. Only then, with a new president—Richard M. Nixon—in the wings, did all American leaders realize that an end to the conflict was still not in sight.

Because of conflicting estimates of South Vietnamese capabilities, one of the first acts of the Nixon administration was to issue National Security Study Memorandum No. 1 (NSSM 1), often called "the 29 questions." It instructed all U.S. agencies involved in the war effort to submit their evaluations of the conflict and their prognoses for its future. Prominent among the specific questions was NSSM 1's inquiry regarding the capability of Saigon's military forces to deal with a residual insurgency with varying degrees of North Vietnamese support. The responses arrived in February 1969 from the various addressees—the Joint Chiefs of Staff (JCS), the Office of the Secretary of Defense (OSD), the Department of State, and the Central Intelligence Agency (CIA), as well as MACV itself.[5] On the matter of South Vietnamese military capabilities, the judgments were relatively uniform. With continued American advice and military assistance, Saigon might eventually be able to handle a residual Vietcong insurgency. However, the South Vietnamese would never be able to deal with a conventional North Vietnamese threat, nor with any combination of an insurgent-conventional challenge on the battlefield without direct American participation in the ground war. Although not included in MACV's formal answers to NSSM 1, the judgments of Abrams' major field commanders within South Vietnam, including those of the III Marine Amphibious Force, the Army's I and II Field Forces, and the Delta Military Assistance Command agreed with these harsh conclusions.[6]

While the NSSM 1 responses were being digested in Washington, Nixon's new secretary of defense, Melvin Laird, traveled to Saigon to talk the matter out with General Abrams and his MACV staff. MACV had made great strides in re-equipping and enlarging the South Vietnamese armed forces, expanding government security programs, and in general consolidating the gains made by allied forces in the wake of the 1968 Tet Offensive. Although allied progress had to be measured primarily in terms of somewhat questionable statistics, the improvement of such figures over previous years was marked. Moreover, the enemy's major attacks during the Tet '69 holidays had gone nowhere. Abrams's conventional units appeared to have been driven permanently from the borders of South Vietnam into their Laotian and Cambodian sanctuaries. But the future course of the war still seemed hazy.

In conversation with General Abrams, Secretary Laird pointed out that, for domestic political reasons, it was advisable to withdraw some American troops in the near future, suggesting a figure of 44,000 within the next three or four months.

Although averse to any reduction of his combat strength, Abrams reluctantly agreed, and, in ensuing talks between Saigon and Washington, the figure was set at 50,000 for 1969. Any additional withdrawals, Abrams insisted, had to depend on further progress in the war effort and in South Vietnamese capabilities.[7]

Returning to Washington, Laird argued his talks with General Abrams had produced a formula for gradually reducing American participation in the ground war, "de-Americanizing" the war, or, expressed positively, "Vietnamizing" it.[8] Both President Nixon and National Security Adviser Henry Kissinger apparently agreed, resulting in the promulgation of NSSM 36, a directive authorizing the Vietnamization of the war according to Secretary Laird's recipe.[9] NSSM 36 instructed military agencies to draw up plans removing all American ground combat forces from South Vietnam within eighteen to thirty months and replacing them with South Vietnamese forces. However, NSSM 36 also specified that there would be no diminution of current levels of combat—that is, no negotiated settlement and no expansion of the ground war. Equally important, there was to be no reduction in American advisory, logistical, technical, financial, or air power assistance to the Republic of Vietnam, all of which was to continue indefinitely.[10]

In the months that immediately followed, negotiations between OSD and the JCS further clarified that the withdrawal increments would be presidential decisions. No "residual support force" with ground combat units was contemplated. MACV could determine the composition of the withdrawing increments but not their size or timing. It also would have primary responsibility for the American role in shaping the South Vietnamese military structure that was to succeed it.[11] In June 1969, President Nixon and South Vietnamese President Nguyen Van Thieu publicly announced the Vietnamization program during a meeting on Midway Island. Subsequently, some 25,000 troops left South Vietnam, the first of fourteen successive American withdrawal increments.

General Abrams had no plans for South Vietnamese troops to fill in behind departing Americans. The existing South Vietnamese expansion and modernization efforts begun in 1968 had been based upon a negotiated settlement resulting in some sort of truce followed by a much more rapid American and North Vietnamese troop withdrawal. Such a scenario emphasized a postwithdrawal pacification strategy and the growth of Saigon's area security capabilities, an aim closely complementing MACV's current efforts to destroy the more elusive elements of the insurgency (the Vietcong local forces, guerrillas, and clandestine political apparatus). With most of the enemy's regular units located outside of South Vietnam's borders, there was little else for the over 500,000 American troops to do. Initially, Vietnamization thus had little impact within South Vietnam. In fact, despite all the publicity over the new policy, both General Abrams and Ellsworth Bunker, the American ambassador in Saigon, expected that some sort of breakthrough in the Paris peace talks might occur at anytime, making any long-range plans to Vietnamize the entire war somewhat pointless.[12]

During the remainder of 1969 and throughout 1970, General Abrams, Secretary Laird, and their staffs argued over the evolution of the South Vietnamese armed forces. Laird demanded that MACV come up with a force structure for Saigon that could stand alone with minimal American support; Abrams responded that South Vietnamese manpower resources were already stretched to the limit and their society lacked the technical infrastructure allowing them to employ the sophisticated weapons used by the Americans. Thieu and his generals joined the debate from time to time, requesting more modern weapons—main battle tanks, heavy self-propelled artillery, and air defense capabilities, for example—and more financial support to combat Saigon's runaway inflation rate that was threatening to destroy military salaries. Abrams, however, remained adamant. While agreeing to activate a few South Vietnamese heavy artillery units to replace departing American batteries along the border between North and South Vietnam, and while also approving elaborate plans to train and activate a large fleet of helicopters for the South Vietnamese Air Force over a three-year period, he believed further efforts of this sort would be counterproductive. Better to concentrate on more mundane matters such as maintenance, inventory control, small unit training, and improved officer selection, assignment and promotion measures that would make the existing force perform better.[13]

In the eyes of General Abrams and his field advisers, the main problem with Saigon's armed forces was not a lack of equipment, but a lack of will to use it aggressively. American advisers had continually criticized South Vietnamese military leadership since the early 1960s. The demise of President Diem in 1963 propelled the military inextricably into the political administration of the nation. But Saigon's factionalized officer corps found it difficult to establish a stable government. The competition between the various military cliques further politicized the officer corps, fostering corruption and militating against the professionalism needed for the tasks at hand. Not surprisingly, promotions and appointments depended on patronage and financial blandishments rather than on ability or professional success.[14] As one adviser commented, "Having a poor South Vietnamese officer relieved was as difficult as getting a politician out of office."[15] Vietnamization offered no cure for such problems.

The establishment of a constitutional government in 1967 was unsuccessful in divorcing the military from politics, and the South's leadership problems persisted throughout the Vietnamization effort. Although Abrams and Bunker labored heavily to have those whom they considered the poorest South Vietnamese generals transferred from the most important combat commands, their influence over their counterparts in such matters was minimal. Vietnamese stubborn reluctance to accept American advice in these areas was almost gospel, and American efforts to identify and promote able South Vietnamese officers were sometimes even counterproductive. As Westmoreland himself once noted, too much American praise was sometimes a "kiss of death" to a Vietnamese officer's career.[16]

For a time the combined American–South Vietnamese "incursion" into Cambodia in 1970 soothed some of these worries. Billed domestically as a "test" of Vietnamization, the militarily successful endeavor seemed to show Saigon's forces had the ability to conduct extended conventional operations with minimal American assistance and with little or no interference from a greatly weakened internal insurgency. Although the Cambodian incursion also appeared to represent a return to the American attrition strategy, the insistence of both Laird and Abrams that Thieu return his troops to South Vietnam immediately after the U.S. disengagement (a request refused by Thieu) argued against any change in American strategy or the thrust of Vietnamization.[17]

Lam Son 719, the purely South Vietnamese incursion into Laos in 1971, could only strengthen the misgivings of Abrams and his field advisers over Saigon's leadership and conventional capabilities. By that time the existing ground force modernization and expansion plans were virtually complete. The old leadership problems, however, remained and were highlighted by bitter squabbles between participating South Vietnamese Army, Airborne, Marine Corps, and Ranger commanders, and also between Saigon and the field commands. This time Abrams, sensing that this was the last opportunity that significant U.S. direct combat and logistical support could be brought to bear, pressed Thieu to throw more units into the battle. The South Vietnamese president, however, declined the advice and elected to withdraw. Heavy losses in his pro-government Airborne and Marine components threatened to undermine the internal stability of his regime. The large commitment of other forces could erode his support from the army's four powerful, but still heavily politicized, corps commanders. In the interests of political stability, the risks of fighting a large conventional battle could not be taken.[18]

Despite the Laotian experience, the form and substance of Saigon's armed forces changed little over the next two years.[19] North Vietnam's employment of main battle tanks in Lam Son 719 prompted General Abrams to authorize one battalion of similar machines for Saigon's army, and Thieu's unilateral decision to activate a new infantry division opposite the Demilitarized Zone led the MACV commander to approve, albeit reluctantly, financial and material support for that unit too. But the heart of South Vietnam's military strength remained in the now eleven standard infantry divisions, which were locally recruited, locally trained, and locally based, with little operational mobility. Dependents, for example, continued to be housed on or near almost all Vietnamese combat bases. Lengthy deployments from those traditional bases were rare. Here was another critical problem that Vietnamization failed to address.

Saigon's Territorial infantry—the Regional Force companies and Popular Force platoons, popularly known as the RF-PF, or "Ruff-Puffs"—were even less deployable outside of the limited areas they were expected to secure. Only the Airborne and Marine units, recruited throughout South Vietnam but trained and home-based around Saigon, could move at will to any threatened area within the country and thus constituted the small nucleus of a truly national army. But as long as American leaders tied Vietnamization to a limited pacification strategy, Saigon's forces appeared properly organized and deployed.

North Vietnam's Easter Offensive in the spring of 1972 appeared to be the ultimate test of Vietnamization. As envisioned by NSSM 36, no U.S. ground combat units were involved, but American advisory, logistical, and air support was critical. As expected, South Vietnamese military leadership proved lacking in many areas, but led by aggressive American advisers such as Major Gen. James F. Hollingsworth and John Paul Vann, Saigon's forces held together and their opponents suffered devastatingly high losses. Yet the timing, scope, and nature of the offensive had come as a surprise to the Americans, who were clearly unprepared for the widespread employment of armor, conventional artillery, and missiles by the North Vietnamese high command. The insurgency, now weakened by years of attrition, was hardly a noticeable factor in the contest. After the initial setbacks at Quang Tri, Tan Canh, and Loc Ninh, Abrams himself was dismayed and believed that an imminent South Vietnamese collapse was possible. Only the inexperience of his foes in conducting extended conventional operations may have saved Saigon that year. Certainly NSSM 36 had not envisioned the evolution of the war into a conventional struggle, which ironically was just the type of conflict American military leaders hoped for seven years earlier.[20]

Despite the success of South Vietnam in repulsing the 1972 offensive with strong American assistance, the conclusion that America had "groomed its ally" for the wrong war and at the wrong time and place is inescapable. The NSSM 36 Vietnamization order tried to turn the clock back to 1964, with the American presence in Vietnam reduced to its pre-1965 advisory era levels. But the war itself had changed dramatically. A South Vietnamese military that resembled a huge territorial police force was no longer appropriate to the threat it faced. Explanations for this situation are numerous but difficult to weigh. U.S. military leaders were wary of providing more technical weaponry than Saigon could handle. Concern about expanding the war also led them to reject more offensive weapons for their ally, such as diesel-engined tanks and armored personnel carriers, long-range aircraft equipped with electronic countermeasures, and an operational air- or sealift capability. In this respect the hundreds of main battle tanks and fighter aircraft hastily transported to South Vietnam prior to the final American withdrawal in early 1973 only underlined the faulty assumptions of NSSM 36, as did the Paris peace accords, which effectively nullified all of its provisions. The settlement that was finally negotiated never provided for a mutual American–North Vietnamese withdrawal. Instead Hanoi was allowed to retain a large military presence in the South.

Clearly Vietnamization had not prepared South Vietnam for the conventional struggles of 1973–75. According to Gen. William B. Rosson, the U.S. Army Pacific component commander who visited General Abrams during the summer of 1972, the MACV commander hoped that the war in Vietnam might gradually fade into a "Korean-type situation" with a small U.S. force remaining behind indefinitely.[21] However, the termination of direct American involvement one year later, the continued weakness of Saigon's political and military leadership, and, perhaps above all, the determination of North Vietnam's leaders to see the war through to the bitter end made such an outcome highly unlikely.

Notes

1. For an extended discussion, see Jeffrey J. Clarke, "On Strategy and the Vietnam War," *Parameters* 16 (Winter 1986).

2. See U.S. Department of Defense, *United States–Vietnam Relations* (Washinton, D.C.: Government Printing Office, 1971), 3, sec. 4, B.4, "Evolution of the War: Phased Withdrawal of U.S. Forces, 1962–1964."

3. Westmoreland to Abrams, 26 November 1967, "Concept of Situation Portrayed During Recent Visit to Washington," History file 25-A45, William C. Westmoreland Papers (hereafter cited as Westmoreland Papers), U.S. Army Center of Military History (CMH), Military History Institute, Carlisle Barracks, Pa.; and the Lyndon Baines Johnson Library, Austin, Tex.; William C. Westmoreland, *A Soldier Reports* (Garden City, N.Y.: Doubleday, 1976), 230–35.

4. For a summary of these planning activities, see Jeffrey J. Clarke, *Advice and Support: The Final Years, 1965–1973* (Washington, D.C.: CMH, 1988), 294–306.

5. For agency responses, see NSSM 1 files in Thomas C. Thayer Papers (hereafter cited as Thayer Papers), CMH; *Congressional Record,* 92d Cong., 2d sess., 1972, 118, pt. 13:16749–836.

6. Kerwin to Corcoran, 25 January 1969, HQ IFFV to COMUSMACV, 27 January 1969, HQ III MAF to COMUSMACV, n.d., "Situation in Vietnam," with enclosure "Answers to Twenty Questions," all in MACV Microfilm Records, Reel 1, RG 334, Washington National Records Center (WNRC), Washington, D.C.; and HQ, USAAG, IV CTZ, 26 January 1969, "Situation in Vietnam," Wheeler to Abrams, Histories Division Vietnam files, CMH.

7. Laird to president, 13 March 1969, "Trip to Vietnam and CINCPAC, 5–12 March 1969," File: Viet 333 Laird, Box 96, RG 330, WNRC; and Wheeler to Abrams, 14 March 1969, and Abrams to Wheeler, 30 March 1969, both in Abrams Papers, HRB, CMH.

8. Historical Division Joint Secretariat, U.S. Joint Chiefs of Staff, "The Joint Chiefs of Staff and the War in Vietnam, 1969–1970," in *The History of the Joint Chiefs of Staff* (Washington, D.C.: CMH, 1976), 102–4.

9. Henry Kissinger, *White House Years* (Boston: Little, Brown, 1979), 271–72; Richard M. Nixon, *The Memoirs of Richard Nixon* (New York: Grosset & Dunlap, 1978), 392.

10. Kissinger to secretary of state, secretary of Defence, and CIA Director, 10 April 1969, "Vietnamizing the War," Histories Division Vietnam files, CMH.

11. See messages in "Force Planning Synopsis," a separate file in Abrams Papers; and U.S. Embassy (Saigon) and MACV, "Vietnamizing the War: A Mission Coordinated Plan," 20 July 1969, both in Histories Division Vietnam files, CMH.

12. See Defense Secretary Melvin Laird's reports from his February 1970 trip to South Vietnam in File: Viet 333 Laird, Box 13, RG 330, WNRC.

13. The long exchange is treated in USMACV, "Command History, 1969," 2:VI-4 to VI-15 and VI-127 to VI-132.

14. For an open South Vietnamese discussion, see Cao Van Vien, *Leadership* (Washington, D.C.: CMH, 1981), 117–23.

15. Author's interview with Lt. Col. Richard O. Brunkow, 26 February 1976.

16. MFR, 10 March 1966, "MACV Commanders Conference, 20 February 1966," History file 4-C1, Westmoreland Papers.

17. Wheeler to McCain and Abrams, 4 May 1970, and Abrams to Wheeler and McCain, 11 May 1970, Abrams Papers; Memorandum for Record, Odeen (OSD/ISA), 15 May 1970, "Meeting with Laird on Vietnam," Folder 75, Thayer Papers.

18. See message traffic between Abrams and Lt. Gen. James W. Sutherland, Jr., February-March 1971, in Abrams Papers.

19. For details, see USMACV, "Command History, 1971," 1:VIII-2 to VIII-27.

20. For general treatments, see Ngo Quang Truong, *The Easter Offensive of 1972* (Washington, D.C.: CMH, 1980); and G. H. Turley, *The Easter Offensive, Vietnam 1972* (Novato, CA: Presidio, 1985).

21. Author's interview with Gen. William B. Rosson, 16 March 1984.

Nixon and the Air Weapon

Mark Clodfelter

Soon after beginning his fourth year as president, Richard Nixon hosted a White House dinner for members of his cabinet. "This is January 20, 1972 and tonight the fourth quarter begins," he told his guests. "The football analogy tells us that the fourth quarter really determines the game."[1] The president habitually compared the key events of his administration to the sport of football, but this prediction would prove especially prescient. The year 1972 would be marked by dramatic trips to Peking and Moscow, the Watergate break-in, and a landslide reelection victory. Yet the game that was perhaps uppermost in Nixon's mind was the frustrating tie in Vietnam.[2]

Nixon entered the White House promising to end the war. Now, three years later, despite the withdrawal of almost 500,000 troops and twelve secret negotiating sessions by National Security Adviser Henry Kissinger, a resolution to the conflict appeared no closer than it had in 1969. Although he remained committed to preserving a non-Communist South Vietnam, the president was at a loss as to how to achieve that goal. The answer came from the enemy. On 30 March 1972, North Vietnamese troops, backed by heavy artillery and over 200 tanks, launched a massive invasion of South Vietnam. The Easter Offensive was a blatant violation of the bombing halt "agreement" negotiated near the end of the Johnson presidency,[3] and it offered Nixon the opportunity to act in Vietnam as he had always wished—by applying large doses of air power against the North. Annoyed by Kissinger's inability to produce results in Paris, Nixon could now play "the Mad Bomber" he had threatened to become ever since he took office.[4] The president also would demonstrate that he—and he alone—could direct America's potent military arsenal to achieve a decisive outcome in Vietnam. He would be George Patton and Vince Lombardi rolled into one, and the peace achieved would be a direct result of his skill and cunning as commander in chief. Air power would enable him to drive the length of the field during the last minute of the game and kick a field goal as time expired, while the hometown fans (the American public) went wild.

The actual scenario did not go quite the way Nixon had envisioned, but enough similarities remained to convince him after the fact that bombing had indeed been the answer to ending the war. "The bombing had done its job; it had been successful," Nixon wrote in his memoirs regarding his "Christmas air offensive," the eleven-day series of raids against the North Vietnamese heartland in December 1972.[5] His memoirs further show his conviction that the intensive bombing of North Vietnam, in concert with the 1970 Cambodian invasion, would have brought the war to a close.[6] More recently, Nixon has stated that his failure to bomb and mine

North Vietnam immediately after taking office was the greatest mistake of his presidency. "If we had done that then," he told NBC's "Meet the Press" in April 1988, "I think we would've ended the war in 1969 rather than in 1973."[7]

While certainly not unique, the president's sentiments reveal much about his understanding of air power in the context of the Vietnam War. Nixon realized that as long as he remained committed to preserving a non-Communist South Vietnam, air power had become the only military tool at his disposal to accomplish that aim. He would not remove all American troops until Hanoi returned American POWs,[8] nor would domestic public opinion allow him to increase the troop total, which had shrunk to 69,000 by May 1972. By that time, however, the situation in Vietnam differed dramatically from what it had been in either 1969 or 1970. The 1968 Tet Offensive had devastated the Vietcong as an effective fighting force and had caused the North Vietnamese Army (NVA), which also had suffered severe losses, to revert to guerrilla warfare as its primary modus operandi until the 1972 Easter Offensive. Because the NVA fought infrequently and refused to mass, "seeking victory at the gnat-swarm stage," bombing North Vietnam would have had meager impact on its army's combat effectiveness.[9] The war's slow tempo from 1969 to 1972 limited Communist supply requirements to only a fraction of the amount required during Tet, rendering most of North Vietnam's transportation targets superfluous.[10] Moreover, the American public would have been unlikely to condone an intensive air campaign against the North, given the aftershock of Tet and the intensifying "peace movement" during the Nixon presidency.

The Easter Offensive transformed a guerrilla war into a fast-paced conventional conflict. The North Vietnamese blitzkrieg needed vast logistical support to sustain it, and the vital supply lines proved highly vulnerable to air attack and airborne mining.[11] Nixon, however, failed to note that the nature of the war had changed. His comments reveal that he achieved success with air power in 1972 more through happenstance than design, and that he had little understanding about air power's capabilities and limitations. His prime motivation in 1972 was a desire to demonstrate that *he* could end the war through hard-nosed determination and thus claim sole credit for achieving peace.

To Nixon, air power offered the means to show that he was "tough," and he placed a high priority on exhibiting his ability to take punishment. As historian Herbert Parmet observed, "His values incorporated recognition of the anybody-can-make-it-if-he's-willing-to-be-enough-of-a-bastard system as the inherent rule determining the game and its winners."[12] Nixon was impressed by Dwight Eisenhower's display of resolve in ending the Korean War, when the threatened use of nuclear weapons helped prod the Chinese into settling the conflict. During the 1954 debate on supporting the French garrison at Dien Bien Phu, then Vice President Nixon recommended bombing, arguing that "it might not be necessary to have more than a few conventional air strikes by the united forces to let the Communists see that we were determined to resist."[13] Nixon also noted that Eisenhower, in October 1967, thought that President Lyndon Johnson had been "a year and a half late" in initiating the bombing of North Vietnam, and that the bombing, once begun, had been too restrictive.[14]

Upon becoming president, Nixon frequently turned to air power to help solve the Vietnam dilemma. On 18 March 1969, he began the secret bombing of Cambodia with B-52s, and these raids continued through May 1970.[15] He also intensified the bombing of the Ho Chi Minh Trail in southern Laos, in an operation known as Commando Hunt. "Protective reaction" strikes against North Vietnam, in response to violations of the 1968 bombing halt "agreement," increased as well,[16] and on 16 February 1971, Nixon ordered the first B-52 raid on northern Laos. These displays of air power had only limited impact on an enemy waging guerrilla warfare, however, and the stalemate on the ground in South Vietnam continued.

In late 1971 the president learned that the North Vietnamese had begun stockpiling supplies for a potential offensive against the South. Nixon responded with Operation Proud Deep Alpha, in which Air Force fighters flew more than one thousand sorties from 26 to 30 December against supply targets south of the 20th parallel.[17] The Air Force further bombed North Vietnam continually for forty-eight hours in mid-February,[18] although attacks that month were limited to avoid disrupting the president's trip to China. More significant than the bombing was the beginning of a massive transfer of aircraft to Southeast Asian bases. Nixon sent 207 Air Force F-4s to South Vietnam and Thailand between 29 December 1971 and 13 May 1972, giving him a total of 374. He also ordered 161 B-52s to Andersen Air Force Base, Guam, and U-Tapao Royal Thai Air Force Base, Thailand, between 5 February and 23 May, creating a combined total of 210 B-52s in the Far East—more than half the bomber fleet of Strategic Air Command (SAC).[19] In addition, he dispatched the carriers *Constellation* and *Kitty Hawk* to join the *Coral Sea* and *Hancock* in the Tonkin Gulf, which gave the Navy a force of 300 attack aircraft by mid-April.[20]

When the North Vietnamese attacked at the end of March, Nixon was primed for action, and he took those around him by storm. After learning that White House press releases had not referred to the North Vietnamese as "the enemy," Nixon strode into Press Secretary Ron Zeigler's office, kicked his desk, and gave him a tongue-lashing.[21] The president was more frustrated by the response that he received from his military chiefs, who informed him that monsoon weather over North Vietnam would temporarily prevent flying. On 4 April he exclaimed to aide H. R. Haldeman and Attorney General John Mitchell: "Try and get the weather, damn it, if any of you know of any prayers say them. . . . The bastards have never been bombed like they're going to be bombed this time, but you've got to have the weather." Mitchell asked if the weather was still bad, and Nixon snapped: "Huh! It isn't bad. The Air Force isn't worth a—I mean, they won't fly."[22] Two days later the president met with Gen. John W. Vogt, Jr., en route to Saigon to take command of Seventh Air Force. Vogt described Nixon as "wild-eyed" as he berated air commanders for lacking aggressiveness. "He wanted somebody to use imagination—like Patton," Vogt remembered.[23]

Nixon concluded that he would have to be that individual. He had long admired the World War II hero, a California native born in Nixon's Twelfth District, and was especially fond of watching the George C. Scott movie version of the general's World War II career. Nixon kept a copy of Ladislas Farago's biography of Patton by his bed.[24] He "relished the general's ability to move troops swiftly to a decisive conclusion," observed presidential speechwriter William Safire.[25] Nixon also relished Patton's tough demeanor, and he emulated it. "The US will not negotiate at the point of a gun," he scrawled on 10 April in notes for a projected speech on the situation in Vietnam.[26] Six days later, he sought to demonstrate his determination to Hanoi.

The weather over North Vietnam had finally cleared on 5 April, and Nixon had ordered fighter attacks against supply concentrations south of the 18th parallel. Yet the bombing did not significantly impede the flow of men and materiel toward the south.[27] "To achieve the necessary military impact," Nixon determined that more drastic measures were necessary.[28] He reasoned that only B-52s, with their enormous 30-ton bomb loads, would make a difference. Moreover, dispatching a vital part of America's strategic triad into the heavy defenses of the North Vietnamese heartland would be, in Kissinger's words, "a warning that things might get out of hand if the offensive did not stop."[29] On 16 April, B-52s from the 307th Strategic Wing at U-Tapao attacked Haiphong's oil storage facilities. It was the bombers' first raid ever against the city, and Nixon was ecstatic. "We really left them our calling card this weekend," he told Haldeman after receiving a report of the strikes.[30]

The president maintained that the air effort's intensity throughout April. B-52s flew four more missions against North Vietnam during that month, although they did not attack Hanoi. On the twenty-fourth, Nixon ordered two more carriers to the Tonkin Gulf. Secretary of Defense Melvin Laird viewed Nixon's actions as "wild," confiding to the joint chiefs that "the President is personally insisting on massive strikes—[he] personally sent the carriers—the President said, 'I sent them—no one else asks for them.'"[31] Nixon also reiterated a familiar theme. On the eve of Kissinger's departure for a 2 May negotiating session in Paris with Le Duc Tho, Nixon barked: "Henry, you tell those sons of bitches that the President is a madman and you don't know how to deal with him. Once reelected I'll be a mad bomber."[32]

When Kissinger returned from Paris after being snubbed by the North Vietnamese, who gloated over the capture of Quang Tri City on 1 May, Nixon decided that the time was ripe to send the B-52s against Hanoi. On 30 April, anticipating that Kissinger's trip would prove fruitless, he had proposed a three-day series of B-52 raids against Hanoi and Haiphong beginning on 5 May. Now he urged that the attacks go as scheduled. Kissinger disagreed, arguing that while bombing was necessary, the "one-shot" nature of the raids would probably not deter Hanoi, while the use of B-52s against the North Vietnamese capital would likely cause severe domestic criticism.[33] In addition, Gen. Creighton Abrams, commander of U.S. Military Assistance Command, Vietnam (MACV), contended that he needed the B-52s in the South to thwart the continued Communist advance. The arguments convinced Nixon to cancel his planned B-52 raids, but he remained committed to pounding the North with bombs. He decided to endorse the proposal of Maj. Gen. Alexander Haig, Kissinger's military assistant, who recommended sustained bombing with fighter aircraft and the aerial mining of North Vietnamese ports. The mining operation, code-named Pocket Money, commenced at 2000 hours on Monday, 8 May (0900 hours on the 9th in Vietnam), one hour before Nixon announced it to the American public on television. The code name for the bombing campaign, which began one day later, befitted the man who saw himself as coach of a nation in need of decisive action—Linebacker.

Nixon realized that his decision contained grave risks, confiding in his diary, "We have crossed the Rubicon."[34] In particular, Operation Linebacker threatened the Moscow summit scheduled for later that month, during which he was to sign a strategic arms limitation treaty. Yet Nixon had concluded that the summit paled in insignificance when compared to the crisis in Vietnam. He told his key advisers that "the summit isn't worth a damn if the price for it is losing in Vietnam. My instinct tells me that the country can take losing the summit, but it can't take losing the war."[35] Intensive bombing also threatened Nixon's bid for reelection. When Special Counsel Charles Colson suggested that the bombing and mining would infuriate the American public and possibly cost the election, Nixon retorted, "So what! It's the right thing to do. If I didn't do it, the Presidency wouldn't be worth getting reelected to."[36] In actuality, besides believing that a display of Pattonesque bravado was necessary to preserve South Vietnam, Nixon had become convinced that he could *not* be reelected without taking strong military actions. During the first week of January 1972, polls had shown the president running neck and neck with Senator Edmund Muskie, the leading Democratic party contender. Nixon had taken a 4-percentage point lead following his tough speech on Vietnam at the end of January, and he now thought that any failure to display continued resolve would cost him the presidency.[37] In addition, he wanted the certainty of reelection to hold over Hanoi's head as a guarantee that more extreme measures would follow if no settlement occurred by November.

Nixon was again disappointed, however, by the military's recommendations. He termed the joint chiefs' proposed air campaign as "timid," and wrote Kissinger:

> I am concerned by the military's plan of allocating 200 sorties for North Vietnam for the dreary 'milk runs' which characterized the Johnson administration's bombing in the 1965–1968 period. . . . Now that I have made this very tough watershed decision I intend to stop at nothing to bring the enemy to his knees. I want you to get this spirit inculcated in all hands and particularly I want the military to get off its backside and give me some recommendations as to how we can accomplish that goal.[38]

Nixon's memorandum reveals much about his understanding of Lyndon Johnson's Rolling Thunder air campaign against North Vietnam—few pilots who flew against the North during the Johnson presidency would have categorized their missions as "milk runs"; furthermore, the targets bombed during Linebacker were virtually identical to those attacked during Rolling Thunder. The difference was that in 1972 the nature of the war had changed from guerrilla warfare to conventional operations. Destroying those targets had a tremendous impact on an army waging a fast-paced conventional war. Still, Nixon's critique contained a kernel of truth. The joint chiefs had all been high-ranking officers during the Johnson administration, and they had experienced firsthand the mind-numbing frustration of trying to conduct an air war constrained by a multitude of political restrictions. Thus, the proposal originally submitted to Nixon was one more suited to Johnson, whose continued restraints had removed a measure of aggressiveness from America's military leaders.

Compared to Rolling Thunder, Nixon's four-month Linebacker campaign was limited by few political controls, and the bombing wreaked havoc on rail lines and roads leading to China. Yet the real keys to halting the Easter Offensive were stiffening ARVN (Army of the Republic of Vietnam) resistance with massive doses of air power in South Vietnam. By summer the North Vietnamese attack had sputtered, and Linebacker began to have a telling effect as the dwindling supply of stockpiled goods failed to satisfy the needs of the NVA. Kissinger persuaded Nixon to resume negotiations in July, and the North Vietnamese accepted the invitation. The president, however, now put little stock in obtaining a negotiated agreement before the election. The overwhelming success of the Moscow summit, which the Soviets had refused to cancel despite the increased bombing, and the foundering campaign of Democratic Party nominee George McGovern left only the magnitude of Nixon's victory in doubt. The president realized that peace in Vietnam was no longer essential to his success in November. "We have reached the stage where the mere *fact* of private talks helps us very little—if at all," he scribbled on Kissinger's 14 August report from Paris.[39] A week earlier, Nixon, believing that bombing was not having the necessary impact, had once again enlarged the air campaign against North Vietnam. At his direction, three of the six carriers in the Tonkin Gulf began devoting all of their strike sorties to Linebacker, while the Air Force started scheduling a minimum of forty-eight strike sorties a day above the 20th parallel.[40] Nixon had decided that *he* would end the war in his own way, and that he would do it by hammering North Vietnam into submission with air power. A negotiated peace before the election, he concluded, would be unlikely to secure the same terms he could obtain after receiving a new mandate.[41] Then he could finally play the Mad Bomber.

Kissinger disagreed with Nixon's strategy, and the discord marked the beginning of a rift that would profoundly affect the president's subsequent applications of air power. "Nixon and I both sought to end the war as rapidly as possible. But there was a nuance of difference between us over the strategy for doing so," Kissinger understated in his memoirs.[42] The national security adviser appeared to score a breakthrough in Paris on 8 October, when Le Duc Tho dropped his demand for a coalition government in South Vietnam and agreed to an in-place cease-fire followed by the withdrawal of remaining American troops. Tho's concessions conformed to the conditions for a cease-fire outlined in the president's 8 May televised address, but Nixon refused to curtail the bombing of North Vietnam significantly until the North Vietnamese set a specific date for signing the agreement.[43] Kissinger meanwhile journeyed to Saigon to obtain South Vietnamese President Nguyen Van Thieu's concurrence on the proposed settlement. On 19 October, for the first time, Thieu saw the draft agreement's text.[44] He was outraged over the provisions allowing North Vietnamese troops to remain in the South and creating a "National Council of Reconciliation and Concord," containing Communist representation, that would monitor future South Vietnamese elections. Thieu saw this last condition as the possible germ of a coalition government, something he was opposed to from the beginning. He deemed the agreement intolerable unless it included sixty-nine changes. Nixon refused to accept the accord without Thieu's endorsement and requested an additional meeting in Paris between Tho and Kissinger. "As a token of good will," the president suspended air attacks above the 20th parallel. "But," he recalled, "there was to be no bombing *halt* until the agreement was signed. I was not going to be taken in by the mere prospect of an agreement as Johnson had been in 1968."[45]

While frustrated by Thieu's refusal to support the accord, Nixon sympathized with the South Vietnamese leader's rationale. Nearly the entire NVA was now in South Vietnam, and Thieu would have to face that force alone after an American withdrawal. Nixon assured him that "there will be no settlement arrived at, the provisions of which have not been discussed personally with you well beforehand."[46] The North Vietnamese also realized that Thieu's concern prevented Nixon from signing the accord. On 26 October, Radio Hanoi broadcast the previously secret record of the Kissinger-Tho negotiations, including the text of the draft peace agreement. North Vietnam condemned "the Nixon Administration's lack of good will and seriousness," and called for a signing of the accord on 31 October, the date originally scheduled.[47]

To counter Hanoi's charges, Kissinger conducted a press conference—his first ever on national television—that produced the declaration, "We believe peace is at hand." A mood of euphoria swept the United States, as most Americans took the announcement to mean that a final peace in Vietnam was only days away. Nixon had warned Kissinger not to discuss the anticipated timing of the agreement, believing that such an admission might be viewed as a "political gimmick" on the eve of the election.[48] By the end of October, however, Nixon's 25-percentage point lead in the polls had removed all doubt about the outcome of the presidential race. Still, Nixon was far from pleased by the actions of his national security adviser. Upon learning that Kissinger, after returning from Paris, had leaked information about the negotiations to Max Frankel of the *New York Times,* Nixon seethed with anger.[49] Furthermore, polls showed Kissinger's popularity following his press conference was almost as great as Nixon's, causing the president to whisper to Charles Colson: "I suppose now everybody's going to say that Kissinger won the election."[50] Nixon, it would appear, had begun to believe Kissinger's success in

Paris would rob him of the acclaim that he deserved for ending the war, and he intended to ensure that the American public knew in no uncertain terms who merited the credit for achieving peace.

In his memoirs, Kissinger acknowledged he and Nixon had indeed begun to spar for the title of peacemaker. "The publicity I received caused him to look for ways of showing that he was in charge," Kissinger wrote, "even while usually endorsing the strategy *I* devised."[51] The national security adviser's ego was at least as large as the president's, and Kissinger noted that his "peace is at hand" press conference was "a moment of unusual pride not leavened by humility."[52] Kissinger could also sense his newfound limelight portended the end of his tenure as presidential assistant. In an interview with Italian journalist Orina Fallaci, published in mid-November, he likened himself to a Henry Fonda–character in Western movies. "This cowboy doesn't have to be courageous," Kissinger explained. "All he needs is to be alone, to show others that he rides into the town and does everything himself."[53] Nixon boiled after hearing about the interview. He concluded that the time had come for his national security adviser to return to Harvard. "Kissinger will be leaving in six or eight months," the president told Colson. "It's not good for a man to stay too long in that position; it will be better for Henry. Time for him to get back to other things."[54]

In the midst of the growing rift with Kissinger and the breakdown of negotiations in Paris, Nixon scored the predicted landslide reelection victory. Yet the victory was not total; the president's coattails were short and both houses of Congress remained firmly under Democratic control. This failure of Republicans to make significant advances in Congress boded ill for Vietnam. Earlier, on 24 July, an amendment insisting on an American withdrawal in return for a prisoner release had passed the Senate by five votes before failing in the House. Nixon was now certain that if he did not end the war by the time Congress convened in early January, then the Democrats would cut all appropriations for South Vietnam, thus leaving Thieu to face a future Communist assault without any American aid.[55] Nixon had no intention of allowing that to happen. Negotiations were to resume in Paris on 20 November—Nixon believed that his commitment to Thieu necessitated an attempt to include the South Vietnamese leader's demands into the peace agreement—but the president had little faith the effort would bear fruit. Moreover, Nixon feared a negotiated settlement without a further display of presidential resolve would portray Kissinger as primarily responsible for ending the war. That, too, Nixon could not allow.

One option remained that would solve all his problems—air power. This time, though, its application would be on a scale heretofore unknown in Vietnam. B-52s would hammer Hanoi, and the relentless pounding would compel the North Vietnamese to sign an agreement permitting him to beat the perceived congressional threat to end the war. At the same time, the bombing would demonstrate to Thieu that any future North Vietnamese violations of the accord would produce similar results. Finally, the air assault would show Nixon, the commander in chief, playing the decisive role in achieving peace and would make Kissinger's concluding efforts appear a mere formality.

Five days before the election, Nixon had hinted of things to come. He ordered B-52s to begin attacking north of the Demilitarized Zone (DMZ), and two days later the North Vietnamese agreed to meet with Kissinger on 20 November in Paris. There, Le Duc Tho shunned most of Thieu's proposed modifications to the agreement and revoked concessions made in October. Kissinger notified Nixon they had two options: They could break off the talks and begin bombing, or they could determine a minimum "fall-back" position on Thieu's main points and present them to Le Duc Tho as a final offer. The second option, if accepted, would produce an agreement "optically" better than that negotiated in October.[56] While Nixon contends his national security adviser recommended the first option, Kissinger asserts in his memoirs that he preferred the second.[57] Apparently, Kissinger still believed he could secure a settlement. He recalled: "I favored resumption of bombing north of the twentieth parallel only if the talks broke down altogether, and we had not yet reached that point."[58] Nixon, meanwhile, was reluctant to begin bombing Hanoi until he could clearly blame North Vietnamese intransigence for the breakdown of talks.[59] The president had another concern as well—Thieu remained opposed to an agreement that did not incorporate all his demands. Nixon had dispatched Haig to Saigon in mid-November, and the general had warned Thieu of the danger from Congress if he persisted in opposing the October settlement. Yet Nixon did not believe that the time had arrived for Thieu to acquiesce to the October terms. The president penned in his diary: "Of course, we may come to the hard place where we simply have to tell Thieu it's this or else, but this does not need to come at this moment."[60]

Nixon realized time *was* running out. After a negotiating session on 25 November failed to make headway, he ordered Kissinger to ask for a recess in the talks until 4 December. Le Duc Tho approved the request, and Kissinger returned to Washington. The national security adviser remained optimistic he could secure an agreement, telling Nixon there was a 70-30 chance that he could have an accord "wrapped up" by the evening of 5 December.[61] Throughout the latest round of negotiations, Kissinger's stock remained high with both the public and the press; *Washington Post* columnist Tom Braden reported on 25 November that Nixon had "undercut" Kissinger's peace efforts prior to the election.[62] The president was not about to tolerate the perception that Kissinger called his own shots at the bargaining table. On 29 November, Nixon scribbled notes for a meeting with Nguyen Phu Duc, Thieu's personal representative at the Paris talks. He began: "Negotiations have been at my personal direction. K[issinger] and Haig have not made one move I have not personally authorized. I am frankly distressed to see stories to [the] effect [that] they exceed authority." The time had come, Nixon determined, to let Thieu know that he could no longer continue to dig in his heels over the specific terms of an agreement. "Your concern is [to get] all [North Vietnamese] troops out of [the] South," Nixon scrawled. "The American people will not support war for that. Congress will not approve. I will not order it." The president stated that Kissinger would return to Paris for one final session to conclude a settlement resembling the October accord. Nixon directed his national security adviser to seek such an agreement without delay, writing "I will not change." If Thieu accepted the accord and the North Vietnamese violated its terms, Nixon would respond with "massive retaliation." If Thieu refused to endorse the settlement, then he "must go alone."[63]

Having decided to give Kissinger a final chance in Paris and Thieu an opportunity to join ranks, the president steeled himself for the difficult days ahead. He viewed his actions as proper but inevitable, given the situation he faced. He noted in his diary, "We enter a very tough week and a very crucial one, but some way I think it's got to come out because the great forces of history—what is really right—are moving us in those directions. Only insanity and irrationality of some leaders may move us in other directions."[64] If "insanity and irrationality" prevailed, Nixon was ready for it. On 30 November, he met with the Joint Chiefs of Staff in the Oval Office. "The President, Kissinger, and Al Haig already were in their armchairs when we Chiefs trooped in, sober of mien, highly beribboned, and, I fear, a little like performing poodles or trained seals," remembered Adm. Elmo Zumwalt, Chief of Naval Operations. Nixon told the Chiefs he was on the verge of a peace agreement in Vietnam, and they should "not worry about the words. We will keep the agreement if it serves us," the president continued, and he instructed the Chiefs to prepare contingency plans in case the North Vietnamese violated the accord. Nixon further stated he would renew mining and bomb Hanoi with B-52s if the North Vietnamese got "hardnosed" and refused to negotiate. The bombing would continue for three to six days.[65]

On 3 December, Kissinger returned to Paris. His hope of concluding a settlement in two days soon vanished. Le Duc Tho withdrew the minor concessions he had made in November while maintaining all his demands for changes. Nixon had anticipated the stonewalling, and smugly observed in his diary: "What happened here is that Henry went back to Paris firmly convinced that he would quickly . . . reach agreement with the North Vietnamese. . . . The North Vietnamese surprised him by slapping him in the face with a wet fish."[66] The president had also just learned both he and Kissinger were to be named *Time* magazine's "Men of the Year," and he smarted over having to share the acclaim with his deputy.[67]

Le Duc Tho offered Kissinger one alternative to hammering out a completely new agreement: sign the original October accord. That choice was unacceptable to Nixon. Although the concessions made by Tho in November were largely cosmetic, both Nixon and Kissinger deemed them significant because they incorporated at least some of Thieu's desires.[68] The president informed Kissinger that if the next meeting did not produce a breakthrough, he would begin bombing Hanoi. As if by cue, Le Duc Tho returned to the table advancing concessions, but at the same time he rejected the previously accepted stipulation respecting the DMZ as a provisional boundary between North and South Vietnam. "This was precisely where Le Duc

Tho wanted us," Kissinger recalled, "tantalizingly close enough to an agreement to keep us going and prevent us from using military force, but far enough away to maintain the pressures that might yet at the last moment achieve Hanoi's objectives of disintegrating the political structure in Saigon."[69]

Believing that Le Duc Tho sought to stall the negotiations until Congress convened in January, Kissinger now called for the bombing option. After his session on 4 December, he wired Nixon: "Start the bombing immediately. These madmen have doublecrossed us. Go on national television tomorrow night and announce to the American people that we're resuming bombing of the North."[70] Nixon agreed he would ultimately have to respond with bombs, yet he wanted to ensure that the North Vietnamese received full blame for the breakdown of negotiations before he began his air attack. He directed Kissinger to continue the talks until reaching an insurmountable impasse. Meanwhile, the president met with Adm. Thomas Moorer, chairman of the joint chiefs. When Nixon asked Moorer for his opinion on resuming the bombing, the admiral responded that he believed that additional air strikes would have an impact on the North Vietnamese only if an agreement were concluded first, and then violated by Hanoi.[71] While Nixon could perhaps take morbid satisfaction in the failure of his twentieth-century Metternich to make good on "peace is at hand," he had to be dismayed by Moorer's doubts about the effectiveness of his projected air campaign.

On 13 December, Kissinger reported that American linguistic experts had discovered that the North Vietnamese had inserted seventeen changes into the completed portion of the agreement's text. Tho proved inflexible regarding the additions. Kissinger called again for immediate bombing, and Nixon agreed that the time had finally arrived for military force. The president recalled his national security adviser to Washington for consultations. On the morning of 14 December, Nixon, Kissinger, and Haig—no member of the joint chiefs was present—met to determine a course of action.[72] Kissinger recommended a return to October's Linebacker operations, while Haig's argument mirrored the president's—B-52s must attack Hanoi. "Anything less will only make the enemy contemptuous," Nixon asserted.[73] He would now demonstrate that he was in complete control of the situation in Vietnam, and he would risk almost certain condemnation from the world press and the American public to make his point. He ordered a three-day series of B-52 strikes against Hanoi to begin on 17 December, which would be the eighteenth in Vietnam.

Nixon's call for a great emphasis on B-52s took Admiral Moorer by surprise. The joint chiefs had devised an air offensive that included B-52s, but not of the magnitude the president envisioned. "In this case," Moorer later explained, "we refined a plan significantly, and in the process, brought into play a heavy use of the B-52s."[74] The admiral notified the commander in chief of Strategic Air Command, Air Force Gen. J. C. Meyer, of Nixon's desired use of B-52s with the stipulation civilian casualties must be avoided. "I want the people of Hanoi to hear the bombs," Moorer told Meyer, "but minimize damage to the civilian populace."[75] SAC then assumed responsibility for developing the new plan. In August 1972, Meyer had anticipated the possibility of an all-out assault by B-52s against Hanoi and directed Lt. Gen. Gerald Johnson, commander of the Eighth Air Force on Guam, to prepare a plan for such an operation. Johnson had forwarded his proposal to SAC Headquarters in November.[76] Meyer, however—for reasons that remain unclear—chose to disregard the Eighth Air Force plan, which called for attacks against Hanoi with multiple bomber formations simultaneously approaching the city from different directions. He ordered his staff at Offutt Air Force Base, Neb., to devise a new operation. Nixon's requirement for the bombing to begin in three days gave SAC planners minimum time to construct the air offensive.

In the interim, the president pondered his decision. Late on the evening of 15 December, he scrawled notes for a news conference that Kissinger was to give the next day. "We had [an] agreement," he wrote. "They have backed off. We must get this nailed down. . . . We will not be pushed around." Nixon refused to announce the coming escalation or the requirements for a bombing halt, believing that such a declaration would delay further talks by appearing to Hanoi as an ultimatum. The time had come, however, to present one to Thieu. "S. V. Nam has not cooperated—(must cooperate)," he penned.[77] Nixon decided to send Haig back to Saigon in a final attempt to gain Thieu's support for a settlement. Haig departed on the eighteenth, carrying a letter stating: "General Haig's mission now represents my final effort to point out to you the necessity for joint action and convey my irrevocable intention to proceed, preferably with your cooperation, but, if necessary, alone." Nixon further warned that an increase in American military pressure against the North would not indicate a willingness to achieve total victory over Hanoi.[78]

Shortly before Haig left for Saigon, the "Christmas bombings" began. Under the code name Linebacker II, three waves of B-52s containing at least forty bombers each attacked storage complexes, rail yards, and airfields on the outskirts of Hanoi during the evening of 18 December. SAC planners had forged an operation containing little versatility; all three waves of bombers attacked by flying the same routes to target at the same altitude. Eighth Air Force staff officers on Guam were shocked by the repetitive routing, and some members of General Johnson's staff predicted losses as high as 16 to 18 percent.[79] Meyer's own prediction was 3 percent, based partly on the Single Integrated Operations Plan (SIOP), which was the plan for thermonuclear war with the Soviet Union. "General Meyer took the SIOP model estimates, tempered them with his own judgment, and that of his staff, and perhaps put some political English on the final estimates he passed out," recalled Brig. Gen. Harry Cordes, SAC's Deputy Chief of Staff for Intelligence.[80] Losses for 18 December actually totaled three B-52s shot down, all by surface-to-air missiles (SAMs), and two heavily damaged, out of an attacking force of 129 bombers.

Nixon sullenly awaited a report of the strikes,[81] and later confessed that sending the B-52s against Hanoi was his most difficult decision during the Vietnam War.[82] But the bravado that he had exhibited in the spring soon reappeared. On the nineteenth, he extended Linebacker II indefinitely. He also railed at Moorer: "I don't want any more of this crap about the fact that we couldn't hit this target or that one. This is your chance to use military power effectively to win this war, and if you don't, I'll consider you responsible."[83] Although disappointed by the downed B-52s, Nixon confessed to his diary: "We simply have to take losses if we are going to accomplish our objectives."[84] Less than twelve hours before the B-52s started bombing, the president had sent a message to Hanoi in which he proposed a return to the agreement's November text with the addition of one or two subsequently negotiated changes. "On that basis," Kissinger would be prepared to meet again with Le Duc Tho any time after 26 December.[85] Besides forcing the North Vietnamese to negotiate "in good faith," Nixon hoped the bombing would convince Thieu that the promise of future support contained teeth. Now, the president believed, it was up to him to ensure the air offensive continued at the level needed to produce results.

Linebacker II's second and third days paralleled its first in both weight of effort and routes of flight. On 19 December, three waves of B-52s again attacked military targets on the outskirts of Hanoi. SAMs damaged two bombers, but none were shot down. On the twentieth, ninety-nine B-52s attacked rail yards, storage areas, and the Thai Nguyen Thermal Power Plant. Against this force the North Vietnamese achieved their greatest triumph of the campaign, destroying six B-52s and damaging a seventh. The losses infuriated Nixon, who "raised holy hell about the fact that [B-52s] kept going over the same targets at the same times."[86] The president contends in his memoirs that he persuaded the "military to change their minds" about the repetitive routing,[87] but his assertion is not entirely accurate. General Meyer also realized a 6 percent loss rate was unacceptable, especially when one considers the B-52s also had the vital role as the manned leg of the strategic nuclear deterrent triad. After another attack against Hanoi on the twenty-first, in which two bombers out of thirty were shot down, he temporarily forbade additional raids against the North Vietnamese capital. Meyer further turned over responsibility for planning the attacks to General Johnson on Guam. Johnson's staff orchestrated a massive raid for 26 December, following a thirty-six hour Christmas standdown, that conformed to the plan they had originally submitted to SAC Headquarters in the fall.[88]

The impetus for the 26 December attack came from Nixon. He had hoped that the North Vietnamese would answer the Christmas-day reprieve by offering to resume negotiations, but Hanoi remained silent. On 22 December, he had requested a return to negotiations on 3 January and had offered to halt bombing north of the 20th parallel for the duration of the talks. Although urged by some members of his staff to continue the Christmas truce, Nixon concluded that only continued pounding would bring the North Vietnamese back to Paris. As a result, he personally ordered a large-scale assault for the twenty-sixth.[89] The raid was Linebacker II's most ambitious. Instead of attacking through the night as had bombers on the first three days, 120 B-52s struck ten different targets in Hanoi and Haiphong by attacking from nine different directions in a fifteen-minute span. A multitude of SAMs streaked through the dark sky, revealing that Hanoi's defenders had used the five-day intermission to bolster their armaments. Still, only two bombers were shot down, a loss rate of 1.66 percent.

On the morning of 27 December, Hanoi notified Nixon that talks could resume in Paris on 8 January. The North Vietnamese asserted that Le Duc Tho's ill-health prevented earlier discussions. Before the president replied, Hanoi sent another message expressing a desire to resume technical talks after the cessation of bombing and emphasizing that Le Duc Tho would meet Kissinger on 8 January. Nixon answered on the twenty-seventh that discussions between Kissinger and Tho's experts must begin on 2 January. Formal negotiations would start on the eighth with a time limit attached, and the North Vietnamese would agree not to deliberate on matters covered by the basic settlement. If Hanoi accepted these procedures, Nixon stated he would end bombing north of the 20th parallel within thirty-six hours. Meanwhile, Linebacker II's fury continued. Sixty B-52s attacked targets near Hanoi on both 27 and 28 December using the varied routing begun on the twenty-sixth. Two bombers, the campaign's final losses, fell to SAMs on the night of the twenty-seventh. On 28 December, the North Vietnamese accepted Nixon's conditions for renewed talks. The president stopped bombing the North Vietnamese capital after a final raid on the night of 29 December.

Less than one month later, Secretary of State William P. Rogers signed an agreement ending America's active participation in the Vietnam War. The accord was essentially that negotiated by Kissinger the previous October, although it did contain cosmetic differences stemming from Thieu's demands. Nixon believed that air power had been the key to securing the settlement. After receiving word on 28 December that Hanoi had accepted his conditions for a return to Paris, he exuberantly told Colson, "The North Vietnamese have agreed to go back to the negotiating table on our terms. They can't take bombing any longer. Our Air Force really did the job."[90]

But *exactly* what had Nixon's application of air power against North Vietnam accomplished? *Was* it the decisive element that ended America's war in Vietnam? Certainly it had hurt the NVA. It did not, however, single-handedly stem the Easter Offensive. The horrendous pounding inflicted upon the Communist forces in *South* Vietnam, largely accomplished by B-52s, was primarily responsible for halting the assault. Linebackers I and II, together with mining, then prevented North Vietnamese troops from receiving the logistical support that was vital as long as they persisted in waging conventional war—which they did throughout the remainder of the year. Had the North Vietnamese reverted to guerrilla warfare in the summer of 1972, as was their pattern after a failed offensive, the Linebacker campaigns would have had a meager impact on their war-fighting capability. Nixon's offer of an in-place cease-fire, in which territory captured would remain under Communist control, probably persuaded Hanoi to continue waging an aggressive war of movement, and thus made both Linebackers extremely effective. In all likelihood, the desire to preserve the NVA helped induce the Hanoi leadership to sign an agreement in January 1973. Observed Gen. Tran Van Tra, commander of Communist forces in the southern half of South Vietnam, after having undergone nine months of continual bombing: "Our cadres and men were fatigued, we had not had time to make up for our losses, all units were in disarray, there was a lack of manpower, and there were shortages of food and ammunition. . . . The troops were no longer capable of fighting."[91] Moreover, the North Vietnamese knew American war aims were limited. Whereas Johnson had sought a free and independent South Vietnam and operations such as Rolling Thunder were to help achieve that goal, Nixon's aim in the Linebacker campaigns was to end American participation in the war, and he had no intention of committing additional troops. Attempting to score an eleventh-hour victory over the United States, they had gambled that Nixon would not respond with Linebacker II. Although the bid failed, Hanoi's leaders remained firmly committed to unifying the two Vietnams. The agreement signed in January 1973 gave them secure bases in the South from which they could pursue that goal.

Other factors were important in securing a settlement. Nixon's 1972 trips to Peking and Moscow, perhaps the greatest accomplishments of his presidency, caused both the Chinese and Soviets to sacrifice support for North Vietnam to achieve warmer relations with the United States. The president's exploitation of the rift between China and the Soviet Union paid immediate dividends in Vietnam: the Soviets refused to ship additional supplies through the mines of Haiphong harbor, and the Chinese, for three weeks after the mining began, prohibited the shipment of Soviet goods to North Vietnam via Chinese railways.[92] In a 17 August 1972 editorial, Hanoi's newspaper *Nhan Dan* bitterly noted that Nixon's detente had saved South Vietnam from defeat. The failure of China and the Soviet Union to provide North Vietnam with adequate assistance, the newspaper stated, equated to "throwing a life-buoy to a drowning pirate . . . in order to serve one's narrow national interests."[93]

Besides limiting Hanoi's support from the Communist superpowers, Nixon's successful diplomacy eliminated the threat of Chinese or Soviet intervention in Vietnam. That prospect had plagued Lyndon Johnson's Vietnam decision-making, and its absence allowed Nixon to remove many of the political restraints on bombing that had limited Rolling Thunder. During both Linebackers, Air Force and Navy chiefs could, for the most part, choose their own targets and attack them as they thought best. Yet Nixon was often disturbed by what he looked upon as his military leaders' lack of aggressiveness, and the proposals he originally received for both Linebacker I and Linebacker II did not suit his desire for intensive bombing. In particular, the joint chiefs failed to realize Nixon wanted Linebacker II to be a massive B-52 assault. Despite the president's guidance on 30 November, Admiral Moorer nevertheless directed planning for an operation similar to Linebacker I, in which Air Force and *Navy* fighters would play a primary role.[94] Even after adding large-scale B-52 raids, the joint chiefs still included significant numbers of fighter attacks in the final Linebacker II plan, most of which were prevented by monsoon weather that did not affect the B-52s flying at high altitudes. As for B-52 planning, General Meyer dismissed the original Eighth Air Force proposal and chose to go with his own scheme. Major George Thompson, a staff officer at SAC Headquarters, recalled that when Linebacker II began the commanders of both Pacific Command (PACOM) and MACV wanted to control the strikes, as they did for B-52 raids over South Vietnam. General Meyer "told them to go to hell," Major Thompson remembered. "This was his war, and this was out of MACV's jurisdiction, and he was not under CINCPAC."[95] The record shows air commanders not only limited their thinking, at least partly as a result of having endured Lyndon Johnson's political constraints on bombing, but that the "Rolling Thunder mindset" also led them to compete for the right to render the "knockout blow" against North Vietnam.

Given these propensities of his military chiefs, Nixon's 1972 imitation of Patton was not entirely unjustified. Yet Nixon viewed bombing as far more than simply a means to end the war—it was a way for *him* to end the war, a way for him to steal the limelight from Kissinger. In that regard, Linebacker II was an unqualified success. Nixon silently withstood a barrage of criticism from Democratic congressmen and the world press, exemplified by a *New York Times* editorial entitled "Shame on Earth," and an accusation from Hamburg's *Die Zeit* that Linebacker II was "a crime against humanity."[96] In truth the Christmas bombings were remarkably accurate, causing, by North Vietnam's own admission, 1,623 civilian deaths in Hanoi and Haiphong.[97] Kissinger had initially disapproved of the heavy use of B-52s and worked hard to dissociate himself from Linebacker II. The national security adviser allowed friends to inform newspapers that he opposed the bombing,[98] and the press responded by heaping all the blame on Nixon. Kissinger's duplicity enraged the president, who ordered Colson to have the Secret Service keep a record of all incoming and outgoing calls at Kissinger's home in Palm Springs, where he retreated throughout much of late December.[99] Nonetheless, in placing the onus of the Christmas bombings squarely on Nixon's shoulders, Kissinger enabled Nixon to maintain that his forceful leadership was primarily responsible for ending American involvement in Vietnam.

Thieu was likely gratified by Linebacker II, but the bombing did not immediately cause him to support an agreement. He held out until literally the last moment. Only after receiving a further browbeating in mid-January from Nixon through Haig, who assured Thieu that Congress would instantly terminate funding after the settlement if he refused to endorse it,[100] did the South Vietnamese leader reluctantly agree to go along. Linebacker II's role in inducing Thieu to support the accord remains a matter of conjecture.

To Nixon and many of the war's air commanders, Linebacker II was the decisive element of American military power that ended a long and frustrating conflict. Yet the results obtained by Nixon's bombing of North Vietnam—which, we must remember, occurred in an election year—were largely fortuitous, owing at least as much to Hanoi's decision to wage conventional war, and Nixon's superpower diplomacy, as they did to Nixon the Mad Bomber. The situation had changed; the circumstances were different; it was not 1962 or 1965 or 1968. The objective had become to put points on the board before leaving the game, and air power helped Nixon manage a last-minute field goal. But seconds remained, and only history will reveal the final score.

Notes

1. Transcript of Nixon's 20 January 1972 speech to his cabinet, in William Safire, *Before the Fall: An Inside View of the Pre-Watergate White House* (Garden City, N.Y.: Doubleday, 1975), 533.

2. Observed Nixon in his most recent autobiographical work: "A day did not pass during my years in the White House that I did not hate the war in Vietnam." See Richard Nixon, *In the Arena: A Memoir of Victory, Defeat, and Renewal* (New York: Simon & Schuster, 1990), 337.

3. Lyndon Johnson had halted all bombing of North Vietnam at the end of October 1968 in exchange for Hanoi's "agreement" to negotiate seriously and to halt the movement of men and supplies across the DMZ, cease attacks on South Vietnam's major cities, and stop attacks on American reconnaissance aircraft.

4. H. R. Haldeman, *The Ends of Power* (New York: Dell, 1978), 121–22. The North Vietnamese "will believe any threat of force that Nixon makes because it's Nixon," Nixon told Haldeman during the 1968 election campaign.

5. Richard Nixon, *RN: The Memoirs of Richard Nixon*, 2 vols. (New York: Warner Books, 1978), 2:259.

6. Ibid., 79.

7. Transcript of NBC's "Meet the Press," 10 April 1988.

8. Kissinger told White House staffers on 26 April 1972, before Nixon's speech on Vietnam: "When we are down to a certain number [of troops], we will stay there until the prisoners of war are released." See "Briefing by Dr. Kissinger to Members of the White House Staff," Folder 2, General Speech Material, Box 44, Al Haig Collection, White House Special Files, Nixon Presidential Materials Project (NPMP), Alexandria, Va.

9. Douglas Pike, *PAVN: People's Army of North Vietnam* (Novato, Calif.: Presidio, 1986), 223.

10. Ibid., 224. The war in South Vietnam following the 1968 Tet Offensive, until the start of the 1972 Easter invasion, was analogous to that waged before Tet. On the eve of the 1968 Tet Offensive, the Communist army in South Vietnam consisted of approximately 245,000 Vietcong and 55,000 NVA troops. This entire force fought an average of only one day in 30 and had a total daily supply requirement of roughly 380 tons. Of this amount, the Communists needed only 34 tons a day from sources outside the South, a requirement that could be transported by seven 2½-ton trucks. This amount was less than 1 percent of the daily tonnage imported into North Vietnam (5,700 tons), which had a capacity to import 17,200 tons a day. See Headquarters USAF, *Analysis of Effectiveness of Interdiction in Southeast Asia, Second Progress Report*, May 1966, Air Force Historical Research Center (AFHRC), Maxwell AFB, Ala., File K168.187-21, 7; Senate Preparedness Subcommittee, *Air War Against North Vietnam*, 90th Cong., 1st sess., 25 August 1967, pt.4:299; Rostow to president, 6 May 1967, Folder 2EE, Box 75, Country File: Vietnam, National Security Files, Lyndon Baines Johnson Presidential Library, Austin, Tex.; and *The Pentagon Papers*, Senator Gravel Edition (Boston: Beacon Press, 1971), 4:146.

11. Nixon's bombing of North Vietnam reduced overland imports from 160,000 tons a month to 30,000 tons a month, while mining decreased seaborne imports from more than 250,000 tons a month to near zero. See U. S. House, Committee on Appropriations, Subcommittee on DOD, *DOD Appropriations: Bombings of North Vietnam*, Hearings, 93d Cong., 1st sess., 9–18 January 1973, 43, and Robert N. Ginsburgh, "North Vietnam—Air Power," *Vital Speeches of the Day* 38 (15 September 1972): 734.

12. Herbert S. Parmet, *Richard Nixon and His America* (Boston: Little, Brown, 1990), 20.

13. Nixon, *RN,* 1:189.

14. Ibid., 357–58.

15. Between 18 March 1969 and 26 May 1970, B-52s flew 4,308 missions against Cambodian targets

and dropped 120,578 tons of ordnance. See Carl Berger, ed., *The United States in Southeast Asia, 1961–1973: An Illustrated Account* (Washington, D.C.: Office of Air Force History, 1984), 141.

16. In 1969, pilots flew 285 sorties against North Vietnamese targets; in 1970, they flew 1,113. See Guenter Lewy, *America in Vietnam* (New York: Oxford University Press, 1978), 406–7.

17. Headquarters, 7th Air Force, *7 AF History of Linebacker Operations, 10 May 1972–23 October 1972,* n.d., AFHRC File K740.04-24, 1.

18. Lavelle to Ryan and Clay, "Daily Wrap-Up," 10 February 1972, in *Pave Aegis and Other Miscellaneous Messages, June 1971–June 1972,* AFHRC File K717.03-219, vol. 5.

19. Ibid., 3–6; *Air War—Vietnam* (New York: Arno Press, 1978), 115–25; James R. McCarthy and George B. Allison, *Linebacker II: A View from the Rock* (Maxwell AFB, Ala.: Air War College, 1979), 11.

20. "The New Air War in Vietnam," *U.S. News and World Report,* 24 Apr. 1972, 15.

21. Seymour M. Hersh, *The Price of Power: Kissinger in the Nixon White House* (New York: Summit Books, 1983), 508.

22. "Nixon Bombing Recorded in Tape," *New York Times,* 30 June 1974.

23. Hersh, 506.

24. Fawn M. Brodie, *Richard Nixon: The Shaping of His Character* (New York: Norton, 1981), 162.

25. Safire, 183.

26. Nixon's handwritten notes, "Vietnam Points to Emphasize," 10 April 1972, Folder: "Monday, 10 April 1972," Box 74, President's Personal File—President's Speech File 1969–1974, NPMP.

27. *Uncoordinated Draft: Linebacker Study, MACV* (20 January 1973), AFHRC File K712.041-19, chap. 2:2.

28. Nixon, *RN,* 2:64.

29. Henry A. Kissinger, *White House Years* (Boston: Little, Brown, 1979), 1118.

30. Nixon, *RN,* 2:65.

31. Elmo R. Zumwalt, Jr., *On Watch: A Memoir* (New York: Quadrangle, 1976), 379–80.

32. Quoted in Hersh, 568.

33. Kissinger, 1176.

34. Nixon, *RN,* 2:81.

35. Ibid., 79–80.

36. Charles W. Colson, *Born Again* (Old Tappan, N.J.: Chosen Books, 1976), 67.

37. Stephen E. Ambrose, *Nixon: The Triumph of a Politician 1962–1972* (New York: Simon & Schuster, 1989), 511–12; Hersh, 510.

38. Nixon, *RN,* 2:85.

39. Kissinger, 1319 (emphasis in original).

40. CINCPAC to COMUSMACV, CINCPACAF, CINCPAFLT, CINCSAC, 090225Z Aug 1972, in *Message Traffic, May-December 1972,* AFHRC File K168.06-229.

41. Ambrose, 595.

42. Kissinger, 1102.

43. On 13 October Nixon reduced the number of daily attack sorties against North Vietnam to 200, but that action produced no reduction in the number of Air Force sorties sent against the North Vietnamese heartland. Three days later, Nixon cut the number of daily strikes to 150, but this measure reduced Air Force strike sorties above the 20th parallel by only 10. See Nixon, *RN,* 2:192–93, and Headquarters, 7th Air Force, *7 AF History of Linebacker Operations,* 32.

44. Tad Szulc, *The Illusion of Peace: Foreign Policy in the Nixon Years* (New York: Viking Press, 1978), 629.

45. Nixon, *RN,* 2:193.

46. Ibid., 188.

47. Kissinger, 1397.

48. Colson, 75.

49. Ibid., 76.

50. Quoted in Hersh, 604.

51. Kissinger, 1409 (emphasis added).

52. Ibid., 1410.

53. Oriana Fallaci, *Interview with History* (Boston: Houghton Mifflin, 1976), 41.

54. Colson, 80.

55. Nixon, *RN,* 2:224, 230; Kissinger, 1416.

56. Nixon, *RN,* 2:226–27.

57. Ibid., 227; Kissinger, 1420.

58. Kissinger, 1421.

59. Nixon, *RN,* 2:234.

60. Ibid., 224.

61. Ibid., 230.

62. Tom Braden, "Vietnam Stalemate," *Washington Post,* 25 Nov. 1972.

63. Nixon's handwritten notes, 29 November 1972, Folder: "November 29, 1972—Vietnam Negotiations," Box 82, President's Personal File—President's Speech File 1969–1974, NPMP.

64. Nixon, *RN,* 2:231.

65. Zumwalt, 412–15.

66. Nixon, *RN,* 2:239.

67. Kissinger observed in his memoirs, "I knew immediately how this would go down with my chief, whose limited capacity for forgiveness surely did not include being upstaged (and being given equal billing as Man of the Year with his Assistant was tantamount to that)" (p. 1455).

68. Ibid., 1429.

69. Ibid., 1435.

70. Quoted in Hersh, 619.

71. Zumwalt, 415.

72. Kissinger, 1447.

73. Nixon, *RN,* 2:242.

74. *DOD Appropriations: Bombings of North Vietnam,* 45.

75. Cordes to McCarthy, n.d., AFHRC File K416-04-13, 3.

76. Interview of Col. Clyde E. Bodenheimer by the author, 7 January 1983, Maxwell AFB, Ala.

77. Nixon's handwritten notes, 15 December 1972, Folder: "December 15, 1972—Vietnam Notes," Box 82, President's Personal File—President's Speech File 1969–1974, NPMP.

78. Nixon, *RN,* 2:245.

79. Interview by the author with a member of General Johnson's staff who preferred to remain anonymous. General Johnson noted in an April 1973 interview that his estimation of losses was "considerably higher" than those predicted by SAC. See USAF Oral History Interview of Lt. Gen. Gerald W. Johnson by Charles K. Hopkins, 3 April 1973, Andersen AFB, Guam, AFHRC File K239.0512-813, 6–7.

80. Cordes to McCarthy, n.d., AFHRC File K416-04-13, 8.

81. Hersh, 621.

82. Nixon, *RN,* 2:242.

83. Ibid.

84. Ibid., 244.

85. Ibid., 245.

86. Ibid., 246.

87. Ibid.

88. McCarthy and Allison, 121; Bodenheimer interview, 7 January 1983. On 21 December, SAC planners likely believed that the acceptable losses of Linebacker II's first two days vindicated the routes of flight they had selected.

89. Nixon, *RN,* 2:250.

90. Colson, 78.

91. Tran Van Tra, *Concluding the 30-Years War* (Ho Chi Minh City, 1982 [in Vietnamese]; reprint ed. [in English], Arlington, Va.: Joint Publications Research Service, 1983), 33, quoted in Gabriel Kolko,

Anatomy of a War: Vietnam, the United States, and the Modern Historical Experience (New York: Pantheon Books, 1985), 444–45.

92. Interview of Walt W. Rostow by the author, Austin, Tex., 23 May 1986. "This was just to let the North Vietnamese know who lived on their border," commented Rostow, who kept in contact with Kissinger after serving as Lyndon Johnson's national security adviser.

93. *Nhan Dan* editorial, 17 August 1972, in Gareth Porter, ed., *Vietnam: The Definitive Documentation of Human Decisions,* 2 vols. (Sanfordville, N.Y.: Earl M. Coleman, 1979), 2:568.

94. McCarthy and Allison, 41.

95. Interview of Maj. George Thompson, USAF, Retired, by the author, 27 October 1982, Omaha, Neb.

96. Tom Wicker, "Shame on Earth," *New York Times,* 26 December 1972; and "Outrage and Relief," *Time,* 8 January 1973, 14.

97. Murray Marder, "North Vietnam: Taking Pride in Punishment," *Washington Post,* 4 Feb. 1973. In contrast, Maj. Gen. Curtis LeMay's B-29s killed an estimated 86,000 civilians in a single raid on Tokyo on the night of 9–10 March 1945.

98. Safire, 668.

99. Colson, 79–80.

100. Nixon, *RN,* 2:261.

Richard Nixon, Vietnam, and the American Home Front

Joan Hoff

It was clearly in Richard Nixon's psychic and political self-interest as president to end the war in Vietnam as soon as possible. Although he came to office committed to negotiating a quick settlement, he ended up expanding and prolonging the conflict. As a result, he could never build a solid home-front consensus behind his handling of the war even though he dramatically reduced U.S. troop involvement through the policy of Vietnamization.

Despite the role of the antiwar movement in the demise of his predecessor in the Oval Office, Nixon never changed his attitudes or policies on Vietnam because of protests. In any case the most intense confrontational activities of the antiwar demonstrators took place between 1965 and 1971, thus affecting the presidency of Lyndon Johnson more than that of Richard Nixon.[1] Nevertheless, the antiwar movement's presence forced him to consider more carefully both the timing and publicity given his military and diplomatic moves than otherwise would have been the case for a wartime president.

In truth, whenever he took action in Vietnam, Nixon faced three "publics" at home, varying in size and influence: (1) a tiny group of eastern intellectuals, journalists—many of whom were influential opinion-makers; (2) students in the antiwar movement; and (3) the general public at large who approved of him as president, but who at the same time became increasingly ambivalent or negative about the war.[2]

Nixon's Vietnam Diplomacy

Nixon viewed the Vietnam War in terms of geopolitical strategy. For both Nixon and National Security Adviser Henry Kissinger, Vietnam symbolized U.S. influence in the Third World which, in turn, formed part of their grand geopolitical design for international relations.

In his book *No More Vietnams*, Nixon argues that the Vietnam War was military, moral, and multinational in scope.[3] Consequently, he first sought to bring military pressure to bear on the North Vietnamese in order to speed up the negotiating process. There is little indication, however, that this approach succeeded because the Vietcong correctly counted on the opposition of the antiwar movement to provide counterpressure. Likewise, Nixon's commitment to the war as a "moral cause" did not ring true as the carnage in that civil war increased despite American troop withdrawals. Finally, the president never succeeded in convincing the country that a rapid departure from Vietnam would "damage American strategic interests" all over the world. So ending the draft and bringing U.S. troops home did not end opposition to the war in Congress. Nixon failed to convince Congress and many Americans that the conflict in this tiny Third World country warranted the military, moral, and multinational importance he attributed to it.

Instead, Nixon allowed his national security adviser to become egocentrically involved in secret negotiations with the North Vietnamese from 4 August 1969 to 25 January 1972, when they finally were made public. In the end, only marginally better terms were reached in 1973 than those that had not been acceptable in 1969. The trade-off between Hanoi's agreement that South Vietnamese President Nguyen Van Thieu could remain in power in return for allowing North Vietnamese troops to remain in place in South Vietnam pales when compared to the additional 20,000 American lives lost during this three-year period—especially considering the inherent weaknesses of the Saigon government by 1973.[4]

On the tenth anniversary of the peace treaty ending the war in Vietnam, Nixon admitted that "Kissinger believed more in the power of negotiation than I did." Nixon also said he "would not have temporized as long" with the negotiation process had he not been "needlessly" concerned with what the Soviets and Chinese might think if the United States pulled out of Vietnam precipitately.[5] Because Nixon saw no way to end the war quickly in 1969 except through overt, massive bombing attacks over North Vietnam that he did not think the general public would tolerate, there was neither peace nor honor for America in Vietnam by the time the war was finally concluded on 27 January 1973. Instead, the war had been expanded into Cambodia and Laos, destabilizing all of Indochina, not simply Vietnam. A plausible argument can be made that Nixon and Kissinger's initial concern about public relations locked them into a compromised military strategy that both prolonged the war and destabilized Indochina.

To most Americans, Vietnam had become a dinner-hour television marathon complete with stylized but disjointed accounts of the conflict, body counts, and an occasional atrocity.[6] Thus, the war in Southeast Asia had to be settled as soon as possible not only to avoid endangering other elements of Nixonian diplomacy and domestic policy but also to relieve an increasingly restive public from its gruesome nightly television dosage.

Polls showing disapproval of the war must be weighed against Nixon's relatively high approval ratings as president. These ratings remained high until Watergate began to affect them in the spring of 1973 *after* the signing of the Paris peace accords ended American participation in the war. But these public opinion polls only tell part of the story about the domestic problems created for Nixon by his prolongation of the Vietnam War and the three publics he faced as long as the war continued.

Nixon Versus Intellectuals and Journalists

From the very beginning of his long public career in 1947, hostility toward Richard Nixon, frequently in the form of vicious humor, always exceeded normal bipartisan political boundaries. Watergate only confirmed his opponents' worst suspicions. In all its various manifestations, this event made all their dire predictions about Nixon over the years appear to be one gigantic self-fulfilling prophecy.

Despite the fact that Nixon's lengthy presence in the political arena had always divided intellectuals, Gallup polls prior to Watergate always indicated that the general public numbered him among the "most admired." Even in the immediate wake of Watergate, he ranked eleventh in a Gallup poll of "Greatest Presidents" and by 1985 that rank had risen to eighth in a nationwide survey.[7] After all, only Franklin D. Roosevelt and Richard Nixon won four out of their five tries as candidates for vice president or president. Any voter younger than forty-six years of age when Nixon resigned in 1974 would have had only one chance to vote in a national election in which Nixon was not running. Columnist Meg Greenfield aptly noted that her generation of Americans who voted for the first time in the 1952 presidential election had spent their entire adult lives voting for or against Richard Nixon:

> The psychological implications of this fact are staggering: half of us have lived our whole adult life as a series of dashed hopes and disappointments, while the other half have passed the same period in a condition of perpetual anxiety over the prospect that he would succeed. . . . What distinguishes us as a group from those who came before and those who have come after is that we are too young to remember a time when Richard Nixon was not on the political scene, and too old reasonably to expect that we shall live to see one.[8]

Since the late 1960s when Greenfield wrote these lines, several other generations of left-of-center intellectuals, scholars, and especially post-Watergate investigative journalists—now in their forties, fifties, and sixties—expressed similar thoughts. It is not unusual for Americans to target political figures, especially presidents, and castigate them. Seldom, however, have so many elite groups of Americans held such negative feelings about a single political figure as they did about Nixon. Writer Victor S. Navasky once concluded: "You can't have voted for Richard Nixon and be a member of the New York intellectual establishment."[9] Their position was adopted by young leaders of the antiwar movement. "It is becoming more obvious with every passing day," wrote columnist David Broder in the *Washington Post* on 7 October 1969, "that the men and the [antiwar] movement that broke Lyndon Johnson's authority in 1968 are out to break Richard Nixon in 1969." Broder wrongly concluded: "The likelihood is great that they will succeed again."[10] But it was not opposition to the war in Vietnam that brought Nixon down. As we all know, it was Nixon himself.

Since the assassination of John F. Kennedy, Americans have figuratively been "shooting down" the man in the Oval Office with great gusto. In 1983, Greenfield argued that the game of "Trashing the President" had become the unofficial national pastime, not only with journalist and intellectuals but also to a lesser degree with the public at large. This practice, she argues, blurred American's ability to make sound judgments about the men who occupy the White House.[11] While Nixon survived criticism of his Vietnam policies at home, his resignation over Watergate in 1974 was viewed by left-of-center intellectuals and journalists and by most members of the then defunct antiwar movement as a vindication of their position.

With the exception of ending the draft and creating an all-volunteer military, practically every action taken by Nixon with respect to Vietnam, including the Vietnamization program for withdrawing U.S. troops, created resentment, suspicion, and opposition from intellectuals and journalists opposed to the war. The dissatisfaction of this powerful, but relatively small, number of upper- and middle-class Americans proved more significant in the steady decline in public approval of the war than did the much more numerous and publicly visible members of the antiwar movement.

General Public Opinion and Foreign Policy

Conventional wisdom would have one believe that since the height of U.S. military participation in Vietnam in the mid-1960s, general public opinion demonstrated a greater ability to influence both foreign and domestic policies than ever before in U.S. history. Conversely, it should be noted that the ability and tendency in Washington to manufacture and manipulate such opinion also increased. More to the point, perhaps, in this debate over the importance of presidential approval ratings is the fact that even mainstream government bureaucrats within the State Department now readily admit the partisan public opinion connection between domestic and foreign policy issues. This relationship was denied in official diplomatic circles when revisionist historians first introduced it in the late 1950s.[12] Nixon was personally well aware of the impact domestic issues could have on foreign policy. After the Watergate revelations began to unfold, his foreign policy became captive to the increasingly negative congressional reaction to this major domestic event. Even before this, he complained to his aides that opponents of the war in Congress often arbitrarily opposed some of his domestic reform bills when they normally would have supported such legislation.[13] Finally, Gallup polls taken since Vietnam indicate that the American public is now much more likely (1) to think about foreign policy issues as important national problems than it was in the late 1940s, 1950s, and 1960s during the height of the Cold War; (2) to question "international activism" (except for short-term military actions such as Grenada and Panama); and (3) to be either more cynical or skeptical about politics and politicians in general.[14] As the military buildup undertaken by the Bush administration during Operation Desert Shield in the Middle East indicated, however, the general public almost always initially reacts favorably to strong demonstrations of strength by the United States.[15]

Because left-of-center intellectuals, journalists, and historians so disliked Nixon,[16] and because he privately expressed concern about his administration's inadequate public relations long before Watergate, it is often concluded that his administration was the most vulnerable to public opinion with regards to the Vietnam War. What is usually forgotten in such conclusions, however, is that as President Nixon was actually less sensitive to public or media criticism than Johnson having been subjected to at least the latter for his entire political career. As one of the most controversial Republican politicians since World War II, Nixon was accustomed to bad press and seldom took criticisms personally the way LBJ did. During his presidency, he thought that such criticism was basically unfair only to the degree that it negatively affected both national security and his domestic programs.

Despite his angry private outbursts and intemperate directness as president (which historians should not take at face value because his closest aides did not), the criticism of eastern elite journalists, intellectuals, and scholars was nothing new to Nixon. It was probably much more difficult for a Democratic president such as Johnson to receive such criticism, and particularly upsetting for a man such as Kissinger whose academic career had been based on courting approval from such groups.[17] With the possible exception of the decisions in February and March of 1969 *not* to begin bombing North Vietnam, none of Nixon's military or diplomatic actions was influenced by any of his three publics. This basic exception notwithstanding, Nixon pursued his most innovative diplomatic ideas regardless of public or media opinion with the dogged determination so characteristic of his entire political career.

In fact, Nixon takes personal pride in his toughness with respect to personal criticism. He consistently denied in public and private interviews that his foreign policy in Indochina or elsewhere was ever influenced, let alone determined by, general public opinion or by his critics in the antiwar movement. A typical example of this attitude can be found in his response to the plans by antiwar leaders for a nationwide Vietnam moratorium on 15 October 1969. He said in a press conference on 26 September: "Now, I understand that there has been and continues to be opposition to the war in Vietnam on the campuses, and also in the nation. . . . As far as this kind of activity is concerned, we expect it. *However, under no circumstances will I be affected whatever by it.*"[18] On the day of the demonstration he reiterated his position: "If a president—any president—allowed his course to be set by those who demonstrate, he would betray the trust of the rest. . . . To allow government policy to be made in the streets would destroy the democratic process. It would give the decision, not to the majority, and not to those with the strongest arguments, but to those with the loudest voices."[19]

Nixon was not totally unjustified in his tough stand on public criticism. After he assumed office in January 1969 his public approval ratings rose to over 65 percent in the spring and summer and then fell to a low of 56 percent just before his major address on Vietnam in the fall of 1969. In the wake of his speech, his approval ratings again rose to almost 70 percent. After another dip in the spring of

1970 with the public announcement of the U.S. incursion into Cambodia on 30 April, Nixon's popularity rose again to over 60 percent.[20] Then, it began to decline throughout the rest of 1970 and into 1971. The 8 February 1971 invasion of Laos did nothing to revive it. However, his trips to China and to the Soviet Union in the first half of 1972 brought it back up to over 60 percent where it remained for the 1972 election, only to plunge with the Christmas bombings of December 1972. Following the announcement of the Paris peace settlement in January 1973, Nixon's approval ratings soared again to almost 70 percent. Thus, in terms of public approval, Nixon survived the Vietnam experience relatively unscathed.

This is not to say that Nixon was impervious to public opinion. In fact, he repeatedly expressed concern to his staff about biased reporting negatively affecting his image and policies. Two examples demonstrate his attitude toward public opinion—namely, the secret bombing of Cambodia and his general reaction to the antiwar movement during his first years in office. In each case the president and some of his advisers confided in each other their concerns about public opinion.

The Secret Decision to Bomb Cambodia

Under President Johnson the Joint Chiefs of Staff (JCS) had repeatedly requested permission to bomb Communist sanctuaries in Cambodia. The last of these requests was to the outgoing Democratic administration on 13 December 1968. The JCS simply reiterated this position to the incoming Republican administration when Nixon, on 21 January 1969, directly asked Gen. Earle G. Wheeler, chairman of the JCS, in National Security Study Memorandum No. 1 (NSSM 1) to provide a "study of the feasibility and utility of quarantining Cambodia against the receipt of supplies and equipment for support of [the] Viet Cong and North Vietnamese Army."[21]

Nixon's carefully guarded decision to bomb Cambodia has to be viewed in relation to the action undertaken by his administration in Vietnam during his first weeks in office. Whether they realized it or not, the JCS had more bargaining power on the question of bombing Cambodia under Nixon than under Johnson. Nixon knew that they were not entirely pleased with his agenda, which included: Vietnamization (turning the bulk of the fighting and management of the war over to the South Vietnamese), the unilateral withdrawal of American troops, stepped up negotiations with the Vietcong and North Vietnamese in Paris, and the establishment of a volunteer military.[22]

Ironically, the JCS found that among Nixon's newly appointed cabinet members, Secretary of Defense Melvin Laird ardently supported American withdrawal from the war by means of Vietnamization and adamantly opposed the bombing of both North Vietnam and Cambodia. Laird believed that bombing would not be popular with Congress, the country, or the United Nations. In the first weeks of March, however, he endorsed the bombing of Cambodian sanctuaries as a better alternative to bombing North Vietnam—an option initially under consideration by the Nixon administration—after the Communists increased attacks against major South Vietnamese cities in February.[23] In this sense, bombing Cambodian sanctuaries became a surrogate for the more drastic option of bombing North Vietnam. At no time, however, did Laird believe that the bombing of Cambodia should be kept secret.

Much to the disdain of John D. Ehrlichman and others close to Nixon, Laird seemed too much the politician on most issues, but particularly this one. Nixon's closest aides attributed Laird's position on getting out of the war through Vietnamization purely to what Ehrlichman pejoratively called "constituency politics"—meaning that Laird was excessively beholden to Congress and the Pentagon.[24] In fact, the greatest weakness of his position was not his personal concern about congressional or military opinion but the fact that his Vietnamization program would take time to implement—a commodity Nixon did not have with respect to his three publics and the war.

By 1969 it would have been next to impossible to court *both* Congress and the Pentagon. Therefore, criticism of Laird for being too politically oriented because he was trying to serve two masters is difficult to accept at face value. Ehrlichman in particular seemed to harbor strong hostility toward Laird for being "impossible to rely on . . . never delivering on a promise . . . in it for himself . . . [and] ingenious to a fault."[25] The impact of such attitudes ultimately weakened Laird's influence within the administration—a condition later exacerbated when Nixon and Kissinger began to deal as much as possible with the JCS and the National Security Council (NSC) behind the backs of both Laird and Secretary of State William Rogers.[26] Nixon's own increasing lack of confidence in Laird was based on the president's opinion that his secretary of defense was a typical Republican "isolationist" wanting to end the fighting quickly "because it was their [the Democrats] war."[27] Others within the administration thought that Laird wanted to end the war rather than win it. Faced with such overwhelming internal opposition, the secretary of defense chose to speak his mind instead of trying to ingratiate himself with Nixon. He asserted that the secret bombing of Cambodia, if it ever were made public, would only further undermine the administration's credibility. Laird therefore sought to document his position as fully as possible.

Laird was the only one to call for a full NSC review of the policy. Among other things, he insisted that "because of the political implications of bombing Cambodia, the entire NSC should review the policy."[28] The NSC meeting on the bombing of Cambodia took place on 18 March, the same day that Laird delivered his own memorandum to the president based on information received from General Wheeler. This was two days after the command decision was made to implement the secret bombing of the Cambodian sanctuaries at a 16 March meeting attended by Rogers, Laird, Wheeler, and Kissinger. At this meeting only Rogers opposed the bombing of Cambodia, and he did so for domestic, not foreign, policy reasons.[29]

Laird's 18 March memorandum provides important insight into the secretary of defense's thinking on the subject. It also forced NSC members to listen one more time to his objections to keeping the Cambodia bombing secret. In his memorandum, Laird noted that while the military had suggested actions "subject to their political acceptability . . . there are international political and legal implications of blockade or quarantine operations" which they did not address. He further informed Nixon that "to assist in this review" he had asked the JCS for more specific information than they had provided for his predecessor about the respective "military effects and risks of each action."[30]

Since General Wheeler authorized the strike on Communist headquarters two days before Laird wrote to the president,[31] one can assume that Nixon decided to approve the secret bombing without the additional information Laird requested from the JCS. It can further be assumed the NSC policy review which did take place was indeed intended by the secretary of defense to set the historical record straight from his point of view and to apply political pressure on the JCS in order to obtain more specific military information. Regardless of precisely when and on what basis the decision was made, the secret B-52 sorties over Cambodia began on 18 March under the general code name Menu with the exact target areas given the unsavory titles of Breakfast, Lunch, Dinner, Supper, Dessert, and Snack. From 17 March 1969 to 26 May 1970, these bombings took place in secret.[32] The question remains—Why?

Some have attributed the secrecy to Nixon's observation of the manner in which Eisenhower, after he was elected president in 1952, had privately threatened to use nuclear weapons if necessary to end the Korean War. This thesis is not very convincing, since there is no documented evidence Nixon ever sent secret nuclear threats to either the North Vietnamese or the Chinese. Moreover, Eisenhower did not suppress information about the escalated bombings he ordered over North Korea in the spring of 1953. More convincing is the argument that fear of triggering new demonstrations and destroying the honeymoon period Nixon unexpectedly experienced from the media until the fall of 1969 influenced the new administration's decision to cover up the initial bombing of Cambodia. Because Nixon's and Kissinger's concerns over public relations apparently prevented them from seriously pushing for the bombing of North Vietnam, they opted to bomb Cambodia and to keep it secret.

President Nixon went on to weather the protests, including the deaths of students at Kent and Jackson State, accompanying the overt bombing and incursion into Cambodia in the spring of 1970 without serious political consequences. (In the following fall midterm elections, the Republicans gained two Senate seats and lost only twelve in the House.) In the spring of 1969, however, Nixon was less sanguine about possibly alienating the general public. He feared further incensing student demonstrators more in his first months in office than he did in 1971 and 1972. By then he had undercut the antiwar movement by following through on his campaign promise to end the draft. Also by August 1972 he had withdrawn all U.S. combat troops from Vietnam, thus removing casualty reports and body counts from the evening news.

Nixon's opposition to antiwar demonstrators and other critics of the war did not trigger secret domestic surveillance and wiretaps. This type of covert and semiconstitutional activity came directly out of Nixon and Kissinger's initial conduct of the war in Vietnam. From May 1969 to May 1970 all domestic FBI wiretap reports were on an elite group of intellectuals and journalists (many of them current or former acquaintances and associates of Kissinger) suspected of being national security risks. Likewise, the initial efforts of the plumbers to "plug" leaks were directed at issues deemed threatening to national security, such as the publication of the Pentagon Papers in June 1971. Because so many of his initial foreign policy moves were secret, including Kissinger's negotiations with the North Vietnamese in Paris, it became imperative that the administration oppose publication of the Pentagon Papers containing the secret Vietnam mistakes and misgivings of previous administrations. The administration had to convince Hanoi that they could keep their own secrets secret. Therefore, it was the secret way in which Nixon chose to conduct his foreign policy that determined how and why he finally tried to deal with domestic dissent through wiretaps and surveillance—not the other way around as is usually argued.

Nixon and the Antiwar Movement

Nixon appears to have paid more attention to general public opinion than to the antiwar movement in reaching his decision not to bomb North Vietnam in his first months in office. But he and his advisers also took the antiwar movement seriously for two reasons. First, Nixon and Kissinger were convinced that protestors were harming their attempts to negotiate a settlement. They believed that antiwar demonstrations indicated to Hanoi that the United States wanted out of the war. Having discussed student unrest with Kissinger "from time to time," Nixon concluded in April 1969 that "this was the heart of matter." Second, some of his advisers, such as Attorney General John Mitchell, Arthur Burns, and Tom Charles Huston, were convinced that there was "ironclad proof" that the student demonstrations in the United States and other countries [shared] reflected communist [characteristics] sympathies because they were being "bankrolled" and coordinated by groups in China and Cuba. Yet his more liberal advisers, such as Ehrlichman and Leonard Garment, insisted to the president that "the conclusion of the intelligence community is that our Government does not have specific information of 'ironclad proof' that Red China or Cuba is funding campus disorders." Nixon repeatedly asked for reports on different groups such as the Students for a Democratic Society, the Women's Strike for Peace, and the Socialist Workers Party on the grounds that they were front organizations and should be exposed as such. The president indicated in one handwritten note to Ehrlichman that this information might have to be used, especially if campus disorder spread to Latin America.[33]

As a result of such divided opinion among his advisers, Nixon essentially followed a three-track policy with respect to student demonstrators. First, he tried whenever possible to discredit antiwar groups as Communist fronts. Second, he approved of meetings between some of his staff and young Republicans concerned with the "liberal drift" of the administration on domestic policy and yet still supportive of the administration's efforts in Vietnam. Third, he tried to tighten the coordination of intelligence information about antiwar leaders, especially those who took their messages abroad such as Black Panther leader Stokely Carmichael. This led Nixon in 1970 to approve the infamous, but never implemented, Huston Plan. He also considered a variety of other tactics, including taking legal action against pacifist groups in the United States that were sending supplies to North Vietnam. Nixon refused implementation of these options even though Kissinger favored them.[34]

Naturally, Nixon agreed with the *Wall Street Journal*'s 27 May 1969 recommendation that the administration take a hard line on campus disorder. Referring back to Abraham Lincoln's attempts to keep the nation together, this publication said that Nixon faced an even harder task because he, unlike Lincoln, "must save the Union not from a civil but a guerrilla war." Nixon had been confronted, after all, with antiwar demonstrators on the day of his inauguration before he had even begun to assume power and responsibility as president. Immediately afterward he inquired about why and how events became so "screwed up" in the police action taken against the protestors. In particular, Nixon wanted to know why demonstrators at his inauguration were not removed before they got out of hand. He thought that "people would have supported strong action."[35] By the fall of 1969 he and his staff, as well as the Washington police and National Guard, were better prepared for the Vietnam moratorium demonstration.

The Nixon administration made few "screw ups" in countering the antiwar movement for the remainder of 1969. In fact, by the end of 1969 the president appeared, unlike LBJ, to have defeated the antiwar movement with his Vietnamization policies and determined criticism of opponents of the war, climaxed with his 3 November 1969 speech to the nation.[36] But when demonstrations over the bombing of Cambodia resulted in student deaths at Kent State on 4 May 1970, the antiwar movement appeared fully revived. As universities all over the countries closed and major demonstrations in Washington were being planned for 9 and 10 May, the president reacted personally as well as officially to the impending student "invasion" of the capital.

After an awkward meeting with a group of students in the White House and an unsatisfactory press conference, Nixon decided abruptly at 4:00 A.M. on 9 May to go to the Lincoln Memorial to meet informally with students camping there in preparation for the post–Kent State demonstration protesting the bombing of Cambodia. Both Herbert Parmet and William Safire described this strangely poignant and pointless act by Nixon in great detail. The president himself dictated a fourteen-page memorandum to H. R. Haldeman about it. "That night . . . turned out to be the most traumatic and most uplifting of his first term," according to Safire. "It was the strangest, most impulsive, and perhaps most revealing night of Nixon's

Presidency." But in the end it was all for naught. The press had a field day with the incident. To Nixon, it was simply distorted and misinterpreted by the media—as usual. Personally for him, it represented one of the few times in his public career that he attempted to talk about "matters of importance—qualities of the spirit, emotion, of the depth and mystery of life . . . [and] to lift them [the students with whom he spoke] out of the miserable intellectual wasteland in which they now wander aimlessly around."[37]

In the final analysis, Nixon did not succumb to any of his three home-front publics on the Vietnam issue, with the one exception where the bombing of North Vietnam was ruled out by the administration in February and March 1969, possibly due in part to concern about general public opinion. It also has been asserted, but not proven, that Nixon timed the Christmas bombings to coincide with the semester break at most colleges and universities. There is strong evidence to support the idea that these bombings were more closely related to Kissinger's faltering negotiations with both North and South Vietnam than the fact that the campuses were deserted.[38] Ultimately, Nixon subdued the antiwar movement by ending the draft and assuaged the general public with his January 1973 peace accords. However, he never came close to ending the criticism and suspicions of his career-long critics—eastern intellectuals, journalists, and opinion-makers.

Notes

1. Melvin Small, *Johnson, Nixon, and the Doves* (New Brunswick, N.J.: Rutgers University Press, 1988), 1–23. The more liberal Nixon aides or advisers were generally more troubled by the antiwar movement than the president himself and they tended to attribute their attitudes to him. Ibid., 20, 171, 242 (nn. 81, 82, 83, 86). These last two footnotes contain reviews of the literature contending that the antiwar movement did significantly affect U.S. foreign policy under Johnson and Nixon and the literature saying that it did not.

2. John Mueller, "A Summary of Public Opinion and the Vietnam War," in Peter Braestrup, ed. *Vietnam as History: Ten Years after the Paris Peace Accords* (Washington, D.C.: University Press of America, 1984), in app., n.p. Throughout this paper general public opinion is distinguished from antiwar sentiment because the former determined presidential approval ratings, while the latter influenced opinion specifically about the war.

3. Richard M. Nixon, *No More Vietnams* (New York: Arbor House, 1985).

4. Joan Hoff, *Nixon without Watergate* (New York: Basic Books, forthcoming), chap. 8.

5. Author's interview with Richard Nixon, 26 January 1983.

6. Lawrence W. Lichty, "Comments on the Influence of Television on Public Opinion," in Braestrup, ed., *Vietnam as History*, 158–59. Summarizing other studies, Lichty points out that "heavy battle" or actual combat scenes constituted only 3 percent of the nightly television coverage of Vietnam from 1965 to 1973. Although between 1966 and 1970 two-thirds of all those discussing the war on TV were "hawks," the coverage became increasingly critical after the Tet Offensive of 1968 and between 1970 and 1973 more than one-half of all the guests interviewed on the major news shows were critical of the Nixon administration's Vietnam policy. For the importance of military casualties (and POWs and hostages) in the minds of civilian leaders since 1968, see Mark Lorell and Charles Kelley, Jr. *Casualties, Public Opinion, and Presidential Policy during the Vietnam War* (Santa Monica, Calif.: A Rand Project AIR FORCE Report, March 1985).

7. George Gallup, Jr., *The Gallup Poll: Public Opinion 1985* (Wilmington, Del.: Scholarly Resources, 1986), 168.

8. Greenfield's spring 1967 statement cited in Earl Mazo and Stephen Hess, *Nixon: A Political Portrait* (New York: Popular Library, 1968), 4

9. Navasky cited in ibid.; Arthur B. Murphy, "Evaluating the Presidents of the United States," *Presidential Studies Quarterly* 14 (Winter 1984): 117.

10. *Washington Post,* 7 Oct. 1969.

11. Meg Greenfield, "Our No-Good Presidents," *Newsweek,* 28 Nov. 1983, 120. Also see Sheldon Wolin, "The State of the Union," *New York Review of Books,* 18 May 1978, 28–31. In this essay Wolin said, "an unnatural rite has become incorporated into the anthropology of American political life: the ritual destruction of the president" (p. 28).

12. William Appleman Williams was one of the first historians to point out this hotly contested relationship in the late 1950s.

13. For details, see Hoff, chaps. 5, 6, and 8.

14. See Ralph B. Levering, "Public Opinion, Foreign Policy, and American Politics since the 1960s," *Diplomatic History* 13 (Summer 1989): 383–93; and John Dumbrell, "Congress and the Antiwar Movement," in John Dumbrell, ed., *Vietnam and the Antiwar Movement* (Brookfield, Vt.: Averbury, 1989), 101.

15. Lichty, 159.

16. All of these groups came of age in the 1950s and 1960s. In particular, post-Watergate investigative reporters and a number of professional historians and other scholars have both internalized and propagandized ideas about the presidency since World War II that naturally led to a dislike and distrust of Nixon. Their ideas are based almost exclusively on romanticized versions of the leadership styles and personalities of either Franklin Delano Roosevelt or John Fitzgerald Kennedy, or both. Poll-taking among historians to determine the best and worst presidents did not begin until 1948. Thus, there has not been a winner or loser in this presidential popularity contest, conducted by historians, who has not been measured against the fun-loving, charismatic, macho model constructed in the last thirty years by Arthur M. Schlesinger, Jr., Richard Neustadt, Clinton Rossiter, Theodore White, and James David Barber. It was not until the enlightened imperial presidential mantel, so revered by the followers of FDR and JFK, fell on the hunched shoulders of Richard Nixon that presidential power became suspect. Then suddenly power, when wielded by a dour rather than a dapper president, was no longer purified as Neustadt had claimed, but took on the sinister overtones that had been carefully concealed in reporting during the shining days of Camelot. The reporting of deficiencies in presidential lifestyles and administrations, which journalists and intellectuals on the fringes of John Kennedy's administration carefully kept from public view, reached their logical extremes in Nixon, except for one—JFK's womanizing ways. And even this, one suspects, was held against Nixon on the ground that a peccadillo now and then would have at least humanized him, if not made him what he always wanted to be—one of the boys. Nonetheless, many of the cleverly concealed warts of the Kennedy administration, such as its passionless belief in technology and technocratic solutions; its disdain for Congress and the bureaucracy; its tendency to isolate the president by surrounding him with a handful of unelected, personal advisers—all can be found in the Nixon administration. For details, see Hoff, chap. 1; and Gary Wills, *The Kennedy Imprisonment: A Meditation on Power* (Boston: Little, Brown, 1981), 184–86; Arthur M. Schlesinger, Jr., *The Imperial Presidency* (Boston: Houghton Mifflin, 1973). For a comparison of Schlesinger's about-face on presidential power from Kennedy to Nixon, see Fred I. Greenstein, ed., *Leadership in the Modern Presidency* (Cambridge, Mass.: Harvard University Press, 1988), 318, n22, 413.

17. Small, 169–73. Walter Isaacson, *Kissinger: A Biography* (New York: Simon & Schuster, 1992), 82–128, 573–86. Kissinger's reaction to such criticism was to "leak" information to his critics to mollify them. He appears to have carefully monitored and even "catered to antiwar critics in the eastern establishment and on eastern campuses" in order to maintain a popularity with the press (if not the public) that Nixon never enjoyed. Stephen Ambrose in the second volume of his biography of Nixon, *Nixon: The Triumph of a Politician, 1962–1972* (New York: Simon & Schuster, 1989), fails to place into this perspective the many negative comments the president made about the press and the administration's public relations in general.

18. Richard Nixon, *Memoirs* (New York: Grosset & Dunlap, 1978), 399 (emphasis added); also cited

in the *New York Times,* 27 Sept. 1969.

19. Nixon, *Memoirs,* 403. This statement was made in a response to one of the many letters the president had received from students criticizing his previous 26 September statement.

20. Fred I. Greenstein, ed., *Leadership,* 319.

21. NSSM 1, 21 January 1969, National Security Archive, Washington, D.C.

22. Hoff, chap. 7; and William Shawcross, *Sideshow: Kissinger, Nixon and the Destruction of Cambodia* (New York: Simon & Schuster, 1979), 19–30. The relevant declassified documents obtained through the Freedom of Information Act (FOIA) upon which this interpretation is based are Joint Chief of Staff Memoranda (JCSM) 558–68, 13 December 1968, 558–69, 29 February 1969, 207–69, 9 April 1969—all with enclosures, U.S. Department of Defense; and author's interview with Melvin Laird, 15 October 1984.

23. See NSSM 19, 11 February 1969, and NSSM 21 and 22, 13 February and 12 March 1969, National Security Archive.

24. Author's interview with John Ehrlichman, 9 April 1984. For a description of Laird's position that is less negative, see Henry Kissinger, *White House Years* (Boston, Mass.: Little, Brown, 1979), 245.

25. Author's interview with Ehrlichman, 9 April 1984.

26. For details, see Hoff, chap. 7.

27. Author's interview with Richard Nixon, 26 January 1983.

28. Laird to Nixon, 18 March 1969, declassified through FOIA, 11 April 1977.

29. Kissinger, 246–67; Seymour M. Hersh, *The Price of Power: Kissinger in the Nixon White House* (New York: Summit Books, 1983), 63.

30. Laird to Nixon, 18 March 1969, declassified through FOIA, 11 April 1977.

31. Wheeler to Abrams, COMUSMACV, Holloway, CINCSAC, Hutchin, CSCINCPAC, and McCain, CINCPAC, 16 March 1969, declassified through FOIA, 11 April 1977. This telegram read in part: "Strike on COSVN headquarters is approved. . . . In the event press inquires are received following the execution . . . as to whether or not U.S. B-52's have struck in Cambodia, U.S. spokesman should confirm that B-52's did strike on routine missions adjacent to the Cambodian border but that he has no details and will look into this question." This statement was repeated in all orders while the bombing of Cambodia remained secret from 18 March 1969 through 26 May 1970.

32. U.S. Department of Defense, "Report on Selected Air and Ground Operations in Cambodia and Laos (White Paper)," 10 September 1973. The secret dual-bookkeeping system that was used to report on the covert bombing of Cambodia was not discontinued, however, until 17 February 1971. According to this "White Paper," the purpose of MENU "was to protect American lives during the preparation for and actual withdrawal of U.S. military personnel from southeast Asia by preempting imminent enemy offensive actions from the Cambodian sanctuaries into south Vietnam and against U.S. servicemen and women" (p. 5).

33. 24 January 1969, 2, Annotated News Summary (ANS) with Nixon's handwritten comments (NHC) to Kissinger, ANS, March, n.d., 1969, 4; ANS with NHC to Klein, April 1969, n.d., n.p., ANS with NHC to Kissinger, May 1969, n.d., n.p., ANS with NHC to Ehrlichman, Box 30, President's Office Files (POF), White House Central Files (WHCF); Burns to Nixon, 26 May 1969, with NHC to Ehrlichman, Ehrlichman to Nixon, 5 June 1970, Box 2, Jack Caulfield to Ehrlichman, 10 October 1969 with NHC, Box 3, POF, WHCF, Nixon to Kissinger, 10 April 1969, President's Personal Files (PPF), Box 1, WHCF, Nixon Presidential Materials Project (NPMP), National Archives and Records Administration (NARA), Alexandria, Va. See also Herbert S. Parmet, *Richard Nixon and his America* (Boston: Little, Brown, 1990), 566, 570–74, passim.

34. March, n.d., n.p., 1969, Box 30, ANS, Haldeman to Cole, 13 March 1969, Ehrlichman to Nixon, 18 March 1969, Box 1, POF, Huston to Haldeman, 12 August 1969, Box 51, 8 and 25 June 1970, 10 July 1970, Box 70, H. R. Haldeman Papers, WHCF, NPMP, NARA. Nixon and his advisers endlessly pondered how to disperse to the states power over issues that did not require federal standards and how to combat subversives inside and outside government. These two issues had little in common; nonetheless, they became perversely linked beginning in the 1960s (and, some would claim, reemerged in the 1980s). This linkage led to increased cooperation among the FBI, the CIA, and urban or state intelligence units which then forged links to monitor first the civil rights and then the antiwar movements. Nixon was prevented by

J. Edgar Hoover from implementing an elaborate scheme (the Huston Plan) for coordinating all counterintelligence agencies from the Army, Navy, Air Force, CIA, and FBI into an Interagency Group on Domestic Intelligence and Internal Security. Temporarily thwarted, Nixon began intensive use of the special domestic unit "Operation CHAOS," established by the Johnson administration for monitoring whether antiwar groups were financed by foreign enemies. Subsequently the Nixon administration initiated surveillance of domestic antiwar and other protest groups through a variety of extralegal means. At one level this was an attempt to channel what was perceived to be waning anti-communism (promoted in part by the Nixon administration's rapprochement with China and detente with the USSR) into a broad mainstream cultural campaign aimed at alleged internal subversion. See Jonathan Schell, *The Time of Illusion* (New York: Knopf, 1976), 59–74, 111–27; Tom Shactman, *Decade of Shocks: Dallas to Watergate, 1963–1974* (New York: Poseidon Press, 1983), 259–84. For a defense of the Huston Plan, see Nixon, *Memoirs,* 473–76. According to Nixon, "The irony of the controversy over the Huston Plan did not become apparent until a 1975 investigation revealed that the investigative techniques it would have involved had not only been carried out long before I approved the plan but continued to be carried out after I had rescinded my approval of it" (p. 475).

35. 22 January 1969, n.p., Box 30, ANS, POF, WHCF, NARA.

36. Joseph A. Amter, *Vietnam Verdict: A Citizen's History* (New York: Continuum, 1982), 173–74, 228–29.

37. Parmet, 1–13. Safire, *Before the Fall: An Inside View of the Pre-Watergate White House* (New York: Ballantine Books, 1977), 249, 257–72; and Nixon, *Memoirs,* 458–69; Nixon to Haldeman, 13 May 1970, Box 229, WHSP, Haldeman Papers, NARA.

38. For the assertion that the Christmas bombings were timed to coincide with the semester break, see John Mueller, "Reflections on the Vietnam Antiwar Movement and on the Curious Calm at the War's End," in Braestrup, ed., *Vietnam as History,* 153. For a more convincing argument about the timing in terms of the actual negotiations, see Amter, 285–90, and Isaacson, 461–90.

Name Index

201